Commercial and Economic Law in the Slovak Republic

Alexandra Andhov
Michal Rampášek

This book was originally published as a monograph in the International Encyclopaedia of Laws/Commercial and Economic Law.

General Editor: Roger Blanpain & Frank Hendrickx
Volume Editors: Jules Stuyck & Evelyne Terryn

Wolters Kluwer

Published by:
Kluwer Law International B.V.
PO Box 316
2400 AH Alphen aan den Rijn
The Netherlands
E-mail: international-sales@wolterskluwer.com
Website: lrus.wolterskluwer.com

Sold and distributed by:
Wolters Kluwer Legal & Regulatory U.S.
7201 McKinney Circle
Frederick, MD 21704
United States of America
Email: customer.service@wolterskluwer.com

ISBN 978-94-035-3010-9

e-Book: ISBN 978-94-035-2913-4
web-PDF: ISBN 978-94-035-2914-1

The Authors

JUDr Alexandra Andhov (née Horváthová), LL.M., S.J.D. (born on 20 August 1987), is Assistant Professor of Corporate Law at the University of Copenhagen. In 2019, Alexandra was a Fulbright Scholar at the Cornell Law School. Before joining the Faculty of Law of the University of Copenhagen, she worked at CMS Cameron McKenna office in Budapest and at Centre for Integrity in Business and Government at CEU Business School. Alexandra graduated from the Faculty of Law at Comenius University in Bratislava in 2010. During her studies, she undertook Erasmus programme at Lund University in Sweden, specializing in European Union (EU) law. She also obtained Diploma in Introduction to English Law and the EU Law from Cambridge University and Diploma in Austrian Private and Procedural Law from Wirtschafts Universität in Vienna. In 2011, she earned an LL.M. degree in International Business Law at Central European University in Budapest, and in 2012 she obtained her JUDr (Doctor of Laws). In 2014, she was a visiting fellow at Cornell Law School in the United States. In May 2015, she defended her S.J.D. dissertation on the protection of retail investor. She is fluent in English, French, German and Hungarian.

JUDr Michal Rampášek (born on 12 March 1987) studied Law at the Faculty of Law at Comenius University in Bratislava (2005–2010). During his studies, he successfully completed a course on Introduction to American Legal System. He also obtained European Certificate on Cybercrime and Electronic Evidence in 2009. In 2010, he obtained his JUDr (Doctor of Laws). He has been registered at the Slovak Bar Association since 2010. He is presently a partner with HAVLÁT & PARTNERS in Bratislava. He is fluent in English.

The Authors

Table of Contents

The Authors 3

List of Abbreviations 15

General Introduction 17

Chapter 1. The General Background 17

§1. Geography 17

§2. Population 17

§3. Political System 19

§4. Population and Employment Statistics 22

§5. Social and Cultural Values 24

Chapter 2. The Economic System 26

Chapter 3. The Legal System 28

Part I. Commercial Law 31

Chapter 1. Concepts and Sources of Commercial Law 31

§1. The Distinction Between Civil Law and Commercial Law 31

§2. Other Sources of Commercial Law 32

§3. Entrepreneur & Entrepreneurial Activity 33

I. Natural Persons 34

II. Companies & Cooperative 35

III. Being a Consumer 35

IV. Legal Consequences of the Qualification of an Act as Entrepreneurial Activity 36

A. Obligations of Merchants 37

B. Rules Applying to Commercial Relationships Only 38

1. Relative Commercial Relationships 39
2. Absolute Commercial Relationships 39
3. Absolute Non-commercial Relationships 40
4. Facultative Commercial Relationships 40
V. The Commercial Activities of Public Bodies 40

§4. Importance of International and Supranational Law 41

Chapter 2. The Economic Operators 43

§1. Personal Status of Merchants 43
I. In General 43
II. Married People 43
III. Foreigners 45

§2. Companies (Partnerships & Corporations & Cooperatives) 46
I. Historical Development 46
II. Notion of Legal Entity under Slovak Law 46
III. Different Types of Companies & Cooperatives 47
A. General Introduction 47
B. Unlimited Partnership (Verejná Obchodná Spoločnost') 48
C. Limited Partnership (Komanditná Spoločnost') 49
D. Limited Liability Company (Spoločnost' s Ručením Obmedzeným) 50
E. Joint-Stock Company (Akciová Spoločnost') 52
F. Simple JSC (Jednoduchá spoločnost' na akcie) 54
G. Cooperative (Družstvo) 55

Chapter 3. The Economic Institutions 58

§1. Professional Organizations 58
I. Free Choice of Profession 58
II. Current Situation 58
III. Trade Associations 59
IV. Budget & Contributory Organization (Rozpočtová a Príspevková Organizácia) 60
V. Organizations with an International Element 60
VI. Chambers of Commerce 61

§2. Commercial Arbitration 61
I. Arbitration Agreement 62
II. Composition of the Arbitral Panel 63
III. Jurisdiction of the Arbitral Panel 64
IV. Award 64
V. Role of the Courts 65
VI. Challenging the Award 65
VII. Recognition and Enforcement of the Award 66

A. Domestic Awards 66
B. Foreign Awards 67

Chapter 4. General Obligations of the Economic Operators 68

§1. All Undertakings: Merchants, Companies, Partnerships & Cooperatives 68
I. Commercial Register 68
A. Formal & Material Publicity of the Commercial Register 69
B. Recorded Data 69
C. Collection of Documents 70
D. Application for Registration 71
E. Electronic Application 72
F. Registration 72
G. Sanctions 72
H. Ultimate Beneficial Owners 73
II. Bank Account 73
III. Prevention of Money Laundering & Terrorist Financing 74
IV. Bookkeeping 76
A. Preliminary Observations 76
B. Scope of Application of the Act 77
C. General Principles 77
D. Accounting Period 78
E. Financial Statement under Slovak GAAP 78
F. Fines 80
G. Auditing 80

Chapter 5. Business Assets, Goodwill and Commercial Property Rights 82

§1. Business 82
I. General Observations 82
II. Transactions Relating to the Business 83
A. Overview 83
B. Sale 83
C. Lease 85
D. Management 86

§2. Intellectual Property 86
I. General Observations 86
A. Overview of IP Rights 87
B. Common Characteristics of IP Rights 88
C. International Treaties 89
II. Patents 90
A. Legislation 90
B. Nature and Duration of the Protection 90

C. Substantive Requirements 90
D. Formal Requirements 92
E. Rights of the Patentee 92
F. Inventions by Employees 93
G. Protection of Biotechnological Inventions 93
H. Supplementary Protection Certificates 94
I. Legal Actions by Third Parties 94
III. Utility Models 95
A. Legislation 95
B. Definition of a Model 95
C. Models Excluded from Protection by the Models Law 95
D. Substantive and Formal Requirements 96
E. Rights Conferred by a Model 97
F. Legal Actions by Third Parties 97
IV. Designs 98
A. Legislation 98
B. Definition of a Design 98
C. Substantive and Formal Requirements 98
D. Rights Conferred by a Design 98
E. Legal Actions by Third Parties 99
V. Plant Breeder's Rights 99
A. Legislation 99
B. Definition of a Variety 99
C. Substantive and Formal Requirements 100
D. Rights Conferred by a Breeding Certificate 101
VI. Trademarks 101
A. Legislation 101
B. Definition of a Trademark 102
C. The Different Signs Which Can Be Registered as a Trademark 102
D. Substantive Requirements 102
E. Formal Requirements 104
F. Rights Conferred by a Trademark 104
G. Legal Actions by the Trademark Owner 105
H. Legal Actions by Third Parties 105
VII. Copyright 106
A. Exclusions from Copyright 107
B. Individual (Moral) Authors' Rights 108
C. Proprietorial (Economic) Authors' Rights 108
VIII. Know-How 109

§3. Trade Name 110

§4. The Protection of Domain Names 111

Chapter 6. Bankruptcy and Related Institutions 113

§1. Bankruptcy (Konkurz) 113
I. Insolvent or Excessively Indebted Debtor 114
II. Creditor's Petition for Bankruptcy (Involuntary Bankruptcy) 115
III. Debtor's Petition for Bankruptcy (Voluntary Bankruptcy) 116
A. Liability of Debtor 116
IV. Commencement of Bankruptcy Proceeding and Bankruptcy Declaration 117
V. Effects of Bankruptcy 117
VI. Lodging of Claims 118
VII. Realization of the Assets 119
VIII. Closure 121
IX. Personal Bankruptcy (Small Bankruptcy) 121

§2. Restructuring (Reštrukturalizácia) 122
I. Trustee's Opinion 122
II. Business Activities of Debtor During Restructuring 123
III. Restructuring Plan 124

Chapter 7. Negotiable Instruments 126

§1. Notion and Basic Features 126

§2. Different Kinds of Negotiable Instruments 126

§3. Bills of Exchange and Promissory Notes 127
I. Introduction 127
A. Notion 127
B. Participants 128
C. Forms 130
D. Principle of Independence of Bill Statements 130
E. Transfer 131
F. Requirements of Promissory Note 131
G. Requirements of Bills of Exchange 132
H. Acceptance of the Bill of Exchange 134
I. Aval 134
J. Payment for the Bill of Exchange 135
K. Protesting the Bill of Exchange 135
L. Bill Notification 136
M. Statute of Limitations 136

§4. Cheques 137
I. Notion 137
II. Participants 137
III. Forms 138
IV. Requirements of Cheque 138
V. Transfer 139

Chapter 8. Organization of Financial Markets 140

§1. Introduction 140
I. General Structure 140
II. Oversight 141
A. Banking, Payment Services, Electronic Money & Foreign Exchange Sectors Oversight 141
B. Insurance, Pension Savings, Financial Intermediation Oversight 142
C. Securities Market Oversight 143

§2. Banking 143
I. Obligation to Register 144
II. Banking Licence 145
III. Corrective Measures and Sanctions 147

§3. Insurance 149
I. Authorization for Companies with Registered Seat in the Slovak Republic 150
II. Authorization for Companies with Registered Seat Outside the Slovak Republic and EU 152
III. Termination of the Authorization 152
IV. Corrective Measures and Sanctions 153
V. The Recent Act on Insurance 154

§4. Securities Market 155
I. Investment Firms 155
II. Collective Investment 157

§5. Pension Savings 159

§6. Takeover Regulation 160
I. Takeover Bid 161
A. Squeeze Out 163

§7. Insider Trading, Market Manipulation & Market Abuse 164

Chapter 9. Commercial Contracts 166

§1. General Principles of Contract Law 166

§2. Sale of Goods 166
I. International Sales Contracts 166
II. Domestic Sales Contracts 167
A. Formation of the Sales Contract 167
B. Obligations of the Seller 168
C. Obligations of the Buyer 169

D. Transfer of Property and of Risk 169

§3. Commercial Services 170
I. Distribution 170
A. Exclusive and Non-exclusive Distribution Agreements 170
1. Distribution Agreement 170
2. Influence of EU Competition Law 172
B. Franchising 173
1. Definition 173
2. Legal Protection of Franchisees 173
II. Middlemen or Intermediaries 175
A. Survey: Definition and Categories 175
B. Brokers 175
1. Definition 175
2. Reciprocal Rights and Obligations of the Parties 176
3. Termination of the Brokerage Agreement 177
C. Commission Agents and Mandataries 177
1. Definition 177
2. Rights and Obligations of the Parties 177
3. Special Rights and Obligations Relating to Commission 178
4. Commission Agent Agreement to Procure the Purchase or Sale of a Security (Stockbrokers) 179
D. Commercial Representation 180
1. Definition 180
2. Rights and Obligations of Parties 181
3. Non-exclusive Commercial Representation 183
4. Exclusive Commercial Representation 183
5. Termination of the Relationship with Commercial Representative 183
6. Distribution Versus Representation 184
E. Financial Intermediation 184
III. Insurance 185
IV. Financial Services 186
A. General Observation 186
B. Leasing 187
1. Contract for the Purchase of a Leased Thing 188
2. Contract on Leasing a Means of Transportation 189
C. Factoring 189
V. Carriage by Land, Sea and Air 190
A. General Provisions 190
B. Carriage by Sea and by Inland Waterways 192
C. Road Transport 192
D. Air Transport 193
E. Rail Transport 194
F. Travel Contract 195

Chapter 10. Secured Transactions 196

§1. Introductory Observations 196

§2. Securities under Civil Law 197
I. Real Securities 197
A. Charge/Lien 197
B. Mortgage 201
II. Personal Securities 202
A. Surety 202
B. Bank Guarantee 203

§3. Securities under Securities Act 204
I. Registration of Charge 205
II. Use of the Securities as Collateral 205
III. Transfer of Securities as Collateral 206

Part II. Economic Law 207

Chapter 1. General Principles 207

§1. State Intervention in Economic Activities 207

§2. Basic Principles of Economic Law 207
I. Freedom of Trade 208
II. Free Movement 209
III. Freedom of Establishment 209
IV. Equality 210

Chapter 2. The Law of Establishment and Supervision of Economic Activities 212

§1. Introduction 212

§2. The Establishment Act for Small-and Medium-Sized Undertakings 213
I. Survey 213
II. Recognition of Foreign Persons 213
III. Foreign Business 214
IV. Participation of Foreign Persons in Slovak Legal Persons 214

§3. The Professions 214

§4. The Establishment of Aliens 215

§5. Licensing Requirements in Various Sectors 215

§6. Supervision of Financial Market 215

Chapter 3. State Incentives for Economic Activities 217

§1. General Remarks 217

§2. Incentives 218

Chapter 4. Competition Law 220

§1. Antitrust Law 220
I. Introduction 220
II. Institutional Provisions 220
III. Scope of Application 221
IV. Substantive Provisions 221
A. Restriction of Competition and Restrictive Competition Practices 221
1. Restrictive Agreements 222
2. Abuse of a Dominant Position 223
B. Concentrations 223
V. Procedure 224
VI. Sanctions 225

§2. The Law of Unfair Competition and Trade Practices 226
I. Introduction 226
II. The Commercial Code 226
A. Survey 226
B. Scope of Application 226

Chapter 5. State Regulation of the Conditions of Commercial Transactions 230

§1. Price and Supply Regulation 230
I. Legislative Framework 230
II. Price Regulation 231
A. Main Areas of Regulation 231
B. Price Interventions of the Government 233
1. Price Authorities 233
2. Breach of Price Discipline 234

§2. Consumer Law 234
I. General Observations 234
A. Representation of the Consumer Interest 235
1. Government Level 235

§3. Consumer Protection Act 236
I. Survey 236
II. Scope of Application 236

A. Seller 236
B. Products and Services 238
III. Substantive Provisions 238
A. Denomination, Composition, Quantity and Labelling of Products and Services 238
B. Price Indication 238
C. Advertising 239
D. Unfair Commercial Practices 240
E. Regulated Trade Practices 241
1. Announcements of Price Comparisons and Discounts 241
2. Clearance Sales 242
3. Financial Services Offers 242
4. Gift Vouchers 243
5. Auction Sales 244
6. Unsolicited Sales 244
7. Pyramid Selling 244
8. Door-to-Door and Distance Selling 245
F. Honest Business Practices 246
IV. Interim Measures 246
V. Sanctions 247

§4. Consumer Sales 247

Selected Bibliography 251

Index 253

List of Abbreviations

AmCham	American Chamber of Commerce
AMO	Antimonopoly Office of the Slovak Republic
BCCSR	British Chamber of Commerce in the Slovak Republic
BSE	Bratislava Stock Exchange
CISG	United Nations Convention on Contracts for the International Sale of Goods of 1980
CSD	Central Securities Depository of the Slovak Republic
EU	European Union
FDI	Foreign Direct Investment
FIU	Financial Investigation Unit
FMS	Financial Market Supervision Unit
GDP	Gross Domestic Product
IAS	International Accounting Standards
IFRS	International Financial Reporting Standards
IP	Intellectual Property
IPO	Industrial Property Office of the Slovak Republic
JSC	Joint-Stock Company
LLC	Limited Liability Company
NBS	National Bank of Slovakia
NGOs	Non-governmental Organizations
OECD	Organisation for Economic Co-operation and Development
OTC	Over the Counter
PFMC	Pension Fund Management Companies
SARIO	Slovak Investment and Trade Development Agency
SCCI	Slovak Chamber of Commerce and Industry
Slovak GAAP	Slovak Generally Accepted Accounting Principles

List of Abbreviations

SME	Small-and Medium-Sized Enterprises
SPMC	Supplementary Pension Management Companies
TFEU	Treaty on the Functioning of the European Union
WIPO	World Intellectual Property Organization

General Introduction

Chapter 1. The General Background

§1. Geography

1. Slovakia is a small country lying in the Central Europe. It covers an area of 49,035 km^2 and 1,652.6 km of the land frontiers. Slovakia borders with the Czech Republic and Austria on the west, Poland on the north, Ukraine on the east and Hungary on the south (Figure 1). The largest city is the capital, Bratislava, and the second largest is Košice. The country has a population of 5.4 million and some 287 inhabitants per square mile.

Figure 1 Map of the Slovak Republic

§2. Population

2. Slovakia is composed of one dominant cultural-linguistic community, speaking Slovak (80.7%), and a small Hungarian-speaking community (8.5%) and Romani-speaking community (2%). Slovak is the official language. Hungarian is widely spoken in the southern regions and Rusyn is used in some parts of the North-east. Minority languages hold co-official status in the municipalities in which the size of the minority population meets the legal threshold of 20%. Some 0.5% are foreigners with permanent residence.

The population of Slovakia was as follows (Tables 1, 2 and 3).

Table 1 Population of Slovakia

Year	*Total Resident Population*	*Male*	*Female*	*Proportion of Women in %*
2017	5,443,120	2,786,867	2,656,253	51.2
2013	5,415,949	2,639,060	2,776,889	51.3
2012	5,410,836	2,635,979	2,774,857	51.2
2011	5,397,036	2,627,772	2,769,264	51.3
2001	5,379,455	2,612,515	2,766,940,	51.4
1991	5,274,335	2,574,061	2,700,274	51.2
1980	4,991,168	2,453,065	2,538,103	50.9

Source: https://www.statistics.sk/.

Table 2 Age Groups of Population in Slovakia

Year	*Total Resident Population*	*Age Group*					
		0–14		*15–64*		*65+*	
		Absolute Value	*In %*	*Absolute Value*	*In %*	*Absolute Value*	*In%*
2012	5,410,836	830,576	15.3	3,870,038	71.6	710,222	13.1
2011	5,397,036	826,516	15.3	3,886,327	72.0	682,873	12.7
2001	5,379,455	1,015,493	18.9	3,705,515	68.9	610,923	11.4
1991	5,274,335	1,31,961	24.9	3,415,721	64.8	543,180	10.3
1980	4,991,168	1,302,072	26.1	3,162,504	63.4	519,388	10.4

Source: https://www.statistics.sk/.

Table 3 Nationality of Slovak Population

Nationality	*Total Resident Population*					
	2012		*2001*		*1991*	
	Abs.	*In %*	*Abs.*	*In %*	*Abs.*	*In %*
Slovak	4,360,313	80.58	4,614,854	85.8	4,519,328	85.7
Hungarian	458,091	8.47	520,528	9.7	567,296	10.8
Roma	107,958	2.00	89,920	1.7	75,802	1.4

Nationality	*Total Resident Population*					
	2012		*2001*		*1991*	
	Abs.	*In %*	*Abs.*	*In %*	*Abs.*	*In %*
Czech, Moravia, Silesian	34,451	0.64	44,620	0.8	52,884	1.0
Ruthenian	33,439	0.63	24,201	0.4	17,197	0.3
Ukrainian	7,626	0.14	10,814	0.2	13,281	0.3
German	4,870	0.09	5,405	0.1	5,414	0.1
Polish	3,343	0.06	2,602	0.04	2,659	0.04
Russian	2,079	0.04	1,590	0.02	1,389	0.02
Others and not declared	398,666	7.37	82,502	1.5	124,205	2.3

Source: https://www.statistics.sk/.

§3. POLITICAL SYSTEM

3. The Slovak Constitution was ratified on 1 September 1992 and became effective on 1 January 1993. Slovakia became an independent state on 1 January 1993 as one of the successors to the Czech and Slovak Federative Republic. The Slovak Republic is a parliamentary democracy. The Constitution has been amended several times. The greatest amendments were introduced in February 2001 resulting from Slovakia's intention to join the European Union (EU). Slovakia has recognized international treaties, changed the electoral law, introduced an ombudsman to the Slovak law system, transferred the right to appoint judges for an unlimited time from the Parliament to the President and has undergone changes in a majority of its institutions. The Slovak Republic became a member of the Organisation for Economic Co-operation and Development (OECD) in 2000, North Atlantic Treaty Organization in March 2004 and the EU in May 2004. In 2007, Slovakia joined the Schengen Area and in 2009 introduced the single European currency, the Euro.

4. The Constitution sets out the principle of separation between the three powers of the state. The President of Slovakia is elected for a five-year term by direct popular election. While the President's powers are largely representational and ceremonial, the Office also holds some important legal powers, including the appointment of the Prime Minister and the ability to veto legislation. However, the President's veto can be overturned by a simple majority in parliament. Most executive power lies with the Prime Minister. The Prime Minister shall be appointed and recalled by the President of the Slovak Republic. On a proposal of the Prime Minister, the President shall appoint and recall other members of the Government and empower them with the administration of Ministries.

5. The National Council of the Slovak Republic represents the legislative branch. It is a unicameral body which holds responsibility for most areas of government policy. The National Council is made up of 150 deputies elected for four-year terms.

The judicial power in the Slovak Republic is executed by general courts and the Constitutional Court of the Slovak Republic. The system of general courts consists of the Supreme Court, eight regional courts, fifty-four district courts, and the Specialized Criminal Court. The Slovak Republic has a two-level court system.

6. District courts are competent courts to try proceedings at first instance over three areas (civil, commercial and criminal). Regional courts hear cases as appeal courts. The Supreme Court of the Slovak Republic has the function of an appellate review court. The Specialized Criminal Court has criminal jurisdiction of a regional court for the prosecution of especially serious crime, corruption and crimes of public officials.

7. The Constitutional Court reviews the constitutionality of laws, the constitutional questions of lower-level courts and national and local government bodies as well as constitutional complaints of natural persons and legal persons regarding violation of their fundamental rights and freedoms.

8. The Judicial Council composing of eighteen members who are either judges, law professors or other legal experts, *inter alia*, submits to the President proposals for appointing and recalling judges (except for the Constitutional Court) and also to appoint members and chairmen of disciplinary senates.

9. Slovakia is composed of eight regions: Bratislava Region, Trnava Region, Trenčín Region, Nitra Region, Žilina Region, Banská Bystrica Region, Prešov Region, and Košice Region. Since 2002, Slovakia has been divided into eight self-governing regions, which are called Higher Territorial Units. The territory and borders of the self-governing regions are identical with the territory and borders of the regions. The main difference is that bodies of self-governing regions are self-governance, with an elected chairperson and regional parliament. According to the law, elected chairman and elected regional parliament are two bodies of the self-governing regions. Administrative and organizational tasks are executed by the Office of Self-Governing Region. The competences that the regions exercise today belonged basically to the central state administration in the past. In the process of decentralization, a high number of competences were transferred to the local and regional level. Today, the self-governing regions have broad powers, basically in the domain of economic management and regional development, education, schools, culture, transportation. Furthermore, each region may enact regulations on regional taxes, fees, healthcare system, etc.

10. In 2011, the Slovak Republic had 2,890 municipalities, of which 138 had city status. Municipalities are territorial and legal entities and represent the local government. Local governments manage their own budgets and assets. The state administration may delegate authority to local governments for particular tasks that are financed by state funds. Municipalities may issue regulations that are binding for all individuals and legal persons within their jurisdiction. Such regulations may be superseded or invalidated only by acts of the National Council. Local government authorities are elected directly by the local population. As the highest executive, the mayor summons and conducts the sessions of local representative bodies, represents the Office and the municipality and decides on all matters of local administration with the exception of those that, according to law, are decided by the municipal parliament.

11. In the Slovak Republic, there is a standard system of political parties with the existence of several political parties that continually compete to acquire power or a share of power. The Slovak political scene supports a wide spectrum of political parties. The latest parliamentary election took place in February 2020, which has changed the previous government. The former coalition comprising of Smer (Direction), the Slovak National Party and Most-Híd led by Prime Minister Peter Pellegrini of Smer was defeated. The former opposition party Ordinary People won the election with 25.02%, followed by Smer with 18.9% and We are Family with 8.24%. The Ordinary People formed a coalition together with three other parties, We are Family, Freedom and Solidarity and For the People.

12. The latest presidential elections were held in March 2019, when the incumbent President Andrej Kiska did not run for the second term. Fifteen candidates contested in the first round on 16 March 2019. Zuzana Čaputová, of the Progressive Slovakia party, finished substantially ahead of the other candidates, receiving 40.6% of the votes. Another candidate who qualified for the second round was Maroš Šefčovič, the Vice President of the European Commission for the Energy Union. In the second round, Zuzana Čaputová received 58.41% of popular vote and became the first female president in the history of Slovak Republic.

§4. POPULATION AND EMPLOYMENT STATISTICS

13.

Figure 2 Development of Economic Activity Rate, Employment Rate and Unemployment Rate in the Slovak Republic from 1994 to 2010

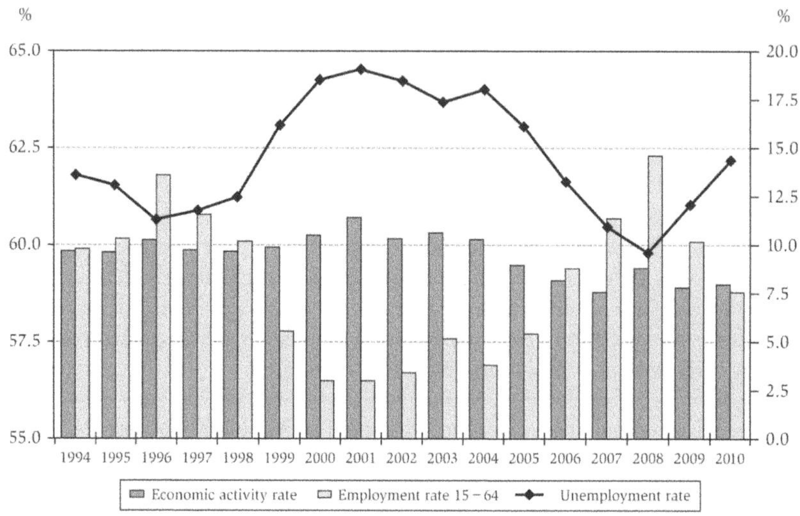

Source: https://www.statistics.sk/.

Figure 3 Unemployment Rate from 2010 to 2018

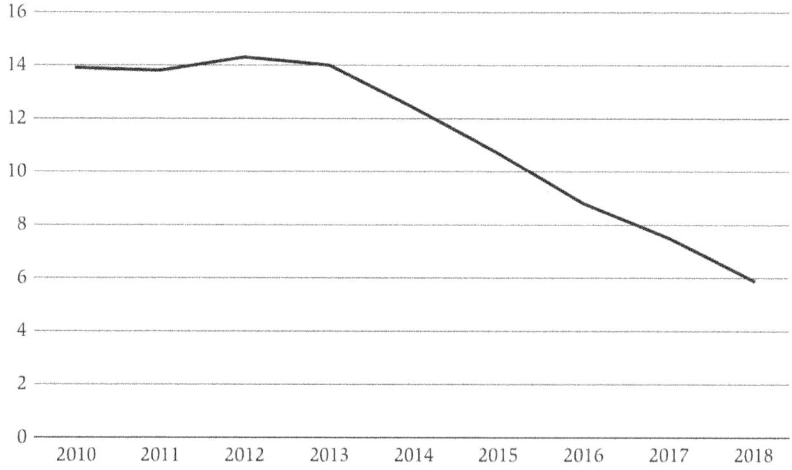

Source: https://www.statistics.sk/.

14. After the period of large rise, the demand for labour force has decreased significantly. However, the period of 2007–2011 was characterized only by a slight decrease in employment by 0.3% – 2,351,400 employed persons in 2011. According to Labour Force Sample Survey, the employment grew, year-on-year, three consecutive quarters. Compared with the 2nd quarter of 2013, the number of the employed rose by 25,800 (by 1.1%) to 2,353,600 persons. After seasonal adjustment, the total employment grew by 11,500 persons (by 0.5%) to 2,349,800 persons, compared with the 1st quarter of 2014. An increase in the total employment was affected mostly by a growth in the number of employees by 25,300 (by 1.3%) to 1,991,800. The number of self-employed (i.e., shareholders, tradesmen, self-farmers, freelancers with the only one or main job) remained at the level of last year, i.e., 359,400 within them, the number of self-employed with employees grew by 4,300 (by 5.9%) to 76,900 and the number of the self-employed without employees declined by 4,300 (by 1.5%) to 282,500 (Figure 2 and Table 4).

15. There were also changes in the structure of employment. The employment continued to grow in services; the share of the services sector increased from 58.5% in 2009 to 60.9% in 2013, while the share of the agriculture sector as well as the share of the industry sector decreased.

16. Decreases in employment were observed between 2009 and 2013 almost in half of economic activity branches, most above in industry, agriculture, construction, other services, accommodation and food services and transportation and storage. High employment growth rise was in information and communication and wholesale and retail trade, repair of motor vehicles and motorcycles. At present, the branch with the highest employment in the Slovak Republic is still industry, with 601,500 persons employed in 2013. The share of the industry in total employment was just 25.8% in 2013, compared with a higher level of 27.1% headed in 2009. The number of persons with higher professional education increased by 28.4% in 2013 compared to 2009 as well as the share of employed with university education from 17.2% to 21.1%.[1]

17. After 2014, we observe a substantial decrease in unemployment across all the sectors in industries, as shown in Figure 3. Currently, the unemployment rate is minimal and reflects the increased economic productivity in Slovakia across all industries.

18. The Slovak Republic remains a country of 'small businesses'. Employment gradually decreased in the public sector (by 5.8%) and increased in the private sector (by 2.6%). This was reflected in changes in the overall structure of employment

1. Statistical Office of the Slovak Republic, Social Development Trends in the Slovak Republic 2014, available online at: http://slovak.statistics.sk/wps/wcm/connect/6fad4776-6fff-4d13-948e-b8e5310fa055/Vyvoj_obyvatelstva_v_Slovenskej_republike_a_krajoch_v_roku_2013.pdf?MOD=AJPERES&CACHEID=6fad4776-6fff-4d13-948e-b8e5310fa055 (accessed 26 Nov. 2015).

by types of ownership. In 2007, the share of the private sector in total employment in the Slovak Republic stood at 71.2%; in 2011, it was at the level of 73.2%.

19. The average nominal monthly wage in the economy in the second quarter of 2014 was EUR 857. In comparison with the second quarter of 2013, it increased by 4.8%. Taking into account the development of consumer prices, real wages increased by 4.9%. Seasonally adjusted wages increased in the 2nd quarter of 2014 compared to the first quarter of 2014 nominally by 1.2%. Nominal wage increased year-on-year in most sectors. Most significantly it increased in administrative services. In the first half of 2014, the average nominal monthly wage in the economy grew by 4.4% to EUR 839. Real wage increased by 4.5%. In 2018, the nominal wage in the economy was EUR 1.013.

Table 4 Units by Legal Form and Size Category by Employees in 2011

Legal Forms	*Total*	*Number of Employees*					
		0–9	*10–49*	*50–249*	*250–499*	*500–999*	*1000 and more*
Total	624,173	422,806	19,491	4,112	405	214	132
Joint-stock companies	5,760	3,369	984	585	124	75	51
Limited liability companies	164,970	127,521	10,827	1,811	170	88	41
Other trading partnerships	1,211	949	68	19	1	-	3
Cooperatives	1,546	805	475	150	10	13	1
State enterprises	21	2	4	11	1	-	3
Subsidized organizations	661	133	295	215	9	3	-
Budgetary organizations	6,463	1,793	3,529	1,059	56	14	5
Natural persons – entrepreneurs	382,213	244,661	2,164	84	2	-	-
Other legal forms	61,328	43,573	1,145	178	32	21	29

§5. Social and Cultural Values

20. The social and cultural values that form the nature of law and industry in Slovakia largely relate to the legal foundations of economic power in a free enterprise economy. Since 1993, Slovakia has continued the difficult transformation from a centrally planned to a modern market-oriented economy of Western society. Life in Slovakia is influenced by traditional values. Becoming more modern and Western, Slovak culture still maintains a high level of tradition. Slovak legal system guarantees four fundamental rights and freedoms, which are the pillars of the economic power. The first is the *right of property*; this right enables the proprietor to dispose of, exploit and benefit from his property, and to make a profit from it. The second fundamental freedom is the *freedom of commerce and industry*. This freedom means that any person can freely engage in commerce, industry or any other activity of his choosing. The third, the *freedom of association*, whereby it is possible for individuals to associate with others in order to engage in industry or commerce, and to that end, to bring in their own capital in order to maximize any profit, which may ensue for eventual division.

The fourth represents *the freedom of labour*. The employee is free to choose his job and his employer and has the consequent freedom to conclude an individual labour contract. By means of this contract, the employee engages himself/herself to work in a position of *subordination*, that is under the command, authority and the control of the employer. Hence, the employer gains power over his/her workers, and they have to carry out – within given limits of course – his/her orders.

21. The Slovak market is significantly influenced by protective labour laws and trade unions, collective bargaining as well as the direct intervention of the state; however, these basic values are still the pillars of the social system and fundamentally determine the development of the labour relations system. The Slovak economic system can be described as socially oriented market economy with active government intervention and regulation. Slovakia has a small, open economy, and therefore needs high export efficiency. The focus of Slovak exports and economic diplomacy, in the area of trade, is the EU, where 82.82% of exports go and from where 62.5% of imports are received (in 2018). Germany continues to be Slovakia's largest trading partner, purchasing 22.01% of Slovakia's exports and supplying 16.02% of its imports in 2014.

22. In summary, Slovakia is a pluralistic and democratic society in which individuals and groups have the freedom to make choices that promote their well-being and in which social conflict is consequently indispensable.

Chapter 2. The Economic System

23. Since 1993, Slovakia has made a significant economic progress. Governments have undertaken broad reforms in all areas of life. The most visible reforms took place in tax system, corporate sector, healthcare or social welfare system. Majority of the former state corporations have been privatized mostly by foreign investors. State only kept the majority shares in the paramount industries – energy and transportation. In 2001–2008, Slovakia recorded the Foreign Direct Investment (hereinafter 'FDI') boom with its business and tax-friendly policies. State opened to join the corporations in joint ventures or grant the foreign investors tax holidays for several years. Moreover, at this time, Slovakian market could be distinguished by cheap and skilled labour, low taxes, flat tax of 19%, 7% on dividends and most importantly its central geographical position in Europe. The main areas of investments were the automotive and electronic sector. FDI inflow cumulatively reached EUR 43.06 billion in 2009. Naturally, the FDI consequently decreased, and in 2013, the FDI declined to EUR 0.45 billion from EUR 2.20 billion in 2012. This trend also continues and FDI in Slovakia averaged EUR 290.61 million from 2012 until 2019.

24. Slovakia consolidated its budget and in 2004 entered the EU. In order to adopt the Euro currency, Slovakia had to undergo further economic reforms and developments and provide the European Council with satisfactory economic indicators. The main fiscal objective was to reduce the general government deficit to fewer than 3% of gross domestic product (GDP) by 2007. The subsequent step was to adjust the general government deficit below 1% of GDP. Slovakia entered into the European Exchange Rate Mechanism in November 2005 and in January 2009 it joined the European Monetary Union.

25. In 2011, the Slovak government adopted a National Reform Programme of the Slovak Republic for 2011–2014. Within this programme, the Government set up six main areas of reform, namely: (i) Pension System Reform, (ii) Fiscal Responsibility Reform, (iii) Reform of the System of Taxes and Social Contributions, (iv) Labour Code Reform, (v) Reduced Administrative Burden, and (vi) Fight Against Corruption and Increased Transparency.[2] Given the current financial and economic stand of Slovakia, the major focus should be devoted to the fiscal consolidation of the government debt and critically address corruption, on both national and regional levels.

26. Since the financial crisis, Slovakian state budget deficit rose to 2.77 billion in November 2012. However, by 2017 the Government stabilized the deficit to 745 million (0.8% of GDP). Measures adopted by the Government since 2012 have

2. For more *see* the programme, available online at: http://www.finance.gov.sk/en/Components/CategoryDocuments/s_LoadDocument.aspx?categoryId=600&documentId=371.

helped to improve tax collection, particularly for Value-Added Tax (VAT). The Government aims to reach budget balance by 2019, in line with its European medium-term objective. According to the OECD, the economy is in a phase of strong, broad-based expansion. Unemployment has fallen below 7%, which is a historical lowest level. However, long-term unemployment remains prevalent in the Eastern part of Slovakia.

27. After the election in spring 2012, the Government led by Robert Fico announced its main economic aim to bring the fiscal deficit below 3% of GDP by 2013, in which it succeeded. In 2010, the Government of liberal Prime Minister Iveta Radičová raised the main VAT rate to 20% as a means of fiscal consolidation. Other taxes remained mostly untouched until 2012 when the new government of Prime Minister Robert Fico removed the flat tax from the beginning of 2013. The corporate income tax rose to 23%, and a progressive personal income tax of 25% is applied once one reaches the income of roughly EUR 35,268.06. Given the current income of the population, the higher personal income tax will apply to the maximum of the 2% of taxpayers.

28. Besides numerous new tax rules and rates, new rates of social, health and pension contributions were introduced based on diverse types of employment relationships. Furthermore, the Government modified the system for the collection of taxes and duties and the pension contributions to private funds will be reduced and diverted to the state budget. The Slovak Republic has one of the fastest ageing populations in the OECD. Currently, the share of elderly persons (65 and over) in the working-age population is one-fifth. However, by 2060 the share will reach almost 60%. The steep population ageing will expose the pension system to strong pressures in the following decades.

Chapter 3. The Legal System

29. The legal system of Slovak Republic is a civil law system influenced by the Austro-Hungarian Empire. Since the eighteenth century, the Hungarian legal system has been applied broadly and thus the Austro-Hungarian codes adopted in the nineteenth century were also applied and enforced on the territory of today Slovak Republic. After the formation of Czechoslovakia in 1918, the Czech legal system and tradition, heavily influenced by the Austrian and German law, interfered with the former Hungarian tradition in Slovakia and started to modify. After the Second World War, the Communist Government in order to reform the basics of the political system had to start with the legal system. The former Hungarian common law in Slovakia and Austro-German Czech law were substantially changed, communist legal principles were adopted and new Czechoslovak legal system was founded.

30. Despite the fact that the governmental establishment had been changing during the existence of Czechoslovakia, the legal order yet remained very similar even after the Velvet Revolution of 17 November 1989 and the subsequent separation. Besides, given the fact that Slovakia and the Czech Republic are Member States of the EU, the substantial similarities between the both legal systems are still present. Moreover, the cross-citation of court decisions could be considered as a daily practice.

31. The independent Slovak Republic was founded on 1 January 1993. The respective Constitution was adopted several months before on 1 September 1992 and since then has been amended several times. The Constitution provides for a multi-ethnic parliamentary democracy and an independent judiciary system. It includes a catalogue of basic rights and fundamental freedoms, general provisions on the state, its institutions and the division of powers. The political system is divided between three classical branches: legislative, executive and judiciary.

32. The legislative power is vested in the National Council of the Slovak Republic, which consists of 150 members elected for a four-year term. The executive power is shared between the President of the Slovak Republic and the Government. The President is the head of the state and represents the Slovak Republic in internal as well as external relations for his five-year term. President can be elected in a direct universal election with possible one re-election. The powers of the President are mostly representative and ceremonial. The highest body of the executive power is the Government with the Prime Minister on its top, who needs to be backed by the majority of the National Council in order to be appointed by the President. The Government decides as a college by an absolute majority of all its members.

33. The judiciary power is divided into two branches: the general courts and the Constitutional Court. The general courts lie in four tiers: (1) fifty-four district courts (trial courts), (2) eight regional courts (courts of appeal), (3) the Supreme Court and (4) the Specialized Criminal Court. District courts are the courts of the first instance, except for administrative and enumerated civil and criminal cases, whereas the regional courts serve as courts of appeal. The Supreme Court is the highest judicial authority in the country and has the function of an appellate review court. The Specialized Criminal Court was established in 2009 as a substitute for the Specialized Court, which was previously revoked due to its unconstitutionality.

34. Judiciary is a self-governed branch, with the Judicial Council on its top. Judicial Council is in charge of the administration of judiciary. It is responsible for selecting, disciplining and removing judges. Judges are appointed for an indefinite term by the President upon proposal by the Judicial Council and can be only removed following disciplinary proceedings conducted by a special judicial ethics panel. The Specialized Criminal Court goes hand in hand with the specialized prosecution, which targets and decides the severe criminal violence and corruption-related crimes. Concerning the personal jurisdiction, the Specialized Criminal Court hears the cases involving high governmental officials, including members of government, parliament, judges, prosecutors or heads of public agencies.

35. Concerning the occupancy of general courts, in civil and administrative matters in district courts, there is always one professional judge who decides the case. In an appellate procedure, there is a senate, composed of three professional judges. Nevertheless, also laypeople participate by sitting as judges in criminal cases in district courts. Local councils elect laypersons.

36. The Constitutional Court is a separate independent judicial body protecting the constitutionality. Thirteen members of the Constitutional Court interpret the Constitution and constitutional laws and decide on the competency conflicts between state authorities, unless such power is delegated to another state authority. Since 2001, the Constitutional Court has also the power to quash decisions of general courts due to the violations of fundamental rights and freedoms.

Part I. Commercial Law

Chapter 1. Concepts and Sources of Commercial Law

§1. The Distinction Between Civil Law and Commercial Law

37. Commercial or entrepreneurial relationships and contracts are in the Slovak Republic governed by both commercial and civil law. In contrast to traditional European concepts, where the commercial law focuses on the business contracts, with limited differences from the general civil law or the law of obligations, Slovak commercial law is to a great extent an independent body of laws, which is in many respects significantly different. The Slovak Commercial Code primarily regulates the status of entrepreneurs, types of business companies, partnerships and cooperatives, business obligations and specific types of contracts between two entrepreneurs and consequent rights and obligations of the parties.

38. Czechoslovak Commercial Code, Act No. 513/1991 Coll. came into effect on 1 January 1992. The adoption of the Commercial Code represented a huge step towards a new economic and political regime. Given the fact that any private property was considered unlawful until 1989, the new regulatory framework had to reflect the possibility to reacquire once seized property, provide for new proprietary remedies for the wrongs inflicted by the former communist regime and establish a possibility to privatize the state ownership in order to provide for fast and effective establishment of economic and business development. Commercial Code was naturally a part of this whole new regulatory system.[3] Since 1992, the number of enacted amendments has been considerable due to the new challenges that Slovakia faced.

39. The Slovak Commercial Code is primarily a legislative act of private law; however, the status of entrepreneurs is also subject to public law. Concerning the contracts and contractual obligations, unless otherwise provided, the Commercial Code governs them. From the Roman law perspective, the Commercial Code functions as *lex specialis* while the Civil Code as *lex generalis*. Thus, if the reference to the character of a relationship between two or more entrepreneurs, their duties or

3. Among a number of other acts, there was, e.g., Act No. 427/1990 Coll. on transfer of ownership of some state property to other legal or natural persons. This Act was called also as a 'small privatization' and allowed a purchase of operating units owned by the state through public auctions. Act No. 92/1991 Coll. was the act which enabled a 'big privatization' during which the large state enterprises were privatized, mostly by voucher privatization.

obligations is to be found in the Commercial Code, this will govern them. Only, in a situation where an issue cannot be resolved by the Commercial Code, will one apply the Civil Code. Naturally, nowadays also the most areas of private life are regulated and therefore the applicability of other acts should be always taken into consideration.

§2. Other Sources of Commercial Law

40. As stated above, commercial relationships may be affected by a number of administrative acts, which provide for certain mandatory duties for the parties. As a result, their application is automatic and in a case that parties did not adhere to some specific administrative procedure, e.g., licensing, their contract may be found void.

41. To determine the sequence of sources and rules governing the commercial relationship, it is important to follow the first paragraph of the Commercial Code, which reads that it is the Commercial Code which governs the standing of entrepreneurs, business obligations, as well as some other relationship related to commerce. Further, the Commercial Code provides that the contracts between entrepreneurs (including natural and legal persons), which are not included within the Commercial Code, are to be regulated by the Civil Code, but the character of the parties as well as the principles of the Commercial Code should be always taken into consideration.

42. Thus, the parties should always follow this systematization of the norms and their relevant provisions:

(1) Mandatory provisions of the Commercial Code.
(2) Contractual obligations between the parties:
   (a) explicitly stated in the Contract;
   (b) referring to the Terms & Conditions of the Contract (section 274 of the Commercial Code);
   (c) referring to extra-contractual clauses (e.g., INCOTERMS);
   (d) referring to business practices that are common within the sector (e.g., Import/Export);
   (e) referring to other factors of the relationship between parties (e.g., Framework Agreement).
(3) Dispositive provisions of the Commercial Code.
(4) Mandatory provisions of the Civil Code.
(5) Dispositive provisions of the Civil Code.
(6) Business practices, unless not referred to within the Contract itself.
(7) Principles of the Commercial Code.

43. Concerning the interrelationship between the contractual terms and conditions agreed by the parties vis-à-vis the business practices, it is of essential importance that the business practices are taken into consideration not only when interpreting the contract but also as the inherent component of any contract. Hence, their interrelationship should be regarded as coordinated – having equal status.[4]

§3. Entrepreneur & Entrepreneurial Activity

44. Slovak legal system defines both the term 'entrepreneur' and the term 'entrepreneurial activity'. According to the definition, the term entrepreneur or merchant (*podnikatel'*) has several meanings. Generally, it is used as a term for all entities engaged in business/entrepreneurial activities. Yet a dividing line should be drawn between individuals – being entrepreneurs and legal entities carrying out business activities. According to the Commercial Code, the entrepreneur is:

(1) a person registered in the Commercial Register;
(2) a person who operates on the basis of Business Licence (*živnostenské oprávnenie*);
(3) a person who operates on the bases of other types of licence;
(4) a natural person who carries out agricultural production and is registered in the evidence under a special regulation.[5]

45. The entrepreneurs under numbers one to three might be both natural and legal persons. According to section 21 of the Commercial Code also foreign persons (non-residents) are authorized to engage in business activities in Slovakia. A non-resident is entitled to conduct business in the territory of the Slovak Republic starting from the date of registration of its enterprise or an organizational unit thereof into the Companies Register to the extent of the scope of business recorded therein. The definition of 'foreign person' is wider than the definition given for Slovak citizens, as Slovakia has to accept any type of entrepreneur, provided it holds authorization in its home state, irrespective of whether it is from or outside of the EU.

46. According to the Commercial Code, 'entrepreneurial activity' means a systemic activity conducted independently by an entrepreneur in his/her own name and his/her own responsibility for the purpose of profit.[6] Thus, before an activity is considered to be entrepreneurial, several conditions have to be fulfilled. Carrying out activities independently in one's own name expresses the independence of the entrepreneur from someone else, and therefore it cannot be seen as any subordinate relationship, as in that case it would be a dependent employment and not independent entrepreneurship. The liability aspect, where the entrepreneur conducts the activity in his/her own name and his/her own responsibility, demonstrates the individual liability of the entrepreneur for his/her own actions. In a case of an illegal action, it

4. Marek, K., Žváčková, L. *Obchodní podmínky, obchodní zvyklosti a vykládací pravidla.* 1. vydání. Praha: ASPI, Wolters Kluwer, 2008, ss 67–68.
5. Section 2 of the Commercial Code.
6. Section 2 of the Commercial Code.

will be the entrepreneur himself being held responsible. Lastly, the main purpose of the entrepreneurial activity is to make profit. Essentially, even in cases where one is unsuccessful, the mere intent is decisive.

I. Natural Persons

47. Natural persons resident in Slovakia are allowed to carry out any business activity under either Business Licence or other types of licence or carry out agricultural production. Natural persons usually decide to form a legal entity in order to legally separate their own personal estate from their entrepreneurial activity. However, in a case a natural person does not dispose of with a sufficient start-up capital, he is still permitted to start his/her own business once he obtains the Business Licence. In such case, he is known as '*živnostník*'. Depending on the specific activities of the individual, the process for obtaining a Business Licence may be either very simple or may take longer if additional concession is required.[7] There are three types of business licences:

(1) Craftsmanship.
(2) Fixed Licence.
(3) Free Licence.

48. In order to obtain the Business Licence for Craftsmanship, a professional qualification in relevant apprenticeship is required (e.g., metalworking, enamelling or watchmaking). In the case of Fixed Licences, other types of qualification than in the case of craftsmanship is required (e.g., installation, repair, testing and implementation of technical equipment *or* production of weapons or ammunition), while concerning the Free Licence, the person has to meet only general conditions, as legal age (18 years), full legal capacity and integrity.

49. It is not only a natural person that is obliged to acquire a Business Licence but also a company registered within the Slovak Commercial Register need to obtain their licences in order to carry out their business activities in the specific field.

50. The other category of entrepreneurs contains those individuals who obtain other than the Business Licence and who are not registered in the Commercial Register. This category as well includes natural persons together with legal persons whose business activity is comprehensively governed by special regulation. These regulations lay down the conditions both for exercising a certain profession and for obtaining the required licence. Within this category, one can find attorneys, court executors, notaries or veterinarians who are registered with a competent authority.

7. For more *see* Act No. 455/1991 Coll. on Business License (*o živnostenskom podnikaní*).

51. Concerning the last type of entrepreneurial activity – the agricultural production – it may be only a natural person who carries out the agricultural production while being registered in the evidence under a special regulation.[8]

II. Companies & Cooperative

52. Under the Commercial Code, a company is a legal entity established for the purposes of entrepreneurial activities. There are four forms of companies and one form of cooperative, which may be established under the Slovak law:

(1) Unlimited Partnership (*Verejná obchodná spoločnosť'*).
(2) Limited Partnership (*Komanditná spoločnosť'*).
(3) Limited Liability Company (*Spoločnosť' s ručením obmedzeným*).
(4) Joint-Stock Company (*Akciová spoločnosť'*).
(5) Cooperative (*Družstvo*).

53. The provisions of the Commercial Code governing various forms of companies stipulate the extent to which the shareholders/partners are liable for the obligations of the company/partnership. The Slovak Republic, as a member of the EU, recognizes also legal entities that are established under the law of the EU, such as the European Company (Societas Europea).

54. A foreign person may, in accordance with the provision of the Commercial Code, participate as a co-founder in the establishment of a Slovak legal entity for the purposes of carrying out business activity. A foreign person may also establish a Slovak legal entity himself or herself and become the sole founder of Slovak legal entity, as long as the law permits a single founder or a single shareholder. A Slovak legal entity may be established only under Slovak law, unless otherwise provided by the law or law of the EU.

III. Being a Consumer

55. According to the Slovak civil law and consumer protection law, a consumer may be also a natural or even a legal person, who acquires goods and/or services for its personal use or for the needs of members of their household. Therefore, it should be kept in mind that the notion of a consumer is established broadly and among legal persons one should understand predominantly civic organizations, foundations or charities. For more on protection of consumers *see* Part II, Chapter 5.

56. Pursuant to the Consumer Protection Act,[9] consumers have the right to products and services in standard quality, as well as a right to complaint, compensation

8. For more *see* Act No. 105/1990 Coll. on Private Business of Citizens.
9. Consumer Protection Act No. 250/2007 Coll.

and information protection of their health, safety and economic interests. A consumer is entitled to file motions and complaints with the supervisory authority – the Slovak Trade Inspection. The Civil Code prohibits unfair terms, i.e., provisions that cause a significant imbalance in the rights and duties of the parties to the detriments of consumers in consumer contracts. Prohibited are also unfair commercial practices. The unfair commercial practices are considered such practices that are: (1) contrary to the requirements of professional diligence, and that (2) materially distort or are likely to distort the economic behaviour of the average consumer in connection with the product or service. Particularly misleading actions and misleading omissions together with the aggressive commercial practices are considered as unfair commercial practices. A list of unfair commercial practices forms part of the Consumer Protection Act – Annex No. 1.

IV. Legal Consequences of the Qualification of an Act as Entrepreneurial Activity

57. While carrying out the entrepreneurial activities, entrepreneurs enter into numerous legal relations every day. They manifest their will towards third persons in order to achieve desired goals. The entrepreneur must be entitled to his/her rights and obligations and he/she must have legal capacity. Furthermore, the action of an entrepreneur must meet certain requirements of a legal act. His/her will must be free, real and deliberate. An entrepreneur cannot claim a 'mistake', given the fact that he/she shall be a professional in a certain field and a mistake per se should be thus limited and, whereas, when it is not limited, the entrepreneur carries the occupational risk, according to the Commercial Code (section 267). The manifestation of his/her will has to be comprehensible, specific and in the prescribed form. At the same time, the subject of a legal action must be possible and permissible.[10]

58. Under the Civil Code, both natural and legal persons have the capacity to acquire rights and assume obligation – i.e., legal capacity. This feature then allows natural and legal persons to enter into disperse legal relations. Concerning the legal persons, according to the Commercial Code, it is the statutory authority of a company which is acting on its behalf. The Commercial Code further elaborates on who is the statutory authority in different forms of companies. In the case of Unlimited Partnership, all of the partners can represent the partnership and act as the statutory authority; in Limited Partnership, it is only the general partner, who is fully liable for the actions of the Partnership. Concerning the Limited Liability Company (LLC), it may be one or more representatives (*konateľ*), while in the case of Joint-Stock Company (JSC) and Cooperative, it is the Board of Directors (*predstavenstvo*), which acts in the name of the legal entity.

10. The general regulation on legal actions can be found in the Civil Code, Act No. 40/1964 Coll. ss 34–51.

59. The scope of the representation by a statutory body is governed directly by the law, which provides that the statutory body represents the company in all matters. Thus, this type of legal representation is unlimited. However, it is possible to limit the representation, either in Articles of Incorporation contractually or by a decision of state authority, though such limitation is deemed unenforceable against third parties, even if they were aware of this limitation. However, in a case that statutory body exceeds its powers, a company is fully entitled to require refunds or in a worst-case scenario sue the statutory body for the breach. In any case, it is the obligation of all companies to specify the form of representation, which will be subsequently registered within the Commercial Register. This form of representation, e.g., whether it is one or more member statutory body and whether they act jointly or separately, will have legal consequences on the third parties, which shall be aware of this and act accordingly. The reasoning behind this shifted liability is that third parties may anytime consult the Commercial Register in order to ensure who and in what form is able to bind a company.

60. In 2018, several revisions of the Commercial Code took place and extended the liability of statutory bodies, members of the statutory bodies, liquidators and legal representatives of companies in the event of failure to file a bankruptcy petition on time. In such cases, the statutory representatives and liquidators are liable for damage caused to the creditors by the breach of this obligation. If no other amount of damages is proven, it is assumed that the creditors have suffered damage to the extent of the unsatisfied claim. Where a bankruptcy petition is not filed in time, even if bankruptcy is not declared, or the execution of similar proceedings against the company is terminated due to lack of assets, the statutory bodies become liable.

61. In a case of direct representation of companies towards the third parties, the statutory authority is a person who manifests the will on behalf of the company and who binds it in connection with third parties. However, there might be circumstances where the authority to represent the company is vested in different person than the statutory authority, so-called indirect representation. The legal ground for such authorization could be either a statutory provision of an act or a decision of a state authority – a statutory representation (in case of insolvency proceeding, a trustee is nominated by the court and from that moment on represents the company) or a contractual representation, where the legal basis for representation is the contract, usually a power of attorney.

A. *Obligations of Merchants*

62. All entrepreneurs have to comply with the statutory time limits related to their obligations. Some responsibilities are only generally set in a statute and some have to be fulfilled by an exact day (e.g., for income tax return for the previous year it is 31 March) or within a limited period. Overall, it is possible to divide the obligations of entrepreneur into the following set of actions:

(1) Register with the Commercial Register.[11]
(2) Registration and reporting requirements, advancement payments arising from the Law on Income Tax.[12]
(3) Registration and reporting requirements under the Law on VAT.[13]
(4) Registration and reporting requirements under the laws governing the excise duties (e.g., mineral oil, tobacco products, beer, wine and spirits).[14]
(5) Reporting obligation under the law governing motor vehicle tax.[15]
(6) Reporting obligation under the law governing the property tax.[16]
(7) Enrolment, reporting requirements and payment obligations of advances to the authorities of health insurance.
(8) Enrolment and reporting requirements to the Social Insurance Agency.
(9) Obligation to conclude a contract due to compulsory insurance for liability for damage caused by motor vehicles.
(10) Obligations associated with the employment of people with disabilities.
(11) Archives and fillings.
(12) Personal data protection.
(13) Combating money laundering.

B. Rules Applying to Commercial Relationships Only

63. According to Slovak law, the rules applying to commercial relationships either stem out directly from the Commercial Code itself in its third part or they are civil law obligations per se but due to the type of the subjects – entrepreneurs – they are perceived as commercial law relationships. Nevertheless, all commercial relationships are based on the following principles:

(1) Principle of equality.
(2) Fair trade practices.
(3) Informality.

64. Based on the above-stated, it is possible to classify commercial relationships into four groups.

---

11. For more *see* Act No. 530/2003 Coll. on Commercial Registry (*o obchodnom registri*).
12. For more *see* Act No. 595/2003 Coll. on Income Tax (*o dani z príjmov*).
13. For more *see* Act No. 222/2004 Coll. on Value Added Tax (*o dani z pridanej hodnoty*).
14. For more *see* Act No. 98/2004 Coll. on Excise Duty on Mineral Oil, Act No. 105/2004 Coll. on Excise Duty on Spirits, Act No. 530/2011 Coll. on Excise Duty on Alcoholic Beverages, Act No. 106/2004 Coll. on Excise Duty on Tobacco Products and Act No. 609/2007 Coll. on Excise Duty on Electricity, Coal and Gas.
15. For more *see* Act No. 582/2004 Coll. on Municipal Taxes and Fees for Municipal Waste and Construction Waste (*o miestnych daniach a miestnom poplatku za komunálne odpady a drobné stavebné odpady*).
16. *Ibid.*

1. Relative Commercial Relationships

65. Relative Commercial Relationships are defined in section 261(1) of the Commercial Code as obligations existing between entrepreneurs, if according to the relevant circumstances it is obvious that they are regarding their respective business activities. The reason why these relationships are deemed 'relative' is due to the fact that their commercial character is based on the subjects – the entrepreneurs in connection with their business activity. Thus, there are three conceptual features of relative commercial relationship:

(1) Subjects are entrepreneurs on both sides of the contractual relationship.
(2) Object is business activity of both subjects.
(3) Explicitness that it is the business activity, which is the subject of the contractual relationship.

The relative commercial relationships may therefore never be unilateral, but only bilateral. In a case that one of the parties would subsequently change its legal status, e.g., terminate its business activities, nothing will change on their reciprocal relationship. There is a second group of relative contractual relationships, where one of the contractual parties is a state or its body.[17]

2. Absolute Commercial Relationships

66. Since 1 February 2013, the Commercial Code has exhaustively been specified in sections 261(6) et seq. contractual relationships, which are always governed by the Commercial Code, irrespective of the subjects.[18] However, when one of the

---

17. *See* for more details Part I, Chapter 1, §3, V.
18. Among these, in the light of s. 261(6), there are the following: (a) among the founders of partnerships and companies, between partners, members and shareholders and their partnership or company, as well as between the partners, members and shareholders themselves, relations concerning participation on the partnership or the company and relations arising from agreements on transfer of ownership interest, the relations between a statutory body (or a members of a statutory body), the supervisory body of a partnership or company and the partnership and the company alone, and also the relations between the partners, members or shareholders and the partnership and the company alone related to the business of the company, as well as the obligations arising between the procurator and the partnership or the company related to the performance of duties by the procurator; (b) between the founders of a cooperative as well as between a member and his cooperative, as regards relations concerning participation on the cooperative and relations arising from agreements on transfer of ownership interest, and relations between the member of a statutory body and a supervisory body of the cooperative and relations between the procurator and the cooperative arising out of the performance of his duties; (c) ensuing from stock exchange deals and brokerage contracts (s. 642), as well as from other contracts for pecuniary interest relating to; (d) contracts for the sale of an enterprise or its parts (s. 476), a credit contract (s. 497), a contract on inspection activities (s. 591), a forwarding contract (s. 601), a contract on the operation of transport vehicles (s. 638), a silent partners contract (s. 673), a contract on opening a letter of credit (s. 682), a contract on money collection (s. 692), a contract on bank deposit (s. 700), a contract on a current account (s. 708) and a contract on a deposit account (s. 716 below); and (e) right from a bank guarantee (s. 313), a traveller's cheque (s. 720) or a promise of indemnity (s. 725).

parties is a consumer, the general protection of consumers under the Civil Code is applicable and the absolute commercial relationships become relative and the consumer enjoys its full protection under the Civil Code and the relevant acts on consumer protection. Given the fact that the EU consumer protection instruments do not recognize the dualism of some of the Member States, it might be advisable for Slovak legislators to abandon the specification of absolute and relative commercial relationship due to the widely accepted notion of consumer protection in the EU.

3. Absolute Non-commercial Relationships

67. Absolute non-commercial relationships are those kinds of contracts, which are concluded between two or more entrepreneurs and are directly connected to their business activities, but laws other than the Commercial Code will govern these relationships (e.g., in the case of real estate, the applicable law is always the Civil Code).

4. Facultative Commercial Relationships

68. According to section 262 of the Commercial Code, parties may agree that the Commercial Code will govern their contractual relationship, unless it is excluded by other provisions, namely section 261 of the Commercial Code. In these cases, such agreement has to be in writing. From the comparative perspective, this provision of the Commercial Code is quite uncommon as it allows persons to apply the Commercial Code to their relationships, which theoretically means that even non-entrepreneurs can agree to fulfil the obligations as stated by the Commercial Code and not by the Civil Code.[19] However, again, the obligatory protection of consumers steps in, thus the relation will be ultimately co-governed by the civil law. This sometimes may render some relationships and their legal character uncertain.

V. The Commercial Activities of Public Bodies

69. The state, regions, districts, towns, and other state authorities participate in many aspects of the economic well-being of a country; it is not otherwise in Slovakia. In principle, the public authorities and the bodies created by them (Slovak Television, Social Insurance Agency or public universities) are under private law considered to be legal entities and the law applies to them without any exception. Naturally, state, regional units as well as other public authorities are governed by specific acts, which identify their main aims and objectives, as well as proceedings that govern their relationships with natural or legal persons. Slovakia has a substantive body of administrative law. Their legal liability is to the same extent enforceable as in a case of privately formed companies. However, in certain cases, e.g.,

19. Such approach was taken in the decision of the Czech Supreme Court from 30 Jun. 2003 sp. Zn. 32 Odo 964/2003.

hospitals, the practical enforceability of a financial award might be problematic due to the fact that some of the institutions may lack funding and thus the court executor cannot proceed with the liquidation of their assets as under the specific law they are protected from proclaiming bankrupt. Moreover, the tax and accountancy laws differ from those applicable to private companies (public JSCs included).[20]

70. Public bodies are included within the second group of Relative Commercial Relationships in the Commercial Code sections 261(2) et seq. The Commercial Code defines which entities of public law in connection with their entrepreneurial activities will be bound by the Commercial Code. They are the following:

(1) State agency (*štátny orgán*).
(2) Municipality (*obec*).
(3) Higher territorial unit (*vyšší územný celok*).
(4) Association of legal persons, where at least of the members is constituted under public law.
(5) Any legal entity incorporated or constituted for the purpose of fulfilling needs of general interest, which have no manufacturing or commercial character and:
   (a) is wholly or substantially financed by a public law entity;
   (b) is controlled by a public law entity; or
   (c) the public law entity appoints or elects more than half of its governing body or inspection authority.

Once one of the contractual parties is one of the above-stated entities and the object of the contractual relationship is directly connected to business activities of the contractual parties, the Commercial Code applies. In the case of state, its regional units and public authorities, it is sufficient if the object of the contractual relationship is to ensure public goods and needs.[21]

§4. Importance of International and Supranational Law

71. In a widely globalized world, where the parties conclude their contracts across the entire world, coming from different legal traditions and different jurisdictions, apprehending the importance of the economic perspective of their relationships, the understanding and application of foreign law is inescapable.

72. Choice of law is one of the manifestations of the contractual freedom and autonomy. In private international law as well as in EU law, this autonomy manifests just the right to choose. Slovakia being the Member State of the EU adopted

20. There is a number of activities which is exempt from tax, for more *see* Act No. 595/2003 Coll. on Income Tax (*o dani z príjmov*).
21. Neither the Commercial Code nor any other statute defines public goods and needs. Therefore, one needs to apply general law doctrine and relevant case law, which suggest that a *'reliable indicator could be the financing from public funds'*.

a number of legal acts, which have direct impact on private parties and the applicable laws. On the national level, the choice of law is governed by the Act on Private International Law,[22] which used to be the main conflicts of law act, governing the relationship with subjects and objects of the contractual relationship with foreign/international element,[23] until the Rome I Regulation[24] and Brussels I and II Regulations[25] substantively replaced it. Now, the Act on Private International Law is still in force but only to a limited extent and not without EU connecting factors.

---

22. Act No. 97/1963 Coll. on Private International Law (*o medzinárodnom práve súkromnom a procesnom*).
23. Under the Slovak law, the foreign/international element is the fact that is directly related to private relationship between two and more parties and has an international character. It can be these following scenarios: (a) person/entity has a nationality, residence or place of business in different state? (b) a legally significant event for the creation and existence of the relationship, which occurred abroad; (c) the object of the relationship is situated abroad; and (d) legal relationship that is ancillary to the main legal relationship is governed by a foreign law.
24. Regulation (EC) No. 593/2008 of the European Parliament and of the Council of 17 Jun. 2008 on the law applicable to contractual obligations (Rome I).
25. The new recast Brussel I Regulation No. 1215/2012 of the European Parliament and of the Council of 12 Dec. 2012 on jurisdiction and the recognition and enforcement of judgments in civil and commercial matters has been applicable since 10 Jan. 2015. It has substituted Council Regulation (EC) No. 44/2001 of 22 Dec. 2000 on jurisdiction and the recognition and enforcement of judgments in civil and commercial matters and Council Regulation (EC) No. 2201/2003 of 27 Nov. 2003 concerning jurisdiction and the recognition and enforcement of judgments in matrimonial matters and the matters of parental responsibility, repealing Regulation (EC) No. 1347/2000.

Chapter 2. The Economic Operators

73. Under Slovak law, the economic operators might be natural persons, companies or even public bodies and institutions. The main aim that the economic operators should follow is the financial profit. Within this chapter, different types of legal entities carrying out business activities will be described and analysed.

§1. Personal Status of Merchants

I. In General

74. The capacity of natural persons to have rights and obligations comes into existence in the moment of birth. However, according to the Slovak law, also conceived baby (*nasciturus*) has the capacity of natural person, if born alive. This capacity lapses by death. Minors have the ability to undertake such legal rights and duties, which are adequate for their intellectual and mental maturity. On the other side, the legal capacity (by one's own actions to acquire rights and assume duties) arises in full by reaching adulthood – turning 18 years old. Before turning 18 years old, one can become adult by entering into marriage, and thus have full legal capacity. Such acquired adulthood will not cease to exist, even in the case of dissolution of marriage or marriage annulment before the eighteenth year.

75. If a natural person due to a mental disorder, which is not only temporary, is not able to carry out legal actions and acts, the court shall deprive him of his legal capacity. In a case that a natural person due to a mental disorder, which is not only temporary, or due to excessive consumption of alcohol or intoxicants or poisons, is able to carry out only limited amount of legal actions, the court shall limit person's legal capacity and specify the extent of person's legal capacity in its decision. Naturally, the court shall modify or revoke the deprivation or the limitation of one's legal capacity if the circumstances change.[26]

II. Married People

76. Married people can exercise a commercial activity without any formal or informal authorization of their spouse. However, according to section 143 of the Civil Code, both of the spouses contribute to their conjugal joint property, and therefore in the light of section 148a of the Civil Code, if a spouse wants to use any part of the conjugal joint property for his or her own entrepreneurial activity, he or she has to obtain consent of the other spouse. After such consent, the entrepreneurial spouse does no longer need any further consent for other business-related legal acts.

26. *See* Act No. 40/1964 Coll. Civil Code ss 7–10.

77. The conjugal joint property could be broadly defined as a set of ownership rights of both spouses to those things that they have acquired during their marriage. The basic characteristic feature of the conjugal joint ownership is that there is no quantitatively determined share of the ownership rights of the spouses. Thus, the spouses have equal property rights to their joint property. However, section 143 of the Civil Code specifies those objects that fall outside of the conjugal joint property. By virtue of law, the conjugal joint property does not include the following:

(1) Objects obtained by inheritance.
(2) Objects obtained by donation.
(3) Objects, which by their nature are of a personal or professional use only of one spouse.
(4) Objects obtained in a restitution procedure by one of the spouses.

78. Concerning the authorization under section 148a of the Civil Code to use the objects of the conjugal joint ownership, it is necessary to point out that there is a dispute among the legal professionals whether the authorization should be general or specific. However, according to the literal interpretation of the provision, it is our belief that the authorization should be general and thus provide consent of one of the spouses that the other spouse is entitled to use any (unspecified) property for the purpose of his or her entrepreneurial activity.[27] Neither the provision of section 148a of the Civil Code nor any other provision specifies the form of such authorization. Therefore, it is sufficient if the consent of a spouse is made orally or even implicitly.[28]

79. The conjugal joint property includes all movable and immovable property, assets and liabilities acquired by either spouse or both spouses during their marriage, since the day, which is listed on their marriage certificate. The conjugal joint property ceases to exist in different ways. First, it can be dissolved by a divorce – the effective date of the judgment of the divorce. In the case that spouses live separately in different households but are not divorced, the conjugal joint ownership continues to exist and all the property that one of the partners acquires, unless specified otherwise by the law, forms a part of the joint ownership.

80. Second, the conjugal joint ownership can be modified by an agreement in the form of a notarial deed or spouses reserve the creation of the conjugal joint ownership as of a day of dissolution of the marriage. In the agreement, both spouses expand or narrow down the extent of their joint ownership or they can even completely dissolve their joint ownership. In a notarial agreement, it is sufficient that spouses divide their joint property and if any property remains within their conjugal

---

27. In Czech Civil Code, since amendment No. 91/1998 Coll., it is possible for a spouse to give the consent to a specific property within the joint property.
28. *See* the decision of Supreme Court of Czech Republic, dated 23 Feb. 1999, file No. 2 Cdon 2072/1997.

joint property, they should define how they will be using it. This settlement agreement shall be then signed in front of a public notary and be registered within the public notarial register.

81. Third, the conjugal joint ownership can be dissolved by a decision of a court. In the case that spouses are unable to find an amicable solution concerning the dissolution of the conjugal joint property, one of the spouses can motion the court to dissolve the joint property once the other spouse has already received his or her Business Licence. Concerning a situation, where both of the spouses obtained their separate Business Licence, any of them may petition the court to dissolve their joint ownership.

82. If the spouses carry out the business activity together and they dissolved their conjugal joint ownership, they shall distribute their revenue in accordance with their written agreement. In a case where such contract had not been concluded, the income is to be distributed equally. In an event, the spouses did not limit or dissolve their conjugal joint property, according to section 147 of the Civil Code, any debt that arises from the activity of the other spouse during the marriage may be enforced or satisfied from the assets of the conjugal joint property. However, in the moment of declaration of bankruptcy, the conjugal joint ownership terminates *ex lege.* If the conjugal joint ownership has not been yet dissolved, the trustee – administrator of the bankruptcy – may perform the settlement instead of the bankrupt, including filing the application of the settlement with the competent court. Any former settlement, which came into force within six months before the declaration of bankruptcy is reviewed and if the settlement is extending the scope of the spouse, which originally belonged only to the bankrupt, such settlement – part of the settlement – is invalid. In the event that the bankrupt married during the bankruptcy proceeding, the law provides that the conjugal joint ownership arises only in the moment of the revocation of the bankruptcy proceeding.

III. Foreigners

83. All EU citizens benefit from the freedom of movement and freedom of establishment, which is applicable, both for natural persons and for the legal persons. Nevertheless, according to section 21 of the Commercial Code, all foreigners may carry out their business activities in the territory of the Slovak Republic under the same conditions and to the same extent as Slovak entities and persons, unless the law stipulates otherwise. In the case of EU nationals, the procedure is to a certain extent simplified.

84. First, it is necessary to understand who is considered to be a foreigner under the commercial law. Foreigners are natural persons resident or legal person established outside of the territory of the Slovak Republic. Entrepreneurial activities of foreigners shall be understood as the foreigner has either a branch or a company located in Slovak territory. The authorization for a foreigner to perform its business activities is valid from the day of the registration of its branch or company in the

Commercial Register. Concerning the foreigners from the EU Member States or OECD states, those who are registered within the registers of these Member States are not required to register with the Commercial Register in the Slovak Republic; however, they are required to obtain Business Licence if they want to provide such activities in the territory of the Slovak Republic. Furthermore, a foreigner may participate in the establishment of a legal entity, establish any legal entity by himself or herself or become a shareholder of an existing legal entity. In this case, all foreigners have the same legal obligations as Slovak nationals. Moreover, a foreigner can transfer the seat of its company to the Slovak Republic. One of the main requirements is that the home state has to allow such relocation. This possibility is much more feasible for entrepreneurs who have their seat of business in the Member States of the EU. However, giving the fact that the EU is not unified as to the rules governing the nationality of a company or an entrepreneur, natural persons, including foreigner, shall broadly research also their home state legal framework before registering with the Commercial Register in the Slovak Republic.

§2. Companies (Partnerships & Corporations & Cooperatives)

85. Under Slovak law, in conjunction with the law of the EU, there are a number of legal entities, which can be established for business purposes. Thus, in the following part, we will refer to them as companies – those legal entities which are established under the commercial law.

I. Historical Development

86. Within the territory of the Slovak Republic, there have been distinct legal orders, which were applicable in different historical intervals. In the twentieth century, there have been several laws, namely law No. 11/1918 of the Collection of Laws and Regulation, the Civil Code of 1950, Civil Code of 1964, which played the role of the basic regulation of private contractual relationships. The Civil Code of 1950 first recognized the capacity of legal persons, which were entitled to rights and obligations. The Civil Code of 1964 then introduced instead of the term 'legal person' the concept of 'socialist organization'. Nevertheless, after 1989, due to the changes in socio-economic conditions, the Civil Code was extensively amended. In 1991 the first Commercial Code, which is still valid, was adopted. Since 1991, the Commercial Code has gone through a number of amendments and changes due to the development of market economy together with the accession to the EU. Nowadays, it could be said that the Commercial Code of the Slovak Republic could be as to its efficiency compared to other commercial codes of Western countries.

II. Notion of Legal Entity under Slovak Law

87. Slovak jurisprudence and practice are based predominantly on positivist theory of the fictitious legal entity, which in simple terms sees the legal entity as a juridical fiction that has no basis in the real world. The general notion of legal persons is to be found in the Civil Code in section 18 and the following provisions. However, the legislator leaves out a specific definition of a legal entity. The Civil Code only stipulates that legal persons also have legal capacity and then it enumerates the types of legal persons that are recognized under Slovak law, *see* Part I, Chapter 1.

88. Section 56 of the Commercial Code defines that a company is a legal entity established for the purposes of carrying out business activities. Both natural and legal persons may become founders of companies and may participate in business activities of such companies, unless the law provides otherwise. Before going to the particularities of different types of companies, the basic concept of legal person and its historical development should be defined under the Slovak law.

III. Different Types of Companies & Cooperatives

89. The current legal framework of the Slovak Republic differentiates between the two main groups of companies, which then subdivide into specific types of companies:

(1) Personal Companies:
   (a) Unlimited Partnership (*Verejná obchodná spoločnost'*).
   (b) Limited Partnership (*Komanditná spoločnost'*).
(2) Capital Companies:
   (a) Limited Liability Company (*Spoločnost' s ručením obmedzeným*).
   (b) Joint-Stock Company (*Akciová Spoločnost'*).
   (c) Simple Joint-Stock Company (*Jednoduchá spoločnost'na akcie*).

In addition to the above-stated, the Slovak Commercial Code recognizes also a Cooperative (*Družstvo*) as a type of a company.

A. General Introduction

90. All companies, irrespective of their character, come into existence on the day, on which they were registered within the Commercial Register. The proposal for registration must be filed within ninety days after the company was established, or after any document, which demonstrates its business activities (e.g., Business Licence) have been issued. If the Articles of Associations or other incorporating documents do not specify that the company was established for a definite period, it is established for an indefinite period. All legal acts concerning the incorporation, establishment, alteration, cancellation or termination of the company shall be in writing. The law further specifies for which the notarial deed is required.

91. Before a company is registered, according to section 64 of the Commercial Code, persons acting on behalf of the company are jointly and severally liable for such actions. If the partners, shareholders or other statutory authorities of the company approve their actions within three months, the company itself becomes bound to third parties. Until the company is registered, it should not take over any other obligations than those associated with the establishment of the company.

92. Any company ceases to exist on the date of its deletion of the Commercial Register, unless the law stipulates otherwise. Before a company is deleted from the Commercial Register, it has to be dissolved with or without liquidation, if its assets are transferred to its legal successor. The liquidation is not required, if the company has no assets or if the notion for bankruptcy proceeding was dismissed, halted or cancelled due to insufficient assets to cover the expenses and remuneration of the trustee in bankruptcy proceeding. If the bankruptcy proceeding is completed and company disposes of any assets, the liquidation is required. If after the bankruptcy proceeding, there are no assets left, the company is directly deleted by a court from the Commercial Register without liquidation. For more on liquidation *see* Part I, Chapter 6.

93. The Articles of Incorporation or Articles of Association or other relevant internal statutory documents specify all obligations of the partners, shareholders and other participating persons within the company. They are generally very flexible legal documents, which govern the relationships between the partners, shareholders and different bodies of companies. The Commercial Code provides for general default clauses, in a case that the involved parties do not wish to specify more or differently their relationships, rights and obligation within the Articles of Incorporation or Association or other relevant internal documents. In the case they do, such specification prevails.

B. Unlimited Partnership (Verejná Obchodná Spoločnost')

94. An Unlimited Partnership[29] is a company, in which at least two persons are participating and carrying out business activities under a common name and are jointly and severally liable for the obligations and debts of the Partnership with all their property. The rights and duties of the partners are governed by the Articles of Association. In an event, partners decide to change the Articles of Association, the consent of all partners is required, unless the Articles of Association provide otherwise.

95. All of the partners are entitled to represent the company and act on its behalf, unless the Articles of Association specify other forms of management of the Unlimited Partnership. If the partners agree that there will be a specific person/s representing the Partnership and managing the Partnership, the remaining partners loose the right to full extent. The managing partner should decide in accordance with the majority decision of partners. Unless the Articles of Association specify otherwise, all partners shall have one vote. Partners may repeal the managing partners if the

29. Governed by ss 76–92 of the Commercial Code.

other partners so decide. In a case that the managing partner is in substantive breach of its obligation according to section 345(2) of the Commercial Code, a court shall revoke its mandate based on a motion of any of the partners, even if such mandate is irrevocable according to the Articles of Association. In any case, the managing partner shall, upon request of any partner, inform on all the matters of the partnership. Each partner is entitled to inspect the documents of the partnership.

96. Partners divide the profit equally, unless the Articles of Association do not specify a different method for profit distribution. A new partner may enter the partnership by a way of modification of the Articles of Association. Any partner can withdraw from the partnership, if at least two partners remain. Concerning the further competition with the partnership, the Articles of Association may specify the extent of non-compete clause. However, the general rule is that during the existence of the partnership, partners shall refrain from competing with the partnership. If the partnership ceases to exist, and the liquidation is carried out, the partners are entitled to a share, according to the value of their paid deposit in the partnership. The rest of the liquidation balance shall be divided equally between the partners. If the liquidation balance is not sufficient to recover deposits paid, the amounts shall be repaid in proportion to the height of the initial deposits. The Articles of Association may modify the form of redistribution of liquidation proceeds.

C. Limited Partnership (Komanditná Spoločnosť)

97. A Limited Partnership[30] is a partnership where the liability of one or more partners for the company's obligations and debts is limited to the amount of any unpaid partner's investment, but not less than EUR 250, and the liability of one or more of the other partners remains unlimited. The former are referred to as a limited partner, the latter as a general partner. The business name of the Limited Partnership should not include the name of the limited partner. If it does, the limited partner loses his limited status and is liable for obligations of the Limited Partnership as a general partner.

98. Only the general partners are entitled to participate in the management of the partnership. In all other matters, the general partners decide jointly and the limited partners decide by the majority of their vote, unless the Articles of Association provide otherwise. During the voting, all partners have one vote, unless agreed otherwise. The general partners represent the statutory body of the Limited Partnership. If the Articles do not provide otherwise, all general partners are entitled to act on behalf of the partnership. A limited partner is liable for the unauthorized obligation entered on behalf of the partnership to the same extent as a general partner – jointly and severally.

99. Concerning the distribution of profits, the Articles of Association provide for the general separation between the general and limited partners. If the Articles are

30. Governed by ss 93–104 of the Commercial Code.

silent on the subject, the profits divide 50:50. These are then divided among the general partners equally and among the limited partners pro rata to their paid-up investments. Any partner can withdraw from the partnership, if at least two partners remain. If all limited partners withdraw from the corporation, the general partners may agree to change their form and become an Unlimited Partnership. If the partnership ceases to exist, and the liquidation is carried out, the partners are entitled to a share, according to the value of their paid deposit in the partnership. If the amount of the liquidation balance is not sufficient, the general partners have a prior right to recover their deposits. The rest of the liquidation balance shall be divided between the partners in an equal manner as the profit. The Articles of Association may modify the form of redistribution of liquidation proceeds.

D. Limited Liability Company (Spoločnost' s Ručením Obmedzeným)

100. The liability of shareholders of a LLC[31] is limited to the amount of unpaid deposits. A sole shareholder may establish a LLC; however, the maximum number of shareholders is fifty. If two or more shareholders establish the LLC, they conclude the Articles of Association. If only one shareholder establishes the company, a Foundation Deed replaces the Articles of Association. A LLC is liable for any breach of its obligation with its entire property, while the shareholder is liable only to the amount of his or her outstanding contribution registered in the Commercial Register. From 1 January 2015, new provisions regarding the LLC were adopted. Before, the minimum capital of LLC in Slovakia is EUR 5,000 and the minimum deposit of a shareholder is EUR 750. LLC, which has registered capital of less than EUR 5,000, may pay out the shares of profit only to three-fourths of the company's net profit. Moreover, a company cannot pay the shares of profit if such action would cause the decline of the company. If the company breaches this provision, the company's creditors can seek repayment of the above claims and if they no longer may obtain their financial claims, the company's managers shall be responsible.

101. In 2018, a number of new provisions have entered into force to provide additional protection to creditors. Therefore, an LLC cannot be established by a person who is listed on the list of tax debtors under a special regulation or on the list of debtors of the Social Insurance Company. There can be special circumstances, under which the Social Insurance Company will grant consent. Such consent then must be attached to the application for entry in the Commercial Register.

102. Company's share/ownership interest reflects the rights and obligations of the shareholders. Its amount is determined at the ratio of the registered capital, unless the Articles of Association stipulate otherwise. Simply, the share or ownership interest of a shareholder is usually set as percentage participation in the LLC. Every shareholder may have only one share or ownership interest in a company; however, one share may belong to several shareholders. In this case, only one person – a representative of the entire group of shareholders – may carry out the rights

31. Governed by ss 105–153 of the Commercial Code.

and obligations arising out of owning a share. Shares of an LLC may not be traded publicly. A transfer of the ownership interest to a person who is not another shareholder of the LLC may be executed only with the consent of the General Assembly, if the Articles of Association do not provide otherwise and in addition the signature of the executive of the company must be officially authenticated.

103. The LLC has several bodies. It is the Articles of Association, which may expand, modify (where allowed by the law) and specify the rights and obligations of shareholders and of company's bodies. In certain cases, the shareholders may agree to adopt as well the Statutes of the company as additional non-compulsory internal document of a company, which in greater detail governs the relationship between different bodies. The Statutes of a company should be understood as general implementing intra-company social contract. They cannot contradict the mandatory provisions of law and of the Articles of Association. On the peak of the company, lies the General Assembly, which decides and determines all key issues of the existence and management of the company, e.g., approval of the annual financial statement, approval of the Statutes of a company, approval of the increase or decrease of the registered capital or the appointment, dismissal and remuneration of Executive/s of the company (*konatel'*). There must be at least one Executive, who acts independently unless the Articles of Association provide otherwise. Any restriction on the authority of Executive is invalid as against the third parties. Executive is required to ensure proper record and accounts keeping, keeping the list of shareholders and inform the shareholders of the company's matters. Executive is required to perform his or her duties with due care and in accordance with the interests of a company and all its shareholders. In particular, Executive is required to obtain all available information related to the subject matter of any decision. Furthermore, Executive maintains all the disclosed information and facts in confidentiality. Executive is prohibited from prioritizing his or her own interests as to the interests of the company. If Executive breached any of the obligations laid down by the law, he or she is jointly and severally liable for the damage caused.

104. In addition to the two above-stated mandatory bodies of an LLC, the shareholders may decide to establish also a Supervisory Board with at least three members. Supervisory Board supervises the Executive/s, it reviews the books and accounts of the LLC and informs the General Assembly on the matters of the company within the period specified in the Articles of Association, otherwise annually.

105. According to the new restatement of the Commercial Code in 2014, concerning a cancellation of shareholders' participation in an LLC, a shareholder may not withdraw from a company.[32] Naturally, a shareholder may sell his share in an LLC or petition the court to revoke its participation in the LLC if his participation in the company may not be justly demanded, unless it is a single-member LLC. In that case, a shareholder may either liquidate the entire company or sell it. Furthermore, unless it is a single-member company, declaration of bankruptcy of shareholder's property (assets), suspension of a bankruptcy proceeding due to insufficient

32. *See* s. 148(1) of the Commercial Code.

assets or a rejection of a bankruptcy petition due to lack of assets has the same effect as the cancellation of shareholder's participation in an LLC by a court. Any company may petition a court to expel a shareholder who is seriously violating his/her obligations despite being requested to fulfil his/her duties properly and was warned in writing about the possibility of his/her exclusion. At least half of all the shareholders of an LLC have to agree with such a petition. Each shareholder, whose participation had been cancelled, has a right for a settlement share. Shareholders, if so provided by the Statutes or Articles of Association, may petition a court and seek company's cancellation for the reasons and under the conditions laid down in the law, Articles of Association or in the Founding Deed, or in the Statutes.

E. Joint-Stock Company (Akciová Spoločnosť')

106. A Joint-Stock Company[33] can be characterized as a company, which obligatorily forms its registered capital from the investments of shareholders with the minimum capital of EUR 25,000. The registered capital is divided into a number of shares with a nominal value, which represents the individual investments of the shareholders. The Joint-Stock Company is liable for its debts and obligations with its entire capital, while the individual shareholder is liable only to the nominal value of his or her shares.

107. JSC may be established by at least one shareholder, if it is a legal person, or by two natural persons. If two or more shareholders establish the company, they conclude the Articles of Association. If only one shareholder establishes the company, a Foundation Deed replaces the Articles of Association. Both the Deed and the Articles of Association have to be in a form of a notarial deed. The Commercial Code recognized two methods of establishing a JSC:

(1) Single time: without the initial public offering. In this case, the shareholders agree that they will deposit in certain proportion the entire minimum registered capital.
(2) Gradual: with the initial public offering. In this case, the shareholders provide the minimum capital requirement in the form of the public offering.

108. The Constituent General Assembly completes the entire process of establishment of a JSC, which may not take place in the case of private JSC. In the case of private JSC, the Constituent General Assembly is replaced by a notarial deed. Either by the Constituent General Assembly or by the notarial deed, the shareholders decide on:

(1) Constitution of JSC.
(2) Approval of Statutes of JSC (which *a contrario* to LLC is obligatory).
(3) Approval of the amount of the contributions to the company.

33. Governed by ss 154–220a of the Commercial Code.

(4) Election of the members of the bodies of JSC (which the General Assembly according to the Statutes is entitled to elect).

As a final step, the Board of Directors of Joint Stock Companies signs the application for registration in the Commercial Register. Their signatures must be officially authenticated.

109. The JSC may be private or public. Majority of Joint-Stock Companies are private. Besides establishing a public JSC *ab initio,* the public Joint-Stock Company is considered to be also a company whose shares or the part thereof were accepted to trading venues within a regulated market located or operated within any of the Member States of the European Economic Area.

110. The Statutes of JSC is the basic document that governs the internal relationships in a company. The Statutes form the part of the Articles of Association or of the Foundation Deed. The two-thirds majority of the General Assembly may amend the Statutes. In addition to Statutes, any JSC has to form a Reserved Fund of at least 10% of its initial registered capital. This fund shall be annually replenished to the amount specified in the Statutes, however, of not less than 10% of the net profits reported in the annual financial statements, until the amount reaches the determined sum by the Statutes, not less than 20% of the registered capital.

111. The JSC has the following bodies:

(1) General Assembly.
(2) Board of Directors.
(3) Supervisory Board.

112. The General Assembly is the supreme body of any JSC, which decides on any matters related to the 'life' of the company. It is held at least once a year and all shareholders should participate. Shareholders can participate personally or by proxy. The General Assembly decides on matters like amendments of the Statutes, increase or decrease of the registered capital, appointment and dismissal of the directors in the Board of Directors, appointment and dismissal of members of the Supervisory Board and others.

113. The Board of Directors manages the company and decides on all matters of company unless the Commercial Code of the Statutes provide otherwise. Unless the Statutes provide otherwise, all members of the Board of Directors are entitled to act on behalf of the company. The Board of Directors shall ensure the proper accounting of the company and submit to the General Assembly for an approval the ordinary financial statements as well as the extraordinary financial statements and the proposed distribution of profits or coverage of the losses in accordance with the Statutes. The Board of Directors is obliged to submit the General Assembly at least once a year the information on the major objectives of the company for the next period and the expected development of assets, liabilities and revenues of the company. Those members of the Board of Directors who have breached their obligations vis-à-vis the exercise of their competence are jointly and severally liable for the caused damages. The members of the Board of Directors shall be not held liable if they prove that they carried out their duties with due care and in good faith.

114. The Supervisory Board oversees the activities of the Board of Directors and the company's business. Members of the Supervisory Board are entitled to inspect all documents and records related to the activities of the company and verify that accounting records are properly kept in accordance with the law and with the instructions of the General Assembly. Only a natural person may be a member of the Supervisory Board. The same person cannot be a member of the Board of Directors and of the Supervisory Board.

115. Concerning the distribution of profits and sharing the losses, the Statutes of the JSC may provide for a specific method. In order to pay out the dividends, the JSC has to prove that it was profitable in the former financial year. Otherwise, the JSC may not distribute its profits to shareholders or its other own resource if such action would cause its bankruptcy and if the own capital identified in the approved financial statements was or would be less than the value of the capital jointly with the Reserved Fund, or other funds generated by the company, which by law or the Articles of Association shall be used for company's performance. Furthermore, the obligatory reserve fund has to be replenished and other obligations under the Statute have to be fulfilled. After these are proved, the General Assembly takes the decision and determines whether all or only a part of the income shall be distributed to the shareholders. Following the decision of the General Assembly, a shareholder can claim its dividends.

F. Simple JSC (Jednoduchá spoločnosť na akcie)

116. Since January 2017, it is possible to establish a new type of a capital company – a simple JSC. The introduction of a simple JSC into the legal order of the Slovak Republic represents one of the regulatory measures to support a development of start-up ecosystem in the country. The Government of the Slovak Republic initiated this support in June 2015. The support of start-up ecosystem is represented by three strategic objectives: (1) creating the most suitable business conditions, i.e., creating a regulatory environment without unnecessary barriers to the operations of start-ups on the market; (2) establishing and providing support services to strengthening the start-up ecosystem, i.e., creating necessary infrastructure for start-ups; and (3) supporting financing in particular during the 'Death Valley' period, when most start-ups fail.

117. The simple JSC represents a hybrid corporate form that combines the elements of a LLC (low capital requirements and simple corporate structure) and a JSC (possibility to seek financing from broader public). This corporate form is designed to be the ideal type of business entity for new entrepreneurs, offering a novel comprehensive business venture solution where flexible corporate ownership, establishment and corporate exit options are introduced. When introducing the simple JSC, the aim was to develop a form, which meets the requirements of organizational simplicity, does not require substantial initial capital investment, yet allows for flexible entry and exit of capital, which is ultimately important for investors. This form is also very flexible in regard to provisions of shareholder agreement, offers employees shares and many additional advantages.

118. The simple JSC has its capital divided into a certain number of shares with a specific nominal value. The company is liable for its obligations with all its assets and property, while the shareholders are not liable for the obligations of the company.

119. In comparison to the original JSC, due to the lower capital requirement, the entire value of the company's capital together with all the deposits have to be paid up before the company may be established. One of the basic conditions in regard to the existence of the simple JSC is that the capital may not be raised by virtue of public offering, neither at the company's establishment nor during its existence. The simple JSC may be transformed into a classical JSC. This transformation is regulated by specific provisions in the Commercial Code. It is important to emphasize that the reverse conversion is not feasible. A classical JSC may not be transformed into a simple JSC.

120. In regard to the organizational structure, the simple JSC has the same set of bodies as the classical JSC: General Meeting, Board of Directors and Supervisory Board (not obligatory). The rules governing these bodies are to a great extent the same as in the case of a classical JSC. The day-to-day operations will be carried out by the Board of Directors, which is the statutory body of a simple JSC. The Board of Directors decides on all issues, unless by virtue of the Commercial Code or the company's Articles of Associations the issues are reserved for the General Meeting to decide.

G. Cooperative (Družstvo)

121. A Cooperative[34] is a community of an unlimited number of persons established for business purposes or for providing economic, social and other needs of its members. The Cooperative must have at least five members; this does not apply if its members are at least two legal persons. There are two types of cooperatives; a small cooperative has less than fifty members. The minimum registered capital of a Cooperative is EUR 1,250.

122. Alongside other companies, the Cooperative is a special form of legal entity, which differs in the following perspectives:

34. Governed by ss 221–260 of the Commercial Code.

(1) Self-help – all members of the Cooperative promote the interests of the Cooperative together with their own interest.
(2) Autonomy – all the members of the Cooperative manage their own affairs independently.
(3) Cooperative Democracy – each and every member has one vote. The preference is given to each of the members and not to their amount of contribution.
(4) Responsibility – the property of the Cooperative is formed by the property of its members, and with those the Cooperative is liable vis-à-vis the third parties.
(5) Mutual support and solidarity – the primary objective of the Cooperative is not the profit, but satisfaction of the needs of its members. This feature of a Cooperative is the most significant.

123. At least five natural persons or two legal persons may establish the Cooperative. To establish a Cooperative, the Inaugural General Meeting must be held. At the Inaugural General Meeting, all members who have submitted their application are entitled to vote. The Inaugural General Meeting shall:

(1) determine the registered capital of the Cooperative;
(2) approve the Statutes;
(3) elect the Board of Directors and the Supervisory Committee.

124. The course of the Inaugural General Meeting has to be certified by a notarial deed, which contains a list of members and the amount of deposits to which they agreed. The final moment of the Cooperative incorporation is its registration with the Commercial Register. The Board of Directors of the Cooperative signs the application for registration in the Commercial Register. Their signatures must be officially authenticated.

125. The Commercial Code provides three mandatory bodies of a Cooperative; unless it is a small cooperative, each Cooperative shall form:

(1) Membership Meeting.
(2) Board of Directors.
(3) Supervisory Committee.

126. Only natural persons older than 18 years can be elected into the bodies of the Cooperative. The term of office of the first representatives in the bodies of the Cooperative is three years. Afterwards, the members can be elected for a maximum of five years.

127. The Membership Meeting is the supreme body of a Cooperative. The Membership Meeting consists of all members of the Cooperative, which participate personally or are represented by proxy. Every member has one vote, regardless of the amount of his or her investment, unless the Statutes provide otherwise. The Membership Meeting generally decides on the major economic and business decision of the Cooperative, like amendments to the Statute, dismissal and appointment of the members of the Cooperative into its bodies, approval of the financial statements and others.

128. Whereas, the Board of Directors is the statutory body of the Cooperative. It generally decides on the daily business of the Cooperative. The Supervisory Committee is the controlling body, which is authorized to inspect all the actions of the Cooperative and discuss the complaints of its members. The Supervisory Committee consists of at least three members and is independent of all other bodies, except the Membership Meeting. The Supervisory Committee is entitled to require any information on the management of the Cooperative. Moreover, the Board of Directors has the obligation without any delay to notify the Supervisory Committee of any facts or events, which may have relevant implications on the economic well-being of the Cooperative and its members.

129. Concerning the distribution of profit and the sharing of loss, it is the Membership Meeting, which determines the individual profit or the participation on loss after the appraisal of the financial statement. Unless the Statutes provide otherwise, the profits are determined based on the amount of the investment of a member. The Statutes or the Resolution of the Membership Meeting may specify other models of profit distribution. However, the Cooperative may not return to their members their contributions or pay them the interests of their contributions, unless the law does not stipulate otherwise.

130. In respect of the liability of the Cooperative, the Cooperative is a separate legal entity and for its obligations and debts is liable with its entire property. The members are not liable for the obligations of the Cooperative.

131. The dissolution of a Cooperative is effective to the date of its deletion of the Commercial Register. This step is preceded by the dissolution of the Cooperative, which may occur in the following ways:

(1) By the Resolution of the Membership Meeting.
(2) Bankruptcy of the Cooperative or a refusal of the application for bankruptcy due to the lack of assets.
(3) Court decision.
(4) Expiration of the period for which it was established.
(5) Achievement of the objectives for which it was established.

Chapter 3. The Economic Institutions

§1. Professional Organizations

I. Free Choice of Profession

132. The term free choice of profession is a widespread and applied freedom in the Slovak Republic. This freedom is encompassed in the Constitution of the Slovak Republic, in Article 35, subsection 1, which reads that:

> Everyone has the right to free choice of profession and to training for it, as well as the right to engage in entrepreneurial or other gainful activity.

Profession is a specific area of business, as the law itself requires the fulfilment of certain requirements as to the education, experience, impeccability, membership in chambers or bars or liability insurance. Special acts that regulate different sectors and professions lay down all these preconditions. Currently, concerning the tax burden, there is only a little difference between the business licensees and free professions.

133. The distinctive feature of a free profession is providing the intellectual-ideological service individually, independently and on the own responsibility of the professional. Furthermore, a majority of free professions require extensive preparation in a form of university degree or state accepted diploma or certificate. Most of the free professions are subject to qualitative entry restrictions, and some of them require registration with a membership organization such as chamber or bar. The Statistical Office of the Slovak Republic keeps records of the free professions that individuals engage in other than in connection with the Business Licence.

II. Current Situation

134. The Business Alliance of Slovak Republic (*Podnikateľská Aliancia Slovenska*), which is a professional membership association of entrepreneurs and employers with the main objective of improving formal and informal rules on business environment in the Slovak Republic in the context of overall social development, declared a decline of business environment in the Slovak Republic in the fourth quarter of 2014. The current index value of the business environment is 61.2 points (in 2012 it was 75.6 points). Compared to the third quarter index of 2014, it dropped by 1.71%. Entrepreneurs criticize especially the constant changes in legislation and the increasing tax burden brought by the amendment to the law on income tax. Deterioration of the situation has also been visible in the application of the principle of equality and in the enforcement of law and judiciary efficiency (Figure 4).

Figure 4 Index of Business Environment in Slovakia (in %)

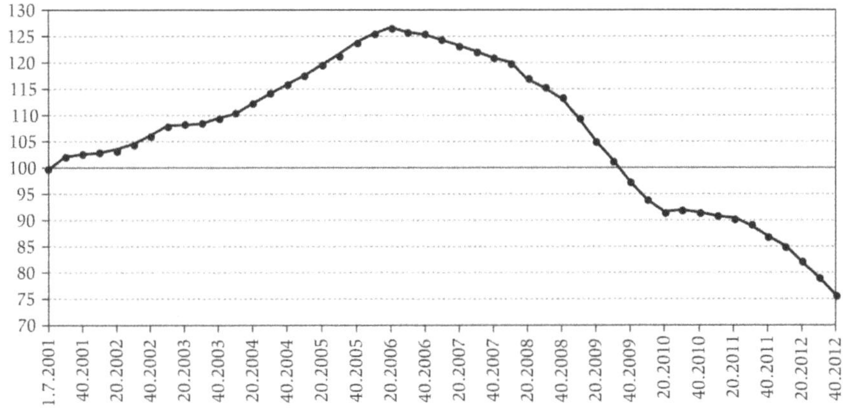

Source: Business Alliance of Slovak Republic (alianciapas.sk).

III. Trade Associations

135. Establishment, legal status and termination of the trade associations (*Záujmové združenie právnických osôb*) are regulated by section 20f of the Civil Code. The trade associations solely comprise legal entities, irrespective of their nature. The purpose of trade associations is to execute the common interest of its members. The members might protect their business interests or other interests, which are not contrary to the law and good morals. The object of the association is to satisfy the common interest and needs of its members. In particular, ensure the coordination of certain common activities, professional services, humanitarian objectives, developing programmes or representing the members before the state authorities and other institutions.

136. A trade association is established in two phases. The first phase consists of the expressed will of the members/founders as to create the association. Members may either conclude a Foundation Deed or during a membership meeting they can by the form of a resolution found an association. Moreover, every association has to have approved Statutes, which need to represent a part of the founding documents. The second phase consists of the expression of the will of the state authority, which grants legal personality to the association. Every association has to be registered by one of eight district offices in the seat of the Region. Registration procedure begins with a written proposal.

137. Trade associations are not per se entrepreneurial entities. However, they may exercise the entrepreneurial activity as a complementary activity, where the profit will be in its entirety used for the development of the main purpose of the trade association. Trade association is rescinded by a removal from a register.

IV. Budget & Contributory Organization (Rozpočtová a Príspevková Organizácia)

138. Besides private legal entities, also the state and its institutions, bodies and organization may form supporting budget and contributory organization in accordance with Act No. 523/2004 Coll. on Budgetary Rules of Public Administration. According to this law, a budget organization is a legal entity created by state, municipality or by a higher territorial unit, whose income and expenditure is linked to the state budget, municipal budget or of a budget of a higher territorial unit. A budget organization manages its funds separately in accordance with the approved budget, which is determined by its founder. A contributory organization is a legal entity as well formed by state, municipality or by a higher territorial unit, which covers less than 50% of its production costs with its sales and which receives a contribution from the budget of state municipality or higher territorial unit.

139. The budget and contributory organizations are set up in order to perform certain tasks of state, state municipality or of the higher territorial unit under special provisions. They may acquire rights and duties on their own name from the day of their formation. However, they may not carry out any executive or decision-making functions.

140. Budget or contributory organization may be established by:

(1) Statute.
(2) Decision of its founder, which is a governmental department, municipality or higher territorial unit, unless stipulated otherwise.

141. Subsequently, budget and contributory organizations cease to exist under the following circumstances:

(1) Demerger.
(2) Merger.
(3) The founder when establishing the budget or contributory organization specifies the date of its cessation.

V. Organizations with an International Element

142. Besides trade associations, the law recognized also the organizations with an international element, which can be established, operate and seated in the Slovak Republic in accordance with Law No. 116/1985 Coll. on the conditions of the activities of organizations with an international element. Under this Act, the organization with an international element is an international non-governmental organization comprised of foreign nationals. These organizations, however, need to be registered in the Slovak Republic. The application shall be submitted to the Ministry of Interior of the Slovak Republic.

VI. Chambers of Commerce

143. The National Council of the Slovak Republic adopted early in 1992 Act on Chambers of Commerce and Industry, whose aim is to regulate the setting-up, status and scope of activities performed by chambers of commerce and industry as public institutions. The Slovak Chamber of Commerce and Industry (SCCI) is a legal entity with its registered seat in Bratislava. Its main focus is to support and protect business operations of its members at home and abroad. The SCCI has concluded over ninety cooperation agreements with chambers of commerce operating in different countries and continents and thus advises on business environment on markets in these jurisdictions. Furthermore, the SCCI as a public institution under Slovak law is able to certify non-preferential European Certificate of Origin, which is a document used in international trade certifying the 'origin of goods'.

144. Besides the SCCI, there are a number of foreign chambers of commerce, as the American Chamber of Commerce (AmCham), which is a service-oriented organization established in Slovakia in 1993 as an independent and self-supporting organization, fully dependent on the contributions of its members. Currently, the AmCham has reached more than 330 international and Slovak companies, where approximately 23% are American, 42% are Slovak and the remaining 35% are companies of other nationalities. The British Chamber of Commerce in the Slovak Republic (BCCSR) was founded in 1998 as an independent, non-profit organization. The BCCSR is comprised of seventy-five corporations, small businesses, mid-sized companies, members and entrepreneurs of diverse sectors within the Central and Eastern Europe region. In addition to these two biggest chambers of commerce, there are a number of other chambers from Australia, Austria, Canada, Denmark, France, Germany, Italy, Japan, Russia, Spain, Switzerland and others. They all contribute to the same aim to cooperate and help the further development of business environment.

§2. Commercial Arbitration

145. Besides the general judiciary, the parties may decide to resolve their dispute in a form of arbitration. The history of arbitration in the Slovak Republic goes back to the Austro-Hungarian monarchy in 1911, when the Civil Dispute Code, Act No. 1/1911 regulated the arbitration (1911 Civil Dispute Code). The 1911 Civil Dispute Code was in force until 1950. The arbitration was allowed in different areas of law, mainly in property and employment disputes. After the Second World War, Civil Procedure Act No. 142/1950 Coll. was adopted, which contained detailed provisions on arbitration. Thus, the arbitration until 1989 was divided into two main types:

(1) International Arbitration, regulated by Act No. 98/1963 Coll.
(2) Domestic Arbitration of state-owned entities, regulated by Act No. 121/1962 Coll.

146. From 1963 until 1996 (in both Slovak and Czech Republic at this time) the arbitration continued to be regulated by the 1963 Czechoslovakian Arbitration Act, which prohibited the arbitration as a means of dispute resolution, for non-state-owned entities. The Slovak Republic, in 1996 by Act No. 218/1996 Coll. on Arbitration reintroduced the arbitration for private parties. In 2002, Act No. 244/2002 Coll. on Arbitration has replaced the 1996 Arbitration Act. This Act is based on the 1985 UNCITRAL Model Law on International Commercial Arbitration and implements all the principles therein together with the principles in the Slovak Code of Civil Procedure, the 1958 New York Convention and the 1961 European Convention. Since its adoption, Act No. 244/2002 Coll. on Arbitration has been amended substantially in 2014.

147. The arbitral proceedings in the Slovak Republic can be besides the court proceeding carried out before and arbitral institution, which administers the arbitration or by ad hoc arbitration panel. The Arbitration Act governs the resolution proceedings of proprietary disputes arising out of commercial or civil relationship, at both domestic and international levels, when the seat of arbitration is the Slovak Republic. The Arbitration Act prohibits the following disputes from being resolved by arbitration:

(1) Establishment, modification or termination of ownership and other rights in rem in movable property.
(2) Personal status.
(3) Relating to the enforcement of judgments.
(4) Incurred during the bankruptcy and settlement proceedings.

I. Arbitration Agreement

148. According to section 3 of the Arbitration Act, the arbitration agreement is an agreement between contracting parties, where they stipulate that all or some disputes, which have arisen or may arise between them in a specific contractual relationship or other legal relationship, will be resolved by arbitration. An arbitration agreement will also apply to legal successors of the contracting parties, unless excluded by the arbitration agreement. An arbitration agreement may be contained in a separate agreement or within a contract. The law requires a written form of the arbitration agreement. The arbitration agreement is deemed to be in writing, also when it is:

(1) contained in the mutual written communication of the parties; or
(2) it has been concluded by electronic means, which allow capturing the content of the legal act and the person who carried out this act.

149. If the parties failed to conclude the arbitration agreement in writing, they may remedy the situation by a declaration of the parties in the minutes before an arbitration panel on submitting to the jurisdiction to the arbitral panel. The content of such minutes is then the arbitration agreement. An arbitration agreement is deemed to be concluded in writing also when so stated in claimant's claim while not objected by the respondent in its reply.

150. Within the arbitration agreement, parties generally specify the applicable law for the arbitration, which may differ from the law, which governs the contract as a whole. Concerning the principle of separability, the arbitration clause that is part of an otherwise invalid contract shall only be considered invalid if its validity is expressly preconditioned on the validity of the underlying contract. Thus, if the contract has a valid arbitration agreement, courts shall have no jurisdiction to decide the dispute unless such matter is determined otherwise by the arbitral panel.

II. Composition of the Arbitral Panel

151. Arbitral panel has to be composed of an odd number of arbitrators. If parties do not specify the number and then fail to agree on the number, the panel should be composed of three arbitrators. In the case, parties agree on an even number of arbitrators, such agreement is invalid and it shall be deemed that the parties did not agree on the number of arbitrators. Besides the number of arbitrators, parties can agree on the identity of the arbitrators or request the arbitral institution or a court to appoint the arbitrators. In case of three arbitrators, each party appoints one and then the two arbitrators decide on the presiding third arbitrator. If any of the party-appointed two arbitrators fails to appoint the presiding arbitrator, it is again the decision of the arbitral institution or court to remedy the situation and appoint the presiding arbitrator.

152. The procedure for challenge of arbitrators is governed by section 9 of the Arbitration Act, which states that all arbitrators have the duty to disclose all facts and circumstances that could in the opinion of the parties compromise the independence and impartiality of the arbitrator. Such disclosure is part of the acceptance of the appointment. If, based on the disclosed facts in the arbitrator's acceptance, the parties fail to challenge the appointment of arbitrator within fifteen days the grounds for challenging the arbitrator will be limited only to the facts revealed after the appointment of the arbitrator. The duty to disclose the relevant circumstances and facts continues throughout the arbitration, and the arbitrator is required to disclose to the parties all the potential compromising facts.

153. In a case, parties agree to challenge the arbitrator, unless otherwise agreed, the remaining members of the arbitral panel shall decide upon the challenge or a third party has to be nominated by the parties. The decision on a challenge cannot be appealed. During the challenge procedure, the arbitral panel may continue in the arbitration proceeding, but may not render an award. The Arbitration Act does not specifically regulate the liability of arbitrators or fees. The liability will be governed by the general Slovak civil law. Fees of arbitrators are either set up by the arbitral institution or in case of ad hoc arbitration; the arbitrator shall specify the fees before accepting the nomination.

III. Jurisdiction of the Arbitral Panel

154. *Competenz-competenz* principle forms a part of the Arbitration Act, as the arbitral panel is competent to rule on its own jurisdiction, including the challenges to the existence and validity of the arbitration agreement. If the arbitral panel concludes that it does not have the jurisdiction to hear the dispute, it shall terminate the entire arbitral proceeding. According to section 21(2) of the Arbitration Act, the latest stage when a party can raise the jurisdiction objection is when taking the first step in the arbitral proceedings on the merits of the claim (usually by filing the statement of defence), unless the dispute is non-arbitrable. In that case, the jurisdiction of the arbitral panel can be challenged at any stage of the arbitral proceeding.

IV. Award

155. The Arbitration Act does not specify a time frame for rendering an award. The arbitral panel thus renders the award on the issues in dispute in accordance with the law agreed by the parties. In the absence of the agreement on the choice of law, the arbitral panel shall apply the law determined by the Slovak conflict of law rules. In case of domestic arbitral proceedings, the parties are by the Act not allowed to choose any other law to govern their dispute, but Slovak law. However, the panel can take into consideration all relevant customs and trade usages. The arbitral panel may apply the rules of equity only if the parties have so expressly authorized the panel.

156. Regarding the formal requirements of an award, award has to be made in writing and signed by a majority of the arbitral panel. In case an arbitrator does not participate in the voting, the remaining arbitrators may decide the case without him. In case of tied votes, the vote of the presiding arbitrator decides. In the case of a missing signature of an arbitrator, the reasons have to be specified. Furthermore, an award must contain essentials:

(1) name of the arbitral institution;
(2) names of the arbitrators;
(3) names of the parties and their representatives;
(4) seat of arbitration;
(5) date of the award;
(6) decision of the arbitral panel on the issues in dispute;
(7) reasons upon which the award was rendered, unless the parties agreed that no grounds have to be included in the award or the award is based on a settlement agreement; and
(8) instructions to the parties on challenge of the award.

157. Moreover, the award has to contain a ruling on costs and should determine which party is obliged to pay such costs and where the award imposes a duty to perform an act, the panel specifies a period for such completion. The verdict of the arbitration award must be specific. If an obligation is imposed, the tribunal shall also determine the period for its fulfilment. The award has to be either announced orally to the parties or must be officially served to the parties.

158. Any arbitrator is entitled to attach his/her dissenting opinion. In an event that one of the arbitrators is absent and a majority decision cannot be made, the presiding arbitrator has a casting vote. The award cannot exceed the legal issues disputed, and the arbitral panel has to limit the scope of the award to the issues submitted by the parties.

159. Parties of the arbitration may agree in their arbitration agreement that the parties have a right to request a review by another arbitrator/arbitrators of an award. If the parties within the arbitration agreement have not concluded such agreement, any review is excluded. Party may request a review within fifteen days of the service of the award. A served arbitration award, which can no longer be reviewed, has for the parties of the arbitration the same effects as a final court judgment.

V. Role of the Courts

160. The Arbitration Act determines those circumstances in which the Slovak courts have the authority to intervene in arbitral proceedings. On the one hand, the courts help to speed up and remedy failures of the arbitral proceeding by appointing arbitrators, granting interim measures and assisting with the gathering of evidence. On the other hand, the courts play a crucial role in the case of challenging and enforcing the awards.

161. The arbitration proceeding represents a *lis pendens*. Once a court becomes aware of a binding arbitration agreement, it is required to stay the court proceedings. Respondent may contest the jurisdiction of the court, latest at the moment when the respondent contests the merits of the claim. In the case that both parties do not wish to resolve their dispute by arbitration, the court may hear and decide the case. Furthermore, the court will hear the case if it establishes under Slovak law that:

(1) case is non-arbitrable;
(2) arbitration agreement is invalid, inoperative or incapable of being performed;
(3) claim falls outside of the jurisdiction of the arbitral panel; or
(4) relevant arbitral institution refused to deal with the case at hand.

VI. Challenging the Award

162. The Arbitration Act in its section 40 provides parties with a statutory basis for challenging the award. Parties cannot strip the court of such authority via any type of contractual agreement. In case of award challenge, it is the general court, which has the jurisdiction to decide on the challenge. The party challenging the award, however, has to prove one of the following circumstances:

(1) Party did not have the competence to conclude an arbitration agreement, the arbitration agreement was not concluded in accordance with the law, according to which the agreement should have been concluded or that such agreement was not concluded in accordance with the Slovak law.
(2) Party was not properly notified of the appointment of an arbitrator, the arbitration proceedings or that the party was not allowed to participate in the arbitration proceeding.
(3) Arbitration award was rendered in a dispute, for which no arbitration agreement was concluded, or which is not within the limits of arbitration agreement, or that the arbitration award goes beyond the scope of the agreement on arbitrator or the arbitration agreement; however, if only a part of the arbitral award was outside the scope, the court annuls the award only in that part.

163. A party seeking to challenge the award before the Slovak courts has to file its petition within sixty days after being served with the award. In a case, a party requested corrections concerning the final award, the period of sixty days begins to run from the delivery of the corrected award.

VII. Recognition and Enforcement of the Award

A. *Domestic Awards*

164. An enforceable domestic award, which was issued within the territory of the Slovak Republic, becomes a res judicata, and after the expiration of a voluntary performance period set out in the award, a domestic award is enforceable in accordance with the provisions of the Slovak Code of Civil Procedure and Act No. 233/1995 Coll. on Court Executors and Execution Activities. Thus, the enforcement of a domestic award is subject to the same requirements and conditions as a court decision.

165. In a controversial decision of the Slovak Constitutional Court, the Constitutional Court ruled that an arbitral award might be subject to constitutional review if it infringes fundamental rights. The Constitutional Court in its decision referred to Article 6 of the European Convention on Human Rights as to the right to a fair trial, and therefore also arbitral award may be set aside when carrying out the constitutional oversight.[35]

35. For more *see* the Constitutional Court Finding III. US 162/2011, available online at: https://www.ustavnysud.sk/documents/10182/992328/40_11a.pdf/5a9b0da2-30d5-461f-88ef-dfb5988bb56f (accessed 31 May 2013). Or *see* the *Constitutional Court Undermines Finality of Arbitral Awards,* 2 Feb. 2012, available online at: http://www.allenovery.com/publications/en-gb/Pages/Constitutional-Court-undermines-finality-of-arbitral-awards.aspx/ (accessed 31 May 2013).

B. Foreign Awards

166. Foreign awards rendered by states that are the signatory parties to the 1958 New York Convention are enforceable in the Slovak Republic in the same way as domestic awards. The Arbitration Act stipulates in its eight parts the requirements and the procedure of how a party may enforce its award in the Slovak Republic. Party seeking the recognition and enforcement of a foreign award has to file a written petition with the court requesting the recognition and enforcement and enclose the original award together with the arbitration agreement with a translation which has been certified by an official or sworn translator, diplomat or consular agent.

167. The recognition and enforcement of a foreign award may be refused only if:

(1) party did not have the competence to conclude an arbitration agreement, the arbitration agreement was not concluded in accordance with the law, according to which the agreement should have been concluded;
(2) party was not properly notified of the appointment of an arbitrator, the arbitration proceedings or that the party was not allowed to participate in the arbitration proceeding;
(3) arbitration award was rendered in a dispute, for which no arbitration agreement was concluded, or which is not within the limits of arbitration agreement, or that the arbitration award goes beyond the scope of the agreement on arbitrator or the arbitration agreement; however, if the parts of the arbitral award rendered in parts which were outside of the scope and those rendered which were within the scope of the agreement are separable, the court may recognize and enforce those parts rendered within the scope of the agreement;
(4) the arbitral tribunal has not been constituted or arbitration proceeding has not proceeded in a way agreed by the parties; if this agreement has not been concluded and if the nomination of the tribunal or the proceeding was in breach with the law of the country where the arbitration took place, in the case these circumstances might have had affected the outcome of the case;
(5) arbitral award has not become final and binding on the parties to arbitration or its enforcement had been suspended by a court of the state, in which or under the law of which the arbitration award was rendered or by which the awards were cancelled.

168. Court rendering a decision denying recognition and enforcement of a foreign arbitration award is always obliged to justify. Against a denying decision a party has always a remedy.

Chapter 4. General Obligations of the Economic Operators

§1. All Undertakings: Merchants, Companies, Partnerships & Cooperatives

169. As was stated in Chapter 1, all entrepreneurs have to comply with the statutory obligations in due time. The general obligations of natural and legal entities do not differ as to the obligations and duties per se; there might be some differences when it comes to specific date limits or the amount of the fees or duties. In this chapter, the most important duties will be described in a greater detail, namely the obligation to register with the Commercial Register, open and operate a bank account, bookkeeping and the obligation of all entrepreneurs of the prevention of money laundering.

I. Commercial Register

170. The Commercial Register together with the Collection of Documents is a public list that contains all data and collection of documents stipulated by the law on the Commercial Register, Act No. 530/2003 Coll. The Ministry of Justice of the Slovak Republic administers the Commercial Register from 1 January 2001 onwards. The Commercial Register records the data of corporations, partnerships, cooperatives and other legal entities or where stipulated by the law. The Slovak Commercial Register registers also other legal entities established under the laws of the EU, business, branches or plants of foreign entities, if stipulated by a specific act. Natural persons with a permanent residence in the Slovak Republic, who carry out business under a trade licence or based on other than a trade authorization (e.g., attorneys), or those who engage in the agricultural production and are registered with a special registry under a special regulation may register with the Commercial Register at their own requests or if it is prescribed by a specific law.

171. The Commercial Register is kept by the district court in the seat of the regional court for legal entities having their registered seat in the circuit of the respective regional court. For natural persons, the competent court is determined under their place of business. If an entrepreneur, who is a natural person, does not have a place of business, he/she is registered by the Commercial Register of the court competent under his/her place of residence. Foreign persons are entered in the court competent under the location of their enterprise or its branch. The court keeping the Commercial Register is referred to as 'registry court'.

172. The information in the Commercial Register is searchable by trade name, identification number, registered office, registration number and name of a person (e.g., business representative or a member of a board of directors). Information is easily accessible, provided in the form of a current excerpt or a full excerpt, which also lists documents contained in the Collection of Documents, which forms a part of the Commercial Register. The online system, available at: http://www.orsr.sk, is free of charge. However, the information obtained on the online website of the

Commercial Register is not legally binding and usable for legal acts. Thus, in order to use the excerpts for legal purposes, one has to require an official copy or excerpt, which is charged. Excerpts usable for legal purposes can be obtained from the competent registry court, any Notary office, at the integrated service point (post office), or through the central portal of public administration (*Ústredný portal verejnej správy*).

A. Formal & Material Publicity of the Commercial Register

173. The Commercial Register is, as stated above, a public register of prescribed data and public collection of documents. This character of the Commercial Register is called also a formal publicity, which expresses the public availability of data and documents without the need to prove legal grounds. Whereas, the term material publicity means that what are the effects of registrations into the Commercial Register, i.e., what significance have the registrations for the registered person and third person.

B. Recorded Data

174. The following data shall be entered into the Commercial Register:

(1) In case of a legal entity business, name and place of business shall be entered and in case of a natural person, first name and surname of a natural person, if different from the business name shall be indicated together with date of birth, social security number, place of residence and place of business if it differs from the place of residence.
(2) Identification Number (*identifikačné číslo organizácie – 'IČO'*).
(3) Business activities or objects.
(4) Legal form of the entity.
(5) First name, surname, date of birth and social security number (*rodné číslo*) of a natural person who is a statutory body or a member of a statutory body, indicating how person/s act on behalf of the registered entity and stating the starting date and the date of the termination of its capacity in the registered entity; if it is a legal entity who is a statutory body or a member of a statutory body of the registered entity, business name, place of business and identification number have to be indicated; in case of a foreign natural person, his/her social security number has to be registered, if assigned.
(6) In the case of registration of a branch or plant, denomination of the branch or plant, address of location, business activities and objects have to be registered, unless a special act provides for broader registration including the first name, surname, place of residence, date of birth and social security number of the supervisor of a branch or plant together with indicating the starting date and the date of the termination of his/her capacity in the registered branch or plant; in case of a foreign natural person, his/her social security number has to be registered, if assigned.

(7) In case of registering an authorized agent (*prokurista*), his/her first name, surname, date of birth, place of residence shall be registered together with the indication how a person acts on behalf of the registered entity and stating the starting date and the date of the termination of his/her capacity in the registered entity; in case of a foreign natural person, his/her social security number has to be registered, if assigned.
(8) In case of registering a member of a supervisory body, his/her first name, surname, date of birth, place of residence shall be registered together with stating the starting date and the date of the termination of his/her capacity in the registered entity; in case of a foreign natural person, his/her social security number has to be registered, if assigned.
(9) Rescission of legal person and legal grounds thereof.
(10) Date of start and end of liquidation proceeding.
(11) First name, surname, place of residence, date of birth and social security number of a natural person acting as a liquidator; in a case of liquidator being a legal entity, its business name, place of business and identification number shall be indicated together with the specification of how a person acts on behalf of the registered entity and stating the starting date and the date of the termination of his/her capacity in the registered entity; in case of liquidator being a legal entity, first name, surname, place of residence, date of birth, social security number of a person acting on behalf of the legal entity as a liquidator; in case of a foreign natural person, his/her social security number has to be registered, if assigned.
(12) Court's decision on the invalidity of registered entity.
(13) Declaration of start and end of bankruptcy proceeding.
(14) First name, surname, number of the trustee, place of business of the Office of natural person, who is to be registered with the Commercial Register as an appointed trustee in bankruptcy proceeding, restructuring proceeding or settlement proceeding; If a trustee is a legal entity, its business name, number of trustee and the place of business is to be registered.
(15) Date of start and end of restructuring or settlement proceeding.
(16) Imposition and termination of forced administration under special regulation.
(17) First name, surname, place of residence, date of birth and social security number of a natural person or in case of legal entity its business name and identification number, if assigned, of an administrator of forced administration and its representative; in case of a foreign natural person, his/her social security number has to be registered, if assigned.

C. Collection of Documents

175. Besides all the above-stated required information, the registered entity and connected natural and legal persons have to enclose all relevant documents to the Collection of Documents, which is administered by the competent registry court, in which jurisdiction the registered entity is established. The documents have to be filed in Slovak language or in a foreign language with a certified translation into the

Slovak language. The Act on Commercial Register further stipulates which documents have to be filed by a foreign entity or its branch or plant. The registered entity or its representative has to specify the kind of a document and the language; otherwise the court will disregard the document.

176. Furthermore, the Act on Commercial Register indicates the specific time limits. The registered entity or its representative has to file required documents with the registry court within thirty days of their execution, unless stipulated by the Act otherwise. This time limit is kept, if the registered entity or its representative files the document by electronic means. The number of copies, in which a document should be filed, depends on the type of a document. Generally, one or two copies are required, unless filed electronically. The content of all filed documents shall correspond with the actual situation.

D. *Application for Registration*

177. The application for registration of a registered entity into the Commercial Register including application of changes of registered data or rescission of data or the registered entity entirely is filed by the applicant – the registered entity itself or by the person entitled to represent the registered entity under the Commercial Code. The application for registration shall be made on the prescribed form and must be enclosed by all documents, which indicate the required data. All the forms are available online. The authenticity of the signature of the applicant must be certified. Withdrawal of the application for registration is not permitted.

178. Concerning the fees for registration, since January 2016, the fees are the following:

(1) In case of a JSC, EUR 750 (in case of an electronic application, EUR 375).
(2) Other legal entities, EUR 300 (in case of an electronic application, EUR 150).
(3) Natural person (entrepreneur), EUR 150 (in case of an electronic application, EUR 75).
(4) Branch of a legal entity, EUR 300 (in case of an electronic application, EUR 150).
(5) Branch of a natural person (entrepreneur), EUR 30 (in case of an electronic application, EUR 15).
(6) Change of the type of legal entity, EUR 330 (in case of an electronic application, EUR 165).

179. If any proposal is submitted in any matter relating to the Commercial Register (i.e., also the application for registration) by electronic means (*see* section E), the fee is decreased to 50% of the fixed amount set out in Act No. 71/1992 Coll. on Court Fees.

180. In case of change or amendment of registered data, irrespective of the number of changes, unless it is a change of the name or postcode of a city/village/

municipality of the registered place of business or of a street or other public places, the fee for such amendment is EUR 66. For issuing an official certificate in a paper form, there is a fee of EUR 6.50 and in case of electronic form a fee of EUR 0.33. The Notary offices charge EUR 1.33 (excluding VAT) per each page of the certificate.

E. Electronic Application

181. Since 1 August 2007, the amendment of Act on Commercial Register has been in effect which provides for an opportunity to submit proposals for incorporation by electronic means. The application for registration is available online and has to be signed by a guaranteed electronic signature of the applicant; otherwise the Commercial Code disregards the application. The enclosed documents to the application may be filed not only in paper form but also electronically by electronic means. The authentication of the signature of the applicant is not required.

F. Registration

182. If all the statutory requirements for registration have been satisfied, the registry court will register the applicant within five working days after the delivery of the application. In a case of a cross-border merger or acquisition, the registration court will register the new entity within thirty days. If the application for registration proposes a specific day for registration, the court shall indicate this date in the Register. If the application does not indicate a specific date or the registration is executed after this date, the court will indicate following after the day of registry. There are no allowed objections to the registration, which was carried out in accordance with the application. After the registration, the court will notify the applicant without any undue delay.

183. If the application for the registration does not meet the statutory requirements, the court will notify the applicant of the rejection of registration. The notice of rejection in paper form contains the specific reasons why the application has not been successful; in addition, it provides the instructions on possible objections against the rejection of registration. The notice of rejection shall be sent without any undue delay to the applicant. The applicant may file the objection with the competent court within fifteen days after the receipt of the notice.

G. Sanctions

184. In the case when the obliged registered person, legal or natural, fails, within the period provided by the law, to comply with its obligation to:

- notify the registration court of any change of its data;
- notify the registration court of erasure of its data;

– submit the registration court required documents;
– indicate on its official business letters and correspondence its business name, place of business, legal form, ID number, registration number or in case of liquidation or bankruptcy or restructuring procedure indicate its business name with the supplement 'in liquidation' or 'in bankruptcy' or 'in restructuring';
– indicate in the application for registration of false information; or
– submit documents, which do not correspond with the actual situation.

Registration court may fine the registered natural person or the person authorized to act on behalf of a legal entity with up to EUR 3,310.

H. Ultimate Beneficial Owners

185. Slovak Parliament adopted Act No. 52/2018 Coll. amending Act No. 297/2008 Coll. on Protection Against Legalization of Proceeds from Crime on Protection against Financing of Terrorism as amended. The changes are implementing Directive 2015/849 of the European Parliament and of the Council (EU) into the Slovak law.

186. Based on the changes, from 15 March 2018, all legal entities registered in the Slovak Commercial Register, which are not a subject of the public service or a special purpose association of assets without legal capacity, are required to identify their beneficial owner(s). It is the obligation of the legal entity to keep its data on its beneficial owner(s) updated.

187. All legal entities registered in the Commercial Register prior to 31 October 2018 must submit and register information about their beneficial owner(s) to the Commercial Register within 31 December 2019, at the latest. This information is a part of non-public part of the Commercial Register and the Register of Legal Entities. The registration procedure is free from fees.

188. As from 1 November 2018, information about the beneficial owner(s) forms a part of the incorporation documents of each newly established legal entity. Beneficial owners have to be stipulated on an application for registration into the Slovak commercial Register. This obligation shall not apply to the issuers of securities admitted to trading on a regulated market.

II. Bank Account

189. In order to register with the Commercial Register, every company has to open a bank account, as when setting up a company. Depending on the type of the registered company, the Commercial Act defines the necessary down payment. Ordinarily, the way of evidencing such down payment is in the form of a bank account.

III. Prevention of Money Laundering & Terrorist Financing

190. Based on the implemented EU legislation, both natural and legal persons have certain duties connected with the prevention and detection of money laundering and terrorist financing activities regulated by Act No. 297/2008 Coll. on Protection Against Legalization of Proceeds from Crime and Terrorist Financing. The Financial Investigation Unit (FIU) (*Spravodajská jednotka finančnej polície*) is entitled to carry out a control under the above-stated act, whether an entrepreneur complies with the obligations, and in case of a non-compliance may fine the entity up to EUR 165,989 and in case of repeated violations up to EUR 331,939.

191. According to section 5 of the Act on Protection Against Legalization, there is an enumeration of the 'obliged persons'; there are mainly the following:

(1) Banks.
(2) Financial institutions, other than banks,[36] insurance companies.
(3) Export-Import Bank of the Slovak Republic.
(4) Operator of gambling plant.
(5) The post office.
(6) Bailiff (court executor).
(7) A trustee carrying out bankruptcy proceedings, restructuring proceedings or proceedings for debt relief under special regulation.
(8) Auditor, accountant or tax adviser.
(9) Natural or legal person entitled to sale or purchase real estate.
(10) Attorney or notary.
(11) Provider of asset management services and services for other businesses, unless it is a natural person defined in the above paragraphs.
(12) Natural or legal person authorized to carry out organizational and economic advisory, public service delivery or shipping.
(13) Natural or legal person authorized to operate auctions or natural or legal person authorized to trade with works of art, collectibles, antiques, cultural sites, cultural objects, precious metals or precious stones, legal or natural person authorized to commercialize articles of precious metal or precious stones, or a legal or natural person authorized to operate a pawn.
(14) Creditor.
(15) Another person, if stipulated by a special regulation.
(16) Any entrepreneur who carries out a transaction valued of at least EUR 15,000, regardless of whether the transaction was conducted within one individual transaction or as multiple successive transactions, which may or may not be interlinked.

36. Among the financial institutions, we understand institutions as CSD, stock exchange, commodity exchange, securities dealer, investment companies, foreign collective investment companies, insurance undertakings and alike.

192. Thus, the number of the 'obliged persons' is fairly extensive and it happens many times that in case of non-specialized entrepreneurs, they do not carry out their obligations under the Act, which are the following:

(1) Develop a written programme of its own actions against money laundering and terrorist financing (Program).
(2) Considering whether the prepared or carried out transaction is 'unusual'.
(3) Report the 'unusual' trades to the FIU.
(4) Ensure staff training at least once a year, which aims to familiarize the employees with the Program.
(5) Ensure that each and every employee has unlimited access to the Program.
(6) Store for the period of five years after the termination of the contractual relationship with a client or after the execution of transaction all data and evidentiary documents connected to it.
(7) Provide the FIU with appropriate conditions for the exercise of control and the necessary assistance, plus refrain from action, which could hamper the exercise of control.
(8) Based on request, provide the FIU with the information and documentary evidence on compliance over the previous five years.

193. It is important to highlight that even a person who ceases to exist is obliged to keep the data and evidentiary documents for the period of five years after its cessation.

194. Section 4 of the Act defines the 'unusual' transaction as an action, which suggests that it may enable the legalization or terrorist financing. The FIU, in order to help the entities to spot such transactions, published guidelines on how to recognize the 'unusual' ones. The guidelines contain both general and specific ways depending on the activities carried out by the parties.

195. Concerning the general methods of detection of unusual transactions, there are the following:

(1) Trading operation apparently deviates from the ordinary scope or nature of a particular type of trade or business of a client.
(2) Transaction has no apparent economic or lawful purpose.
(3) Refusal to identify itself when entering into a business relationship.
(4) Amount of funds, with which the client operates, is manifestly disproportionate to the nature and scope of its business or property.
(5) Refusal to provide information about the upcoming transaction.
(6) Commercial transaction with no obvious relationship to the ordinary business activities of a client.
(7) Business partner misses the required documentation, which is ordinary in the legitimate trade.
(8) Use of falsified or stolen identification documents.

196. Furthermore, as to the specific methods of detection of unusual transaction, the FIU indicates the following:

(1) In case of real estate activity:
   (a) business partner acquires the real estate for a third party;
   (b) urgent transfer of the real estate property for a price that is significantly different from the normal market price;
   (c) gifting the estate to third parties; or
   (d) property transfer for a symbolic value (e.g., EUR 1).

197. The obliged person – an entrepreneur – is required to postpone the unusual transaction if by its execution the seizure of proceeds of crime funds intended to finance terrorism may be substantially hampered. It should be noted that this obligation naturally is closely connected to the particularities of one's business. In case the obliged person is a bank, a transfer of money or providing of a credit is simple, while in case of an external auditor, the completion of such obligation is close to impossible.

198. As to the most common obligations under this Act, any entrepreneur who carries out a transaction of more than EUR 15,000 in cash shall identify the business partner and verify its identification with an official document. Any obliged persons, under section 5 of the Act, have an ongoing obligation to identify any business partner when carrying out a transaction of more than EUR 2,000.

IV. Bookkeeping

A. Preliminary Observations

199. Since 2005, the International Accounting Standards (IAS)/International Financial Reporting Standards (IFRS) have been effectively applied by EU-listed companies in the EU. In 2002, the EU adopted the IAS Regulation for companies listed in the EU securities market, including different investment vehicles as banks, pension funds or insurance companies, which ought to prepare their consolidated financial statements in accordance with the IFRS (*see* Regulation (EC) No. 1606/2002 of the European Parliament and of the Council of 19 July 2002 on the application of IAS). The Slovak Republic, being a Member State of the EU, adheres to the IAS. At present, the bookkeeping as such is regulated by the Act on Accounting No. 431/2002 Coll.[37] In addition to the EU legislation and the Act on Accounting, the Ministry of Finance by a form of a decree stipulates general chart of accounts and details of accounting procedures in the double-entry bookkeeping system for

37. The Act on Accounting reflects all the required EU measures on accounting as: Fourth Council Directive 78/660/EEC on annual accounts of certain types of companies; Seventh Council Directive 83/349/EEC on joint accounts; Council Directive 86/635/EC on annual accounts of banks and other financial institutions; Council Directive 91/674/EEC relating to annual accounts; and consolidated accounts of insurance undertakings.

different types of entities. The Slovak Generally Accepted Accounting Principles (Slovak GAAP) stem out from the accounting legislation in force in the Slovak Republic.

B. Scope of Application of the Act

200. Slovak legal entities and foreign entities whose branch or plant is registered in the Commercial Register are obliged to perform the double-entry bookkeeping in line with Slovak GAAP, unless they are not obliged to prepare their financial statements according to the IAS/IFRS standards. Natural persons, certain types of entrepreneurs under a separate regulation, a contributory organization established by a municipality or a higher territorial unit, civic associations and other not-for-profit organizations and their branches with a limited yearly income have the option of choosing either the double-entry or single-entry bookkeeping.

201. Under the Slovak GAAP, an accounting unit must record its accounting entries using a prescribed chart of accounts, which contain the following categories:

- Class 0: Non-current assets.
- Class 1: Inventory.
- Class 2: Financial accounts.
- Class 3: Debtor and creditors, other assets and short-term liabilities.
- Class 4: Capital accounts and non-current liabilities.
- Class 5: Expenses.
- Class 6: Revenues.
- Class 7: Closing an off-balance sheet account.
- Class 8 and 9: Internal accounting.

202. Furthermore, the Slovak GAAP prescribes a three-digit ledger account code (synthetic accounts) for each class of asset, revenue, expense and liability and optional sub-ledger accounts (analytical accounts). In addition to the prescribed chart of accounts, entities are entitled to create other synthetic account codes for balance sheet accounts. Concerning the time limit for record-keeping, in case of financial statements, entities shall retain them for a minimum of ten years, while other accounting documentations as invoices, ledgers or chart accounts shall be retained for a minimum of five years.

C. General Principles

203. Under the Act on Accounting, accounts have to be maintained and financial statements must be prepared in accordance with certain general principles as 'true and fair' view, going concern, materiality, comprehensibility, comparability, reliability, compliance, completeness, supportability and individual valuation. The general accounting principles of an accounting unit have to be consistent from year to year, and in case of change in an accounting estimate, it should be not presented retrospectively. Among the basic accounting principles of Slovak GAAP are the following:

(1) Assumption on the going-concern basis.
(2) Use of accruals and matching concepts.
(3) Prudent valuation of each asset takes place on cost basis:
    (a) Fixed assets are valued at acquisition cost, net of depreciation.
    (b) Merchandise or raw materials, finished products and work in progress are valued at the lower cost or net realizable value.
    (c) Cost on inventories may be established either on a specific identification, weighted average or FIFO (first-in, first-out) basis.
    (d) Some of the financial investments may be valued based on equity method.
(4) Valuation of debtors and creditors at their nominal amount.
(5) Value adjustment for impaired fixed assets, financial investments, obsolete and slow inventory and doubtful receivables.

204. Financial statements have to be prepared on the going-concern principle unless legal requirements or other relevant circumstances require otherwise. In the case of liquidation, special accounting principles are applicable.

D. Accounting Period

205. The accounting unit shall record accounting entries during the accounting period continuously. The accounting period is in the most cases equivalent to the calendar year, but it also may be equivalent to the financial year, which is a period of twelve consecutive calendar months not identical with the calendar year. Each accounting unit should announce the change of its accounting period to the relevant tax authorities in writing within thirty days of the unit's establishment or fifteen days prior to the change of the accounting period. Any change is effective only from the first day of a calendar month.

E. Financial Statement under Slovak GAAP

206. Under the Act on Accounting No. 585/2003 Coll. all the accounting unites are obliged to prepare financial statements and consolidated financial statements, if required by the law, for each financial year. The individual financial statements should be prepared not later than six months after the end of the reporting period, while the consolidated financial statements should be prepared during the subsequent accounting period. All publicly listed companies are obliged to prepare quarterly and half-yearly financial statements as well as consolidated financial statements.

207. The individual financial statement consists of balance sheet, profit and loss statement and notes to the financial statement together with a cash-flow statement.

The attached notes shall contain detailed information assessing the unit's assets, liabilities, financial position and financial results after the accounting period. Moreover, it shall indicate the applied accounting principles, valuation methods and depreciation rates. All the details on the forms are available on the website of the Ministry of Finance of the Slovak Republic.

208. The following entities were, from 1 January 2006, required preparing and submitting the individual financial statements in accordance with IFRS:

(1) Companies and partnerships under the Slovak Commercial Code (unlimited partnership, limited partnership, LLC and JSC) while two of the following conditions are met in at least two consecutive accounting periods:
  (a) Total value of assets excluding provisions exceeded EUR 165,969,540.40.
  (b) Net turnover exceeded EUR 165,969,540.40.
  (c) Average number of employees exceeded 2,000.
  (d) In an event that in the following accounting period, the requirements fail to exist, the unit is still required to prepare its financial statements in accordance with the IFRS.
(2) Bank, insurance company or other entities providing financial services.
(3) Entity, which is required to prepare IFRS financial statements under special Government or EU legislation.

209. All consolidated financial statements are to be prepared in accordance with the IFRS. Concerning the cross-border ownership, if a company is owned by a parent company with a seat in the EU (having 100% or at least 90% of ownership and an agreement with other shareholders who agreed with the joint consolidated financial statements), the company is not required to prepare consolidated financial statements and issue an Annual Report on the consolidated financial statements if:

(a) parent and its subsidiaries are included in the consolidated financial statement prepared and submitted by its parent in accordance with EU legislation;
(b) consolidated financial statements prepared by the parent company are audited and published in accordance with EU legislation;
(c) subsidiary discloses in its notes of the individual financial statement the name and seat of its parent company, which prepares the consolidated financial statements and information that the subsidiary did not prepare any consolidated financial statements;
(d) moreover, a parent company is not required to prepare consolidated financial statements if the aggregated data contained in the most recent individual statements of the entities representing the consolidated entity in each of the two preceding accounting periods fulfilled at least two of the following conditions:
  – total asset value of the aggregated entity was less than EUR 17,000,000;
  – net turnover of the aggregated entity was less than EUR 34,000,000; or
  – average number of employees of the aggregated entities in the accounting period did not exceed 250.

(e) parent company is not required to prepare consolidated financial statements if the subsidiaries are not significant; i.e., they are not significantly affecting the financial position and the results of the consolidated entities.

210. All accounting units are required to submit one copy of its financial statements to the relevant tax authority together with its corporate income tax return. Moreover, each unit has to publish its financial statement and Annual Report by filling with the Commercial Register, the LLC, JSC, cooperative and a state company within thirty days after their approval the limited partnership and the unlimited partnership within seven months after the end of the accounting period. The consolidated financial statements must be filed with the Commercial Register within one year after the end of the accounting period. Those accounting units that prepare their individual financial statements in accordance with IFRS have to publish their full financial statements and Annual Reports on the Internet and in the *Commercial Bulletin* (*Obchodný vestník*).

F. Fines

211. The Act on Accounting defines for which breaches of the Act or omissions an accounting entity may be fined. In case of a substantial breach, a company may be fined up to 3% of total gross assets, while in less serious cases up to 1% of its total gross assets. If the value of total gross assets is impossible to assess, the total penalty may rise up to EUR 3.3 million.

G. Auditing

212. Not all of the business entities are required to have their individual financial statement audited. The Act on Accounting stipulates precisely which entities have to undertake this obligation:

(1) Business entities that are obliged to create issued capital (limited liability companies, JSCs and cooperatives), if they met any of the two following requirements at the balance sheet date in the year preceding the relevant year:
   (a) Total value of the entity's assets exceeded EUR 1,000,000.
   (b) Entity's net turnover exceeded EUR 2,000,000.
   (c) Average number of employees exceeded thirty.
(2) All publicly listed companies.
(3) All entities, which are obliged to prepare their individual financial statements in accordance with IFRS.
(4) Certain organizations that are designated by taxpayers as beneficiaries of income tax, if the annual amount of the tax donations exceeded EUR 33,193.92.
(5) Other entities, if stipulated by the law.

All consolidated financial statements must be audited.

213. An audit has to be carried out by the end of the accounting period following the period for which the financial statements were prepared, unless stated otherwise. The auditors have to be members of the Slovak Chamber of Auditors, having five years of experience and passed the qualifying examinations.[38]

38. For more on the audit and auditors *see* Act No. 540/2007 Coll. on Auditors, Audit and Oversight of Audit, which is in force since 1 Jan. 2008 and is based on the 8th EU Directive.

Chapter 5. Business Assets, Goodwill and Commercial Property Rights

§1. Business

I. General Observations

214. Currently Slovakia stands at 42nd position in the ranking of 190 economies on the ease of starting a business (in 2016 it was on 77th position and in 2014 its position was 83rd).[39] This information is useful for assessing how easy it is for an entrepreneur in Slovakia to start a business. The interesting observation is that the World Bank has defined Slovakia as a 'high-income' country.

215. Business in Slovakia may be established as:

- natural person not entered in the Commercial Register or a natural person entered in the Commercial Register; or
- legal entity in the form of a commercial company.[40]

216. Under Commercial Code, an entrepreneur is:

- individual or legal entity entered in the Commercial Register;
- individual or legal entity doing business on the basis of a trading licence;
- individual or legal entity doing business on the basis of a licence other than a trading licence (e.g., doctor, tax advisor, lawyer, translator, hairdresser, etc.); and
- individual engaged in agricultural production, and therefore registered in the relevant list.

217. The Commercial Code sets out the following basic types of commercial company:

- Unlimited partnership is a legal entity made up of at least two partners, who guarantee its liabilities with all of their assets jointly and severally.
- Limited partnership is a personal company with two groups of partners – general partners and limited partners. The general partners guarantee the liabilities of the partnership jointly and severally with all of their assets, and they are entitled to act on behalf of the company. The limited partners guarantee the liabilities of the partnership on a restricted basis, up to the amount of their unpaid contribution as entered in the Commercial Register. They may take decisions only over changes to the Memorandum of Association, and they are not entitled to act on behalf of the company as statutory bodies of the company.
- LLC generates basic capital from the mandatory contributions of the partners and guarantees against a breach of its liabilities with all of its assets. The partners

39. Available online at: http://www.worldbank.org/content/dam/doingBusiness/media/Annual-Reports/English/DB2019-report_web-version.pdf.
40. For more *see* ss 42–51.

guarantee up to the amount of their unpaid contribution, as entered in the Commercial Register. The value of the mandatory basic capital must be of EUR 1. Yet the Commercial Code introduced also another LLC company with the initial capital of EUR 25,000. Thus differentiating between the two companies: (1) with initial capital between EUR 1–EUR 25,000 and (2) above EUR 25,000, the Commercial Code lays down specific provisions concerning the two.
- JSC is a capitalized commercial trading company with an obligation to generate basic capital, the amount of which is recorded in the Commercial Register. As a legal entity, it is responsible for its liabilities through all of its assets. The shareholders are not liable for the obligations of the company. The value of the company's basic capital must be at least EUR 25,000.
- Cooperative is a community of an unrestricted number of persons for the purpose of securing business or economic, social and other needs of its members. Members are not liable for the obligations of the cooperative. The value of the cooperative's basic capital must be at least EUR 1,250. Cooperative must have at least five members (or at least two legal entities).

II. Transactions Relating to the Business

A. *Overview*

218. The conditions applying to transactions relating to the business in Slovakia are set out primarily in the Commercial Code and subsequently also in the Civil Code. This is a result of the existing dual model of the Slovak law of obligations in civil and commercial relations. There are specific contract types regulated in the Civil Code as well as in the Commercial Code. Several are identical, and the scope of their application depends on the nature of their subjects. However, there are generally applicable contract types in these codes, regardless of the nature of subjects. Specific contracts regulated in both codes may fall under the category of consumer protection and may be qualified as consumer contracts, provided that they satisfy legal requirements.

B. *Sale*

219. The Commercial sale contract is regulated in the Commercial Code, which states that the contract is established by agreement of the contractual parties on essential elements of the contract.

220. Essential elements of the sale contract are:

(1) determination of the parties;
(2) specification of the subject matter;
(3) amount of goods;

(4) obligation of the seller to deliver the subject matter of the contract (movable goods) to the buyer and to transfer the respective property rights to the buyer; and
(5) obligation of the buyer to pay the selling price.

221. The sale contract may be concluded in written or oral form; the Commercial Code does not specify the exact form of the contract. In Commercial sale, the contractual parties have to be entrepreneurs. The Commercial Code expressively states that public law subjects (e.g., state body, self-governing region, municipality) may also be a party to Commercial sale contract even though they are not entrepreneurs.

222. Subject matter of the Commercial sale contract can be only movable goods. In case of the immovable things, provisions of the Civil Code generally apply. However, the Commercial Code must be applied in case of contract of sale of an enterprise involving immovable things as parts of the enterprise, and contract of sale of a thing leased (also lease contract or contract on financial lease).

223. The price must be expressed in money. If as the substitute for the goods, other goods were delivered, this would not be a sale contract, but a contract of exchange. The Commercial Code regulates two ways of determination of the price. In the sale contract the price must be: (i) set directly by certain amount of money, or (ii) the manner of its subsequent determination must be set; i.e., the price must be determinable.

224. As regards the transfer (sale) of the immovable property, under section 46 of the Slovak Civil Code, any agreement relating to the transfer of immovable property must be concluded in writing. Immovable property ownership rights are acquired upon registration at the Land Registry (Cadaster). The Slovak law requires the signature of seller on a contract to be authorized. The transfer is effective; i.e., the buyer acquires the title to the immovable property from the date the decision of the proper Land registry office on approval of registration becomes final. The Land registry office is obliged to issue the decision within thirty days following the submission of the application. However, subject to the payment of the fee in amount of EUR 265.50, Slovak law allows the party to request the Land registry office to decide in speedy procedure within fifteen days following the submission of the application for additional fee.

225. An owner's title to immovable property may be verified by inspecting the ownership certificate extract, which is a public document or via online Cadastral Portal https://www.katasterportal.sk/kapor/. Cadastral Portal enables authorized access to land register data, obtain basic information instantly and without visit to the respective Land Registry, for the authorized subjects obtain summary and detailed information without complicated correspondence. Land register data publication on the Internet is supposed to bring enhanced database, improvement of property and legal relations transparency, decrease of corruption and increase of the credit of the Slovak Republic abroad. However, ownership documents obtained through Cadastral Portal cannot be used for legal purposes. They have only informative character.

226. There are also still some limitations on the acquisition of the immovable property for foreigners. Since the entry of Slovakia into the EU in 2004, any person or legal entity from another EU Member State may freely acquire immovable property in Slovakia, even though they are not resident in Slovakia or are not established in the country. However, the freedom to acquire agricultural land and forestland by non-residents is limited by the Foreign Exchange Act 1995 (Act No. 202/1995 Coll. as amended). The non-residents cannot acquire the agricultural land and forestland unless they inherited it or they are Slovak citizens. Regarding the agricultural land, if the non-resident is a citizen of any EU state, has temporary permit in Slovakia and farms at least three years on the agricultural land, he/she may acquire the agricultural land.

C. Lease

227. General provisions of the Civil Code govern lease, while specific provisions of other laws apply to leases of non-residential premises, flats, as well as forest and agricultural land. Commercial leases are governed by Act on lease and sublease of non-residential premises (Act No. 116/1990 Coll. as amended) as well as by the provisions of the Civil Code.

228. Premises may only be rented as commercial premises if they have been classified as commercial premises in the decision of the respective building office authorizing the use of the building or the premises. Further, only the activities stated in the decision of the building office may be exercised on the premises. It is therefore important to check the authorized activities for the premises before concluding the lease.

229. A lease contract must be concluded in writing and must contain the following essential elements:

(1) Definition of the parties and the relevant premises.
(2) Subject matter of the lease and its purpose.
(3) Amount of the rent, due date and method of payment.
(4) Duration of the lease (definite or indefinite period).

230. A lease contract, which does not include all the elements, is invalid. The parties may freely determine all other provisions.

231. A commercial lease may be concluded for a definite or an indefinite period of time.

Unless otherwise stated in the lease contract, a commercial lease for an indefinite period may be terminated from the first day of the month following the month of delivery of the notice. A lease agreement signed for a definite term terminates upon expiry of the agreed term. It may also be terminated before the end of the term by three months' notice solely on the grounds provided by the Act on lease and sublease of non-residential premises.

232. If the tenant continues to use the leased premises after the end of the term and the landlord fails to file a petition with the court for the premises to be handed over within thirty days, the lease agreement is renewed on the same terms and for the same time if the lease was concluded for less than one year or for a one year if the lease was concluded for one year or longer.

233. The transfer of the lease by the tenant without the prior consent of the landlord is not permitted. A tenant may sublease non-residential premises (or a part) only for a definite period and only with the landlord's consent. The rights and duties of the tenant also apply to the subtenant.

D. Management

234. Management means a very wide term within the Slovak legal framework; therefore it is necessary to distinguish between a director (manager) in the position of: (i) a statutory body (or a member of statutory body) of company as defined in the Commercial Code, or (ii) a managing employee as defined in the Labour Code (Act No. 311/2001 Coll. as amended). Generally, the statutory body, i.e., the executive director in the LLC or a board of directors in the JSC, directs activities of the company and makes decisions in all matters not vested to competencies of company's other bodies (e.g., general assembly or Supervisory Board) and acts for and on behalf of the company.

235. A director represents a company and its interests towards third persons. The director manages activities of the company, acts for and on behalf of the company and decides on all matters concerning the company. He/she is liable to perform his/her function with due professional care.

§2. Intellectual Property

I. General Observations

236. Intellectual property (IP), very broadly, means the legal rights, which result from intellectual activity in the industrial, scientific, literary and artistic fields. IP is also characterized as legal protection for commercially precious products of human intellect. The law protects IP for two main reasons. One is to give statutory expression to the moral and economic rights of creators in their creations and the rights of the public in access to those creations. The second is to promote creativity and the dissemination and application of its results and to encourage fair trading, which would contribute to economic and social development.

237. Generally speaking, IP law aims at safeguarding creators and other producers of intellectual goods and services by granting them certain time-limited rights to control the use made of those productions. Those rights do not apply to the physical object in which the creation may be embodied but instead to the intellectual creation as such. IP is traditionally divided into two branches, 'industrial property' and 'copyright'. The first one includes rights connected mainly to industrial designs, trademarks and patents. The other one protects artistic and literary work, as well as the rights of performers and broadcasting organizations.[41]

A. *Overview of IP Rights*

238. Industrial property rights protect technical or aesthetic inventions and trademarks. This mainly concerns patents for inventions, designs, industrial models, trademarks and geographical origin.

239. Industrial property rights are divided into two groups:

(1) Industrial property rights to results of creative intellectual activity, and
(2) Industrial property rights to designation.
Industrial property rights to results of creative intellectual activity:
 (a) Patent rights (rights of inventions) and supplementary protection certificates – which are granted following the performance of formal/legal and factual research for discoveries which are new, which include inventive effort and which are industrially useful. Patents apply for twenty years, with the payment of continuation fees.
 (b) Designs – are understood to include the appearance of a product or parts thereof, consisting mainly of the characteristic lines, outlines, colours, shape, structure or materials of the product itself or its ornamentation. Registration of a design applies for five years from the date of submitting the design application. The validity period of a design registration may be extended up to four times on the basis of an application from the design owner, up to a maximum of twenty-five years.
 (c) Utility models – if there is a new technical solution, which is the result of inventive effort and is industrially useful. The protection lasts for four years from the submission of the application for the utility model and may be extended twice, for three years each time, on the basis of an application from the utility model owner.
 (d) Semiconductor topographies – topographies which result from creative intellectual effort by the originator and which do not currently exist in semiconductor products. The protection of a topography ends ten years after the end of the calendar year in which it commenced.
 (e) Animal and plant variety rights (plant breeder's rights) – the exclusive right for production, promotion, sale, import and export of the variety.

41. *Intellectual Property Handbook* Ch. I (WIPO 2004).

Industrial property rights to designation:

(a) Trademarks – verbal, pictorial, spatial or combined markings, which make it possible to distinguish the goods or services of one person from the goods or services of another person. The protection period of a trademark is ten years from the date of submitting the trademark application. The owner may apply to extend the protection period of a trademark by renewing the registration for a further ten years following payment of an administrative fee.

(b) Trade name – the name under which a company is recorded in the Commercial Register. The name must not be interchangeable with the name of another business.

(c) Designation of origin and geographical indications protects designations of origin for products and geographical indications for products.

240. Rights similar to Industrial property rights:

(1) Rights similar to Industrial property rights that are results of creative intellectual activity:
   (a) Innovations (right of innovative drafts).
   (b) Right to new ways of prevention, diagnosis and treatment of humans and animals and protections of plants against pests and diseases.
   (c) Know-how.
(2) Rights similar to industrial property rights on designation:
   (a) Logo.
   (b) Domain names.
   (c) Protection of personality and protection of the name and reputation of the legal entity.

241. Copyrights and related rights (also known as literary and artistic rights) protect original literary and artistic works, and also musical compositions, television programmes, computer programs, databases, advertisements and multimedia platforms.

B. Common Characteristics of IP Rights

242. IP Rights include all intangible assets, which are eligible to be subject of dispositions (in private relationships) of its owners and have certain potential proprietorial (or at least moral) value regardless of whether they are the result of the creative intellectual activity or not.

243. Common Characteristics of IP Rights are the following:[42]

42. Vojčík, P. Intellectual Property Rights. Aleš Čeněk, Plzeň, 2012, pp. 30–31.

(1) Special laws regulate subjects of the IP (Patent Act, Design Act, etc.), but there are also rights without special regulation (e.g., logo, domain names, know-how, etc.).
(2) Subjects of the IP may but also may not be a result of the creative intellectual activity. Regarding the subjects, which are the result of the creative intellectual activity (e.g., copyright work), special law protects also the creator (author or originator). Regarding the subjects, which may not be the result of the creative human intellectual activity (e.g., trademark, business name), industrial property law does not protect their creators. Trademark may, however, be a copyright work.
(3) Special laws usually regulate creating and using of the subject of protection including rights of the authors or originators. In certain cases the laws regulate only using of the subject of IP (e.g., in case of trademarks). Creation of the trademark, if it is a copyright work, may be protected by the copyright.
(4) Subjects of the IP have value and may be evaluated.
(5) Subject of the IP may be only such intangible asset, which may be in individual property of the natural or legal persons, i.e., persons may obtain exclusive rights to it.

C. *International Treaties*

244. IP is governed by several conventions introduced by two main organizations – the World Intellectual Property Organization (WIPO) and the World Trade Organization (WTO). Slovakia as EU Member State has adopted the following conventions, leading to better harmonization of national regulations in this field. Namely, Slovakia has ratified the following international multilateral treaties:

(1) Madrid Agreement Concerning the International Registration of Marks.
(2) Common Regulations under the Madrid Agreement Concerning the International Registration of Marks and the Protocol Relating to That Agreement.
(3) Budapest Treaty on the International Recognition of the Deposit of Microorganisms for the Purposes of Patent Procedure.
(4) Convention Establishing the WIPO.
(5) Nice Agreement Concerning the International Classification of Goods and Services for the Purposes of the Registration of Marks.
(6) Paris Convention for the Protection of Industrial Property.
(7) Strasbourg Agreement Concerning the International Patent Classification.
(8) Lisbon Agreement for the Protection of Appellations of Origin and Their International Registration.
(9) Locarno Agreement Establishing an International Classification for Industrial Designs.
(10) Madrid Agreement for the Repression of False or Deceptive Indications of Source on Goods.
(11) Patent Co-operation Treaty.
(12) Trademark Law Treaty.

(13) Protocol Relating to the Madrid Agreement Concerning the International Registration of Marks.
(14) Agreement on Trade-Related Aspects of Intellectual Property Rights (TRIPS Agreement).
(15) WIPO Performances and Phonograms Treaty.
(16) WIPO Copyright Treaty.

II. Patents

A. *Legislation*

245. Slovak patent law is governed by Act No. 435/2001 Coll. on patents, supplementary protection certificates and on amendment of other acts (the Patent Act) as amended and by Decree of the Industrial Property Office of the Slovak Republic (IPO) No. 223/2002 Coll. implementing Act No. 435/2001 Coll. the Patent Act. Further patent legislation includes Paris Convention for the Protection of Industrial Property, Patent Co-operation Treaty, Strasbourg Agreement Concerning the International Patent Classification, Budapest Treaty on the International Recognition of the Deposit of Micro-organisms for the Purposes of Patent Procedure, and TRIPS Agreement.

B. *Nature and Duration of the Protection*

246. Slovak law defines patent as a protective document granted by the state giving the patent owner the exclusive right for exploitation of his/her invention during the fixed period. By publishing the patent the owner gives to the public valuable technical information. Under the Patent Act patents are granted for inventions, which are new, involve an inventive activity and are susceptible of industrial application after performing preliminary and substantive examination. The so-called deferred examination with the publication of applications after the expiry of eighteen months is implemented. The full examination is carried out upon the request of an applicant, which must be filed within thirty-six months from the filing date of the patent application. It is also possible to patent chemical products and medicaments.

247. The term of the validity of a patent is twenty years as from the filing date of the patent application. The prerequisite of the duration of the patent protection is the payment of maintenance fees.

C. *Substantive Requirements*

248. Patents are granted to the inventions, which are new, involve the inventive activity and which are susceptible of industrial application. Patentable are not only the new products, devices and technologies but also chemical substances, medicines, microorganisms used in industrial production as well as biotechnological processes and products resulting from them. The first criterion is the criterion for patentability of the subject matter. The subject of protection are inventions in all areas of technology, and therefore the evaluation of this criterion should be established whether the solution is an invention or not.

249. The scientific theories, computer programs, plant or animal varieties, the new methods for prevention, diagnosis and treatment of human and animal body processes for cloning human beings and use of human embryo for industrial or commercial purposes are not patentable. The new plant or animal varieties, the new methods for prevention, diagnosis and treatment of human and animal body could be protected under other special legislation.

250. The novelty of the invention is one of the basic substantive requirements of patentability. An invention is considered to be new if it does not form part of state of the art. This fundamental substantive condition applies absolutely and objectively, which means that everything that was available to public by any means of disclosure anytime before the day from which an applicant enjoys priority right, anywhere and any method is not new.

251. To grant patent is not enough that the subject of the application is new. Patentable invention must differ from the state of the art by more than a novelty. It must also include a so-called inventive activity. An invention is considered as a result of an inventive activity if it is not for a person skilled in the art obvious from state of the art. The inclusion of 'inventive activity' as the criteria of patentability is aimed to distinguish patentable invention from other formally new and beneficial inventions (not every formally new and useful invention is a result of an inventive activity). Patentable is the invention, which is a certain contribution to the state of art as a whole. The Patent Act does not include definition of inventive activity. The Act only defines the method of its practical evaluation; i.e., invention includes an inventive activity when it is not apparent to the person skilled in given field in obvious manner from the state of the art. For obvious is considered everything that does not go beyond the skills of professionals in the given technical field. Patentable inventions thus lie beyond the normal routine engineering work. The last of the conditions of patentability is industrial applicability. An invention is considered to be industrially applicable if its subject matter can be produced or utilized in any branch of industry, particularly in any branch of industry and agriculture.

252. The possibility of the production or use of the invention in any industry is such a general condition that its practical fulfilment usually makes no problems. Prerequisite for industrial application is that object based on the invention can be reproduced at any time, i.e., manufactured or otherwise benefited. The invention must be objectively feasible. Unfeasible are usually proposals containing substantial errors, or contrary to objective scientific and technological developments (e.g., *perpetuum mobile*, etc.).

D. Formal Requirements

253. The right to file a patent application has the inventor. Co-inventors of an invention have the right to a solution within the extent to which they participated in creating an invention.

254. The patent application must include a request for granting the patent on prescribed form, description of the invention, patent claims defining the subject matter for which the protection is sought, and drawings and the abstract. The patent application may be filed with the IPO (Office) in Banská Bystrica or with the branch of the Office in Bratislava.

255. Filing of the patent application and its registration by the Office in the register of the patent application is followed by the preliminary examination that eliminates from the ongoing procedure applications containing matters apparently unpatentable (for instance, therapeutic methods), lacking unity or containing defects preventing them from publishing. The Office notifies an applicant of all the deficiencies. If the patent application meets all the requirements, it is published eighteen months after the priority date in the *Official Journal*. As from the date of publication, whoever can file the observations against the patentability of the invention that will be considered by the Office in the procedure of the full examination.

256. The Office on request of the applicant or the other person carries out the full examination of the patentability. This request must be filed within thirty-six months from the filing date and relevant administrative fees must be paid. The patent is granted on the basis of the full examination after if it is found that the invention meets all legal requirements for patentability. In other words, if the invention meets the criterion of protection, criterion of novelty, criterion of inventive activity and criterion of industrial application – every single criterion and all together – the patent protection can be granted. If the requirements of patentability are not met, the Office invites the applicant to remedy the application within certain time period. The Office, subject to the request of the applicant, can extend this time period. If the applicant during the administrative procedure does not remove the defects of the application, the Office will stop the patent application procedure.

E. Rights of the Patentee

257. The patent owner has the exclusive right for the invention. It means that no one may use it without his/her consent. The patent owner has exclusive right to exploit an invention, to grant consent for the exploitation of an invention, to assign a patent to another person or to establish right of lien to a patent. Consent of the owner to use the patent by the other person is given by the licence agreement. The patent can be also sold or transferred to the other person – legal or natural person. The transfer and licence agreement have effect in respect of the third party after registering into the Patent register. Contractual right of lien begins on the day of entry into the Patent register.

258. Without the consent of a patent owner the following is prohibited:

(1) Producing, exploitation, offering or placing on the market, or for this purpose storing or importing a product, which is a subject matter of a patent.
(2) Exploitation of a production process, which is a subject matter of a patent or offering such protected process for exploitation to another person.
(3) Producing, exploitation, offering or placing on the market, or for this purpose storing or importing a product directly obtained by a protected process.
(4) Supplying or offering for delivery to a person not entitled to exploit an invention any means enabling him/her to carry out an invention, if a person infringing right has been informed or with regard to circumstances he should have been informed that these means are intended or suitable to carry out an invention.

F. Inventions by Employees

259. Under the Patent Act if an inventor has created an invention within the framework fulfilling tasks from an employment, similar relationship or from membership relation, right to a solution passes to an employer, until parties to this relationship agreed otherwise. Right of being an inventor remains unaffected.

260. An inventor who has created an invention is obliged to inform an employer about this fact immediately in writing, and at the same time he is obliged to submit any materials necessary for assessment of an invention. An employer is entitled to exercise right to a solution towards the inventor in writing, within a time limit of three months from the above-mentioned notification of the inventor. If an employer fails to exercise right to a solution patent in writing within the time limit, this right passes back to an inventor. An employer, as well as an inventor, is obliged to preserve confidentiality about invention towards third parties. An inventor is entitled to an appropriate remuneration from an employer.

G. Protection of Biotechnological Inventions

261. The Patent Act states that patents are also granted for biotechnological inventions concerning a product consisting of or containing biological material or to a process by means of which biological material is produced, processed or utilized, including cases when invention relates to:

(1) biological material, which is isolated from its natural environment or is produced by means of a technical process, already occurred in nature;
(2) plant or an animal, if technical feasibility of an invention is not reduced to a particular plant or animal variety;
(3) microbiological or other technical process or to a product obtained by such process;

(4) element isolated from a human body or produced by other means of a technical process, including a sequence or partial sequence of a gene also in the case when the structure of such element is identical with a structure of a naturally existing element.

H. Supplementary Protection Certificates

262. Supplementary protection certificates are granted for medicinal products and for plant protection products pursuant to Regulation (EC) No. 469/2009 of European Parliament and of the Council concerning the creation of a supplementary protection certificate for medicinal products and Regulation (EC) No. 1610/96 of European Parliament and of the Council concerning the creation of a supplementary protection certificate for plant protection products.

263. A supplementary protection certificate may be granted for any medicinal product or plant protection product, which was, prior to being placed on the market, subject to an administrative authorization procedure provided that following conditions are met in the Slovak Republic on the filing date:

(1) Medicinal product or plant protection product is protected by a valid basic patent (Slovak or European with a designation for the Slovak Republic).
(2) Valid authorization to place the medicinal product or plant protection product on the market as a medicine or preparation for plant protection has been granted.
(3) Product has not already been the subject of a certificate.
(4) Authorization referred to in (2) is the first authorization to place the product on the market as a medicinal product or plant protection product.

The certificate takes effect at the end of the lawful term of the basic patent for a period equal to the period which elapsed between the date on which the application for a basic patent was lodged and the date of the first authorization to place the product on the market in the Community, reduced by a period of five years. The duration of the certificate may not exceed five years from the date on which it takes effect.

This period may be exceeded for another six months in case of medicinal products on which studies pursuant to experimental paediatric plan have been performed.

I. Legal Actions by Third Parties

264. Opposition: Any person may file oppositions on patentability of a subject matter of an application with the Office after the publication of an application.

265. Request for Revocation: The Office is obliged to revoke a patent if during proceedings started on third-party request or ex officio it is proved that:

(1) requirements for its granting have not been met;
(2) invention has not been disclosed and described in a patent so clearly and fully so that it could be carried out by a person skilled in the art;
(3) subject matter of a patent exceeds content of an application as filed. This also applies in case if the subject matter of a patent granted on the basis of a divisional application exceeds contents of an application as filed;
(4) scope of protection following from patent was exceeded;
(5) owner is not entitled to a solution;
(6) requirements for its granting pursuant to regulations valid in the time of its granting have not been met.

III. Utility Models

A. Legislation

266. Slovak Models law is governed by Act No. 517/2007 Coll. on Utility Models as amended and Decree of the IPO No. 1/2008 Coll. implementing Act No. 517/2007 Coll. on Utility Models.

B. Definition of a Model

267. Utility model is a form of protection of new technical solutions, which are results of an inventive activity from any technical field.

C. Models Excluded from Protection by the Models Law

268. According to the Models Act the following is not deemed to be a technical solution:

(1) Discoveries, scientific theories and mathematical methods.
(2) Aesthetic creations.
(3) Plans, rules and methods for performing mental acts, playing games or trade.
(4) Activities.
(5) Computer programs.
(6) Presentation of information.

269. Under the Models Act the following cannot be protected by utility model:

(1) technical solutions, commercial exploitation of which would be in contradiction with public order or good manners; prohibition of a technical solution

exploitation as such is not considered to be in contradiction with public order or good manners within the meaning of this provision;
(2) plant and animal varieties;
(3) essentially biological processes for production of plants or animals;
(4) methods of surgical or therapeutic treatment of human or animal body and diagnostic methods and methods of disease prevention used on a human or animal body;
(5) technical solutions concerning products consisting of biological material or containing biological material or a process by means of which the biological material is produced, processed or used;
(6) methods for production of chemical substances;
(7) methods for production of pharmaceutical substances; and
(8) medical use of substances and compositions of substances.

D. Substantive and Formal Requirements

270. Every utility model application is subject to an examination procedure by the Office. Those utility model applications, which are not technical solutions, are not industrially applicable (cannot be repeatedly used in industrial activities) or belong to exclusions from the protection, are excluded from further proceedings. Only a technical solution may be subject to the protection of the utility model. The Models Act does not define the term of technical solution; however, the Act states what does not fall under the technical solution and cannot be protected by utility model.

271. A technical solution is considered to be new if it does not form a part of state of the art. State of the art means everything made available to the public by any means of disclosure before the day from which an applicant for a utility model enjoys priority right. Technical solution is considered to be industrially applicable if its subject matter can be produced or used in any branch, particularly in any branch of industry and agriculture.

272. When formal and material irregularities of a utility model application documents are corrected, the Office is obliged to perform a research on state of the art on a technical solution subject matter. The research result must be communicated to an applicant, an application together with the research result is published and publication must be announced in the *Official Journal.*

273. If proceedings on an application have not been suspended or an application has not been refused within examination and no oppositions against entry of a utility model into the Models register have been filed or oppositions against entry of a utility model into the Models register have been refused, or proceedings on oppositions have been suspended, the Office enters a utility model into the Models register and an applicant becomes a utility model owner. The Office issues a certificate on entry of a utility model into the Models register to an owner and entry of a utility model is announced in the *Official Journal.*

E. Rights Conferred by a Model

274. A utility model owner has an exclusive right to exploit a technical solution protected by utility model, to prevent third parties from exploitation of a technical solution protected by utility model without his/her consent, to provide his/her consent with exploitation of a technical solution protected by utility model (licence agreement), to assign a utility model to another person or to establish a lien to a utility model. A utility model is effective from the day on which an announcement of entry of a utility model is published in the *Office Journal*. The transfer and licence agreement have effect in respect of the third party after registering into the Models register. Contractual right of lien begins on the day of entry into the Models register.

F. Legal Actions by Third Parties

275. Opposition: The Models Act provides that any person is entitled to file opposition against entry of a utility model into the Models register with the Office after the publication of an application within three months from this publication for a reason that a subject matter of an application fails to meet conditions of protection.

276. Request for cancellation: Next, after the registration, the Models Act states that the Office may cancel a utility model from the Register on request of a third party. Request for cancellation must contain legal and factual statement of reasons and concurrently evidence, submitted by a requester for cancellation and on which the request for cancellation is based, has to be submitted or indicated. The Office invites a utility model owner to respond to request for cancellation within a specified time limit. If a utility model owner fails to respond within a specified time limit, the Office cancels the utility model from the Register. If it is not possible to decide on the basis of written filing of a requester for cancellation and a utility model owner, the Office appoints a date of the oral hearing. The Office cancels the utility model, if:

(1) subject matter of a utility model is not suitable for protection;
(2) applicant was a person, who was not entitled to utility model protection;
(3) application fails to meet condition of only one technical solution or a group of technical solutions may be interconnected to create a single technical concept;
(4) subject matter of a utility model extends the content of an application as filed;
(5) several utility models with identical subject matter have been registered for the same applicant;
(6) conditions for entry of a utility model into the Register in accordance with regulations valid in the time of its registration have not been met.

IV. Designs

A. *Legislation*

277. Slovak Designs law is governed by Act No. 444/2002 Coll. on Designs as amended and Decree of the IPO No. 629/2002 Coll. implementing Act No. 444/2002 Coll. on Designs.

B. *Definition of a Design*

278. Design means the appearance of a whole or a part of a product resulting from the features of, in particular, the lines, contours, colours, shape, texture or materials of a product itself or its ornamentation. Design protects the outward appearance of a product. Subject of a protection is an image of the appearance of the product or its part. The scope of protection relies on the image of the design as it is filed in the Register. Registered design does not protect technical, constructional, functional, material or other entities of the product, though this would be obvious in certain performance or even generalized.

C. *Substantive and Formal Requirements*

279. Design is eligible for the protection if it is new and has individual character and is deemed to be identical if its features differ only in immaterial details. A design is considered new if no identical design has been made available to the public before the date of priority. Design has a specific character if the overall impression on informed user is different from the overall impression of the published design released the day before filing an application or the day before the rise of priority right.

280. Design application is a subject of examination; i.e., Office examines whether the application meets the requirements of the Act. In case when the design can be registered, the Office enters design into the register of designs and publishes it. The applicant becomes its owner. Owner of the registered design will receive a certificate on registration.

D. *Rights Conferred by a Design*

281. Registered design owner has an exclusive right to exploit registered design, to prevent third parties from exploitation of registered design without his/her consent, to provide his/her consent with exploitation of registered design, to transfer registered design to another person or to establish a lien to registered design. The transfer and licence agreement have legal effects towards third parties from the day of entry in the Register. The contractual right of lien begins on the date of entry into the Register. The validity of the registered design is renewed by the Office pursuant to the request for renewal of the validity of the registered design filed by the owner of the registered design or one of the co-owners of the registered design repeatedly for up to four periods of five years, up to a total term of twenty-five years from the date of filing the application.

E. Legal Actions by Third Parties

282. The Designs Act empowers the Office to cancel registered design based on the proposal of the third party from the Register, if:

(1) registered design does not correspond to the definition of design;
(2) it ascertains that design has been registered contrary to conditions for registration;
(3) its owner is not entitled to design;
(4) distinctive sign is used in registered design, which confers to owner of this sign right to claim prohibition of using such sign before the priority date of registered design;
(5) registered design constitutes an unauthorized use of a work protected pursuant to copyright law;
(6) registered design constitutes unauthorized use of any features mentioned in an international convention or other symbolic features, flags or escutcheons to which an international convention is not related and which are of particular public interest in a Member State.

V. Plant Breeder's Rights

A. Legislation

283. Slovak Plant Breeder's Rights are governed by Act No. 202/2009 Coll. on the Legal Protection of Plant Varieties, together with European legislation – mainly Council Regulation (EC) No. 2100/94 on Community plant variety rights and Commission Regulation (EC) No. 874/2009 establishing implementing rules for the application of Council Regulation (EC) No. 2100/94 as regards proceedings before the Community Plant Variety Office.

B. Definition of a Variety

284. The Act does not define the term variety. In this case, the Act refers to Council Regulation (EC) No. 2100/94 on Community plant variety rights. Under the Regulation, variety means a plant grouping within a single botanical taxon of the lowest known rank, which grouping, irrespective of whether the conditions for the grant of a plant variety right are fully met, can be:

(1) defined by the expression of the characteristics that results from a given genotype or combination of genotypes;
(2) distinguished from any other plant grouping by the expression of at least one of the said characteristics; and
(3) considered as a unit with regard to its suitability for being propagated unchanged.

C. Substantive and Formal Requirements

285. Breeder's certificate, i.e., plant variety rights, is granted for varieties that are:

(1) Distinct.
(2) Uniform.
(3) Stable.
(4) New.
(5) Designated by a denomination.

286. Distinctness: A variety is deemed to be distinct if it is clearly distinguishable by reference to the expression of the characteristics that results from a particular genotype or combination of genotypes, from any other variety of common knowledge as of the date of filing. The variety is generally known if at the date of filing it is already registered in the State Variety Book or in the common catalogue of varieties.

287. Uniformity: A variety is deemed to be uniform if, subject to the variation that may be expected from the particular features of its propagation, it is sufficiently uniform in the expression of those characteristics, which are included in the examination for distinctness, as well as any others used for the variety description.

288. Stability: A variety is deemed to be stable if the expressions of the characteristics, which are included in the examination for distinctness as well as any others used for the variety description, remain unchanged after repeated propagation or in the case of a particular cycle of propagation, at the end of each such cycle.

289. Novelty: A variety is deemed to be new if, at the date of application, variety constituents or harvested materials of the variety have not been sold or otherwise disposed of to others, by or with the consent of the breeder, for purposes of exploitation of the variety:

(1) Earlier than one year before the above-mentioned date, within the territory of the Community.
(2) Earlier than four years or, in the case of trees or of vines, earlier than six years before the said date, outside the territory of the Community.

290. The term of the Breeding certificate runs until the end of the twenty-fifth calendar year or, in the case of varieties of vine and tree species, until the end of the thirtieth calendar year, following the year of grant. Ministry of Agriculture and Rural Development of the Slovak Republic for the purposes of the Plant Variety Act undertakes the same activities as the Community Plant Variety Office in Angers.

291. If the applicant files a national application first and then the European one, the applicant has to inform the Ministry. Ministry then suspends the proceedings until the decision of the Community Plant Variety Office, and if the Office issues the breeding certificate, it will not continue in proceedings until the end validity of a Community plant variety rights.

292. It means that in the case of new plant varieties, a double legal protection, i.e., simultaneous protection in Slovakia and at EU level, is excluded. The Ministry cannot grant the Breeding certificate to the variety that is protected by special regulations, particularly by the Regulation. This means that one and the same variety cannot be granted both national and EU protection simultaneously.

D. Rights Conferred by a Breeding Certificate

293. The rights arising from granted Breeding certificate include:

(1) Exclusive right to exploit the variety at Applicant's own expense.
(2) Right to give consent for Applicant's commercial exploitation to others under a licence agreement, consent for use may relate in particular the right to produce or reproduce (multiplication); conditioning for the purpose of propagation; offering for sale; selling or other marketing; export; import; stocking for any of the purposes.
(3) Right to transfer the Breeding certificate.
(4) Right to seek legal protection against unauthorized interference with the rights to the new variety.

294. The contract for the transfer of the Breeding certificate must be in writing; the authenticity of signatures of the transferor and the transferee must be authorized to be valid. The contract for the transfer of the Breeding certificate enters into force on the date of registration in the Breeding certificates register.

VI. Trademarks

A. Legislation

295. Act No. 506/2009 Coll. On Trademarks governs the Slovak trademark law.

B. Definition of a Trademark

296. A trademark is verbal, figurative, three-dimensional or combined sign which is capable of distinguishing goods and services on the market.

C. The Different Signs Which Can Be Registered as a Trademark

297. A trademark may consist of any sign capable of being represented graphically and consisting particularly of words, including personal names, letters, numbers, drawings, shape of goods or their packaging or their mutual combinations, if such sign is capable of distinguishing goods or services of one person from goods or services of the other person.

D. Substantive Requirements

298. Distinctive Character: The basic requirement of the trademark is its distinctive character. In order for a sign to be classified as distinctive, it must produce a sufficiently direct and specific connection with the goods or services, which would enable the public concerned immediately to perceive, without further thought, a description of the goods and services or one of their characteristics.

According to the case law signs, which have no distinctive character in particular are those which, from the perspective of relevant public, are commonly used in the trade, for the presentation goods or services, or in respect of which there are at least specific indications that allow the conclusion that they could be used in that manner. In addition, signs with no distinctiveness are not capable of performing the essential function of the trademark, that is to identify the origin of goods or services in order to enable the consumer who acquires goods or services covered by the trademark at a later acquisition, to perform the same choice if he had a positive experience, or to perform different choice, if he had a negative experience.

Distinctiveness of the sign provides identification of the origin of goods and services. A sign with no distinctive character particularly consists of a letter or numbers in a standardized format, the simple representation of the products or from simple geometric figures. There is no distinctive character of signs that have exclusively descriptive character, i.e., providing information about the goods and services. A sign consisting of one colour is not distinctive for any goods or services and may be registered only under very specific conditions. It should be absolutely the unusual colour relative to those goods and services as well as it is necessary to demonstrate acquired distinctiveness for the goods or services. A combination of two colours is to be assessed in relation to the declared goods and services, depending on the manner and the ratio of displayed colours.

A sign is not distinctive, if it is a combination of colours, which has only decorative nature (e.g., car colour, colour of T-shirts), if the colour is a characteristic of the goods (e.g., for paints), if the colour is a descriptive designation or its use is required in terms of technical functionality (e.g., red for fire extinguishers, different colours used for electrical cables) in the case of a sign usually or commonly used on the market, or if it expresses characteristics of goods (e.g., yellow for lemons). In the case of a combination of three or more colours, a rule applies that the higher the number of colours, the sign has smaller distinctive character because a customer can hardly remember a larger number of colours and their order.

Slogans are rated as non-distinctive signs, if they mean only compliments for product or service, or if they are more or less a challenge to their purchase. Another situation occurs when a slogan contains funny connection of verbal elements that give a humorous meaning or consists of witty rhymes. Examples of original slogans are: 'Nibbles so right, tastes so healthy, so easily disappear!', 'Healthy tip to sweet hit'. An example of non-distinctive slogan could be: 'We are here for you!', 'We will help you', etc.

299. Exclusions: The Trademarks Act excludes the following signs from the registration:

(1) Signs which do not conform with requirements of the Trademarks Act.
(2) Signs which has no distinctive character.
(3) Signs which consist exclusively of signs or indications which may serve, in trade, to designate the kind, quality, quantity, intended purpose, value, geographical origin or the time of production of goods or of rendering of service, or other characteristics of goods or service.
(4) Signs which consist exclusively of signs or indications which have become customary in the current language or in the bona fide and established practices of trade.
(5) Signs, which consist exclusively of a shape of goods, which result from the nature of the goods or are necessary to obtain a technical result, or give substantial value to goods.
(6) Signs which are contrary to public policy or to accepted principles of morality.
(7) Signs which are of such nature as to deceive the public as to nature, quality.
(8) Signs which contain signs registered in accordance with an international convention without the consent of a competent authority.
(9) Signs which contain signs using of which is contrary to provisions of other legal enactments or with obligations of the Slovak Republic resulting from international treaties.
(10) Signs which include signs of high symbolic value, particularly religious symbol.
(11) Signs which include badges, emblems or escutcheons or other than those covered by an international convention without the consent of the competent authority.
(12) Signs which are subject of application not filed in good faith.
(13) Signs which contain geographical indication and are filed with respect to wines or for spirits not having that origin.

E. Formal Requirements

300. By filing the trademark application the applicant enjoys the priority right against any person who subsequently files an application for registration of a trademark identical or confusingly similar to that mark for identical or similar goods or services. The Office is obliged to examine whether the application complies with the conditions laid down by the Trademarks Act.

301. Before the entry of the trademark in the Trademarks Register, any person may submit observations in the written form to the Office; the Office must take into account the observations in proceedings leading to the decision on the entry of the trademark in the Trademarks Register. The person who submitted the observations will not become a party to the proceedings. If the application meets all registration conditions, the Office publishes the application in the *Official Journal*. If within the period of three months from the publication no opposition against the entry of the mark in the Trademarks Register is filed, the Office registers the trademark in the Trademarks Register.

302. The term of protection of the registered trademark is ten years as from the filing date of the trademark application. Upon the request of the trademark owner and subject to payment of administrative fee, the Office will renew the term of protection for another ten years.

F. Rights Conferred by a Trademark

303. A trademark owner has the exclusive right to affix his/her goods or services with the trademark for which it is registered or use it in connection with those goods or services. Further, the owner is authorized to use the ® mark with the trademark.

A trademark owner has the right to:

(1) exploit the trademark;
(2) give consent for commercial exploitation to others under a licence;
(3) transfer the trademark;
(4) establish a lien to the trademark;
(5) seek legal protection against unauthorized interference with the rights to the trademark.

304. The transfer of the trademark and licence agreement becomes effective towards third parties upon its entry in the Trademarks Register. The right of lien on the trademark is established upon its entry into the Trademarks Register.

305. The owner is entitled to prevent all third parties not having his/her consent from using in the course of trade:

(1) any sign which is identical with the trademark in relation to goods or services, which are identical with those for which the trademark is registered;
(2) any sign where because of its identity with, or similarity to, the trademark and the identity or similarity of the goods or services covered by the trademark and the sign, there exists a likelihood of confusion on the part of the public; the likelihood of confusion includes the likelihood of association between the sign and the trademark;
(3) any sign which is identical with, or similar to, the trademark in relation to goods or services which are not similar to those for which the trademark is registered, where the latter has a reputation on the territory of the Slovak Republic and where use of that sign without due cause takes unfair advantage of, or is detrimental to, the distinctive character or the reputation of the trademark.

G. Legal Actions by the Trademark Owner

306. In case of infringement or jeopardizing trademark rights, the owner of the trademark has the right to apply to the court for an order that the goods, materials or tools infringing or jeopardizing trademark rights were:

(1) recalled from the channels of commerce;
(2) definitively removed from the channels of commerce;
(3) prevented from further infringement or jeopardizing the rights; simple removing of unlawful using of sign on faked goods are not considered as a provision preventing further infringement;
(4) destroyed in a suitable manner.

307. The trademark owner has also the right to apply to the court for a decision to order the party infringing or jeopardizing his/her rights to provide information on the origin and distribution networks of the goods or services or circumstances of placing the goods or services on the market.

H. Legal Actions by Third Parties

308. Observations: Any person is entitled till the registration of the sign to submit written observations against entry of the sign into the Register; the Office must take into account observations in deciding on entry of the sign into the Register. The Office is obliged to inform the applicant about the observations and is obliged to request him/her to respond within the prescribed time limit. The Office must inform the applicant and the person who submitted observations about results of observations assessment.

309. Oppositions: After the publication of the application in the *Official Journal*, an opponent (section 7 of the Patent Act) is entitled to file oppositions to registration within the period of three months from the publication date.

310. Request for Revocation: The Office is obliged to revoke the trademark on the request of a third party:

(1) If the trademark has not been properly used for goods or services in respect of which the trademark is registered within the continuous period of five years in the territory of the Slovak Republic, unless proved otherwise by the owner of the trademark or there are no legitimate reasons for non-use, the trademark is considered not used in the territory of the Slovak Republic within the continuous period of five years. The Office will not revoke the trademark, if the use of the trademark commenced or was resumed following five years of non-use and filing the request for revocation of the trademark; the use which commenced or which was resumed following five years of non-use of the trademark within three months preceding the filing of the request for revocation is disregarded where the preparations for the commencement or the resumption of the use occurred only after the owner becomes aware that a request for revocation of the trademark might be filed.
(2) If by the consequence of acts or inactivity of the owner the trademark has become the common name in the trade for products or services for which it is registered.
(3) If the trademark, in consequence of the use made of it by the owner or with his/her consent in respect of the goods or services for which it is registered, is liable to mislead the public, particularly as to the nature, quality or geographical origin of those goods or services.

311. Upon a request of a third party, the Office is obliged to revoke the trademark on the basis of the court decision declaring that:

(1) trademark containing the name and surname or the image of the natural person, or its pseudonym, infringes the rights to protection of personality;
(2) trademark containing the name or the trade name of the natural or the legal person interferes with its reputation;
(3) trademark infringes earlier copyright;
(4) using of the trademark is an act of unfair competition.

VII. Copyright

312. Slovak copyright and rights related to copyright are based on the classic European standards, meet the terms of degree of approximation and achieve the compatibility with EU criteria required by the EU. Copyright is defined as exclusive right connected to the creation of creative literary, scientific or artistic activity. Slovak copyright law belongs to continental copyright group, and the Slovak copyright law was influenced by both French and German legal science.

313. Act No. 618/2003 Coll. on copyright and related rights as amended governs Slovak copyright law. Copyright is further divided into two partial entitlements (copyrights): individual moral authors' rights (*droit moral*) and proprietorial (economic) authors' rights. Copyright arises already in moment of creating of the work and to prove the copyright no formal registration is required, as the rights arise directly from the Act.

314. Author: The author is a natural person who has created the work.

315. Work: Copyright applies to literary work or other works of arts and a scientific work, which are the unique outcome of the creative activity of the author, especially:

(1) Literary work and computer program.
(2) Literary work expressed by speech, a presentation or otherwise, especially exhibition and lecture.
(3) Theatrical work, especially a dramatic work, a dramatical-musical work, a pantomimic work and a choreographic work, and other works created for the purpose of its releasing.
(4) Musical work with text or without text.
(5) Audiovisual work like, especially, cinematographic work.
(6) Painting, a drawing, a graphic design, an illustration, a sculptural work and other works of fine arts.
(7) Photographical work.
(8) Architectural work, especially a work of architecture and town-planning work, a landscape work and an interior-architectural work and a building design work.
(9) Work of applied arts.
(10) Cartographic work in analogue or other forms.

316. The subject matter of copyright is also the work of a collection, especially an anniversary volume, journal, encyclopaedia, anthology, broadcast programme, exhibition or other databases.

A. *Exclusions from Copyright*

317. Copyright does not apply to:

(1) idea, manner, system, method, concept, principle, discovery or information that has been expressed, described, explained, depicted or incorporated in the work;
(2) text of legal regulation, official decision, public charter, publicly accessible register, official records, Slovak technical norm including a draft documentation thereof and translation of such works, daily reports and a speech and address presented during official proceedings.

B. Individual (Moral) Authors' Rights

318. The author has the following rights to:

(1) label or not to label his/her work with his/her name or pseudonym and to request that his/her name or pseudonym is given in all reproductions of his/her work in the proper manner during every use of the work in public, namely according to the manner of use;
(2) decide about making releasing his/her work;
(3) the inviolability of his/her work, especially to protection against any unauthorized alteration of, or other intervention into his/her work, and also against any defamatory manipulation with his/her work, which would result in violation of his/her dignity and good reputation. If not ensuing otherwise from the nature of the work or of its utilization, the author has the right of author's supervision (author's alteration) over the manipulation with his/her work; in the case of architectural work, the author's supervision is the supervision over the building construction.

The author cannot waive his/her rights. These rights are not transferable and terminate by the death of the author.

C. Proprietorial (Economic) Authors' Rights

319. The author has the right to use his/her work and the right to grant authorization to every use of his/her work, especially:

(1) make a reproduction of the work;
(2) distribute an original work or its copy to the public by sale or other forms of assignment of title;
(3) distribute an original work or its copy to the public by rental or lending;
(4) alteration, translation and adaptation of work;
(5) inclusion of the work into a work of collection;
(6) public exhibition, presentation of the work.
(7) public performance of the work.
(8) communication of the work to the public.

The rights are not transferable, but they are the subjects of inheritance. The author may not waive the rights. These rights last for the life of the author and for seventy years after his/her death.

320. Copyright contract law: The Copyright Act includes two kinds of contracts: licence contract and contract for work. By means of a licence contract, the author grants the licensee his/her consent with the use of his/her work (licence). The licence contract must contain the manner of use of the work, the scope of the licence, period of licence validity granted by the author or the manner of its determination and remuneration or the manner of its determination, if free of charge provision of the licence was not agreed upon between the author and the licensee. The licence contract must be in writing; otherwise it is invalid.

If not stipulated by the contract that the author has granted the exclusive licence, it means that the non-exclusive licence was granted. The licensee is entitled to grant a third person his/her consent to use the work within the licence granted to him/her (sublicence) only with the author's consent. The licensee may transfer the licence by means of an agreement only with the prior author's written consent.

The author by contract for work undertakes to create a work for the client. The parties may agree upon remuneration for creating a work. The author is obliged to create the work personally. Neither by concluding a contract for work nor by transfer of the object through which the work is expressed, the client acquires the right to use this work, if not specified otherwise, except if the client concludes a licence contract with the author, simultaneously with the conclusion of the contract for work or after its conclusion.

321. Employee work: If not agreed otherwise, the author's economic rights to an employee work are exercised by the employer in his/her own name and on his/her own account, regardless of termination of his/her employment contract. If the employer has been carrying out the author's economic rights to an employee work it means that the author had given his/her consent to release this work and that the employer can perform the work in public under his/her name, if not stipulated otherwise; however, individual (moral) rights of the author to an employee work are not prejudiced.

VIII. Know-How

322. The Slovak law does not specially regulate know-how, and its protection is particularly in its confidentiality. This concept is not even defined in any applicable laws despite the fact that mainly contracts, agreements and covenants often deal with this term. The Civil Code determinates the subject matter of the civil relationships as follows: Things and, if their nature admits so, rights or other property values can be subject to civil relationships. Know-how is considered to be 'other property value', and under legal theory it has to comply with the following characteristics:[43]

(1) it is an intangible asset, which is expressed in a form enabling its perception and cognition;
(2) it consists of knowledge, information, and experience in various fields, particularly economic;
(3) it has essential importance (is useful) for its user;
(4) it is not generally known or available;
(5) it has its value (price) which can be expressed in money;

43. Vojčík, P. *Know-How and Its Protection.* Bulletin of Slovak Advocacy. 10/2009, pp. 12–16.

(6) it is usable by others; and
(7) it is not protected by special regulations.

323. Know-how is related to the trade secret. The fundamental difference lies in the fact that trade secret is a specific institute of commercial law and the know-how may be its possible subject matter. Know-how can stand separately and not be part of the assets of the business. It may be the property of a natural or legal person not engaged in business. The right to protection of know-how belongs to the (natural or legal) person that has acquired the know-how by its own activity or activities of its employees or other persons, by its own means (financial or otherwise) or its methods. The right to protection belongs also to the person who legally acquired know-how. Owner of the know-how has a protection against anyone who illegally obtained the know-how, illegally possess it, sell it or use it illegally in its favour.

324. The most interesting feature of know-how is its evaluation in money. Even though know-how is considered intangible, its value for the pragmatic purposes of any corporation should be expressed in money. Decree No. 492/2002 of the Ministry of Justice of the Slovak Republic lays down fairly complex formulas in order to formally establish the capitalization of know-how. These formulas take into consideration: (i) years, during which the know-how was used; (ii) the definable resources that are created by using the know-how; and (iii) determine the contribution which falls on know-how generating the resources.

325. Violation of the rights to know-how can lead also to unfair competition. In a competitive environment, one competitor may unduly use the know-how of the other competitor (contrary to good morals of competition), which is capable of causing harm to the other competitor or to a consumer.

§3. Trade Name

326. The Trade (Business) Name is regulated in the Commercial Code. The trade name is characterized as the designation under which an entrepreneur is entered in the Commercial Register or as was established (if not registered in the Register) and the trade name of an individual (sole proprietor) is the person's first name and surname. Business name should not be open to confusion with the name of another entrepreneur and not give the false impression of an entrepreneur or a scope of business. Commercial names of several entities may reflect joint ownership interest of shareholders, if they are mutually distinguishable.

327. To distinguish the business name of a legal entity, different indication of legal form is not enough. In case of a natural person, stating different place of business is sufficient to distinguish. If an individual has the same first and last name as another entrepreneur in the same place of business, it is required to add to its business name amendment stipulating additional name or type of business so that the business names can be mutually distinguished.

328. The legal regulation of commercial names is based on several principles, such as:

(1) principle of exclusiveness, which means that a new commercial name must differ sufficiently from existing commercial names;
(2) principle of stringency, which means that the commercial name must meet the requirements of distinctness;
(3) principle of truthfulness, which requires that any information included in the commercial name and indicating a particular line of business reflects the entrepreneur's current business activity;
(4) principle of legality, which requires that the commercial name does not contradict the law;
(5) principle of public interest, which means that the commercial name may not include any inadmissible expressions (e.g., vulgar terms).

329. If rights are affected or threatened by unauthorized use of a trade name, the owner may seek to prevent unauthorized user from such conduct and removal of consequences resulting from the infringement of the right, in particular, may seek:

(1) destruction of unlawfully manufactured goods infringing the right to the trade name or its withdrawal from circulation or from other forms of use; or
(2) destruction of materials and implements used in the infringement of trade name or threat of infringement of the trade name or its withdrawal;
(3) provide information on the origin and distribution of goods and services infringing the trade name including;
(4) data about owner, manufacturer, distributor, supplier or seller of goods infringing the trade name or service provider infringing the trade name;
(5) data about produced, delivered, made, taken or ordered quantity or price of goods or services infringing the trade name.

330. Further the owner may claim the infringer to hand over the unjust enrichment and a just satisfaction. If unauthorized use of the business name caused harm, it may also seek damages.

§4. The Protection of Domain Names

331. The domain names are not currently regulated by any generally binding legal regulation. Their legal existence is primarily created only based on contracts between applicants and registrars (so-called soft law). Subsequently, protection of domain names may fall under law of trademarks, law of trade names and law of unregistered signs in economic competition. These traditional rights on designations have limited territorial scope; however, domain names have territorially unlimited, i.e., global scope. In the field of domain names alternative dispute resolutions are frequently used. Within the registration contracts, all applicants have to consent with such clauses (arbitration clauses) in majority of the top-level domain names (e.g.,.com,.net,.eu,.cz, etc.).[44]

332. Exception of the above-mentioned is, e.g., the Slovak top-level domain.sk, since the SK-NIC – Slovak top-level domain registry – did not till to date include such clause into its contracts or rules and therefore disputes regarding the.sk domain are decided by proper Slovak general court. Under Slovak case law, right conferred by the trademark that is protected on the territory of the Slovak Republic, according to Trademarks Act, may be violated only by the holder of the domain. Plaintiff may defend its rights by action to refrain or removal against defendant, who in this case may be only the holder of the domain. Under valid court decision SK-NIC may perform in particular the following:

(1) SK-NIC unilaterally withdraws from a domain contract, which cancels record of domain in the database of SK-NIC and removes records of domain from the primary name server.
(2) SK-NIC will block the ability to change the domain record in the database of SK-NIC. In the case of transfer of the domain to the plaintiff (or his/her legal representative), SK-NIC unblocks the possibility of performing change in the holder of the domain to the plaintiff clearly identified in the court decision.

333. Despite the majority of the top-level domains lack generally binding legal regulation,.eu top-level domain is regulated by Regulation (EC) No. 733/2002 of the European Parliament and of the Council of 22 April 2002 on the implementation of the.eu Top-Level Domain and Commission Regulation (EC) No. 874/2004 laying down public policy rules concerning the implementation and functions of the.eu Top-Level Domain and the principles governing registration. This Regulation is directly effective and binding for all public bodies and private persons in all EU Member States. The Prague-based Arbitration Court attached to the Czech Chamber of Commerce and the Agricultural Chamber of the Czech Republic provides the alternative dispute resolution for.eu domain name disputes.

---

44. Návrat, M. *Computer Program, Database and Domain Name in Intellectual Property Law*, in Švidroň, J., et al. eds, *Intellectual Property Law in Information Society and in System of Law* 450–459 (Bratislava: VEDA 2009).

Chapter 6. Bankruptcy and Related Institutions

334. The purpose of the Act on Bankruptcy and Restructuring No. 7/2005 Coll. (Act on Bankruptcy), which came into effect on 1 January 2006, is to arrange the financial relations of debtor in case of its bankruptcy, either in a form of a restructuring or of the complete foreclosure of its assets and property in bankruptcy. The common feature of both of these forms of procedures is to arrange the financial relations in a way to achieve the maximum satisfaction of debtor's creditors within the shortest possible time. Furthermore, the explanatory report to the Act on Bankruptcy states that it is the purpose of the Act to avoid loss on the value of the bankrupt's property in the period just prior to the commencement of bankruptcy proceedings and during the proceeding, to increase the responsibility of all parties involved in the proceedings, mainly the trustees as well as to avoid the existing absence of the conflicting provisions of international private and procedural law in the area of bankruptcy.

335. The Act on Bankruptcy and Restructuring has several times been revised since its adoption; lastly the amended provisions came into effect on 29 April 2015, while already new changes are to be expected from 1 October 2015 to 1 January 2016. If necessary, those changes will be reflected upon in the following parts. These amendments have been, however, adopted in the wake of political scandal, when one of the biggest Slovak companies – *Váhostav* – which is very closely connected to the governing party has declared bankruptcy. It should be mentioned that the Act on Bankruptcy and Restructuring is in compliance with Council Regulation (EC) No. 1346/2000 of 29 May 2000 on insolvency proceedings.

336. Thus, there are two types of insolvency proceedings under the Slovak Act on Bankruptcy:

(1) Bankruptcy, and
(2) Restructuring.

337. The Act on Bankruptcy recognizes besides the basic two proceedings also other proceedings such as Debt Clearance, Personal/Small Bankruptcy for natural persons – non-entrepreneurs or small businesses – special treatment for insolvent financial institutions, including banks or insurance providers.

§1. Bankruptcy (Konkurz)

338. The purpose of bankruptcy proceeding is to resolve the debtor's insolvency by liquidating its assets in order to satisfy the unfulfilled claims of the debtor's creditors. The Act on Bankruptcy specifies the circumstances under which the debtor is obliged to file for insolvency and when creditor is entitled to require the initiation of bankruptcy proceeding.

I. Insolvent or Excessively Indebted Debtor

339. In order to file for bankruptcy, one of the two circumstances has to take place:

(1) debtor is insolvent; or
(2) debtor is excessively indebted.

340. Under section 3 of the Act on Bankruptcy, an insolvent debtor is the one who is unable to perform within thirty days after the maturity day at least two financial obligations to more than one creditor. If the financial obligation cannot be recovered by form of an execution or the debtor has not fulfilled an obligation imposed on him by a notice, the debtor is considered to be insolvent. When assessing the insolvency of a debtor, the Act defines one claim as all claims, which originally belonged to one creditor during the ninety days prior to the filing of a petition for bankruptcy. In other words, this is the case to prevent a situation, when a creditor assigns some of its claims to the other entity/entities to achieve the plurality of claims and creditors, necessary to force bankruptcy. Moreover, monetary obligations that a debtor does not recognize or refuses to negotiate for some other reason do not count as overdue obligations.

341. However, an excessively indebted debtor is a debtor, who has more than one creditor and the value of its liabilities exceeds the value of its assets. Only those entities, which are required to keep financial statements as companies or sole entrepreneurs can be excessively indebted, as the excessive indebtedness is determined by reference to a debtor's financial statements. In determining the value of assets and liabilities, the accounting or expert opinion is taken into consideration, whereas the expert opinion has priority before the accounting. Naturally, during the assessment, the consideration is given to the expectable results of future asset management or expectable results of further operation of the company. When calculating the liabilities, the amounts associated with subordination (payments for a mother company) and subordinate claims are not taken into account.

342. Subordinate claims, according to section 408a of the Commercial Code, are those which stem from subordinate relationship between two entrepreneurs (subordination agreement), where the parties agree that in the event of bankruptcy of a debtor or in case of dissolution with liquidation, the claims of creditor will be satisfied only after the claims of other creditors are satisfied. The contract that includes a subordination must be in writing. The subordination relationship has to exist for more than three years. It is impossible to modify the subordination agreement. Parties are unable to withdraw from the agreement before the expiry of the time for which it was concluded for. Furthermore, parties cannot change the date of the expiry, and in the case, the agreement was concluded for definite time to change it for indefinite.

343. The subordination agreement ceases to exist by:

(1) expiry of the period for which it was concluded, however, if before the expiry of the agreement, the debtor's bankruptcy is initiated, a settlement is allowed or the debtor goes into liquidation, the agreement may not cease to exist before the repeal of bankruptcy, fulfilment of the settlement or the termination of liquidation;
(2) expiry of three years from the receipt of the notice of termination, if the agreement was concluded for an indefinite period, however, if before the expiry of the agreement, the debtor's bankruptcy is initiated, a settlement is allowed or the debtor goes into liquidation, the agreement may not cease to exist before the repeal of bankruptcy, fulfilment of the settlement or the termination of liquidation;
(3) dissolution of the debtor without liquidation, if it is a bank.

II. Creditor's Petition for Bankruptcy (Involuntary Bankruptcy)

344. Creditor is entitled under the Act on Bankruptcy to file a petition for bankruptcy if it can reasonably expect debtor's insolvency, i.e., if debtor is in delay for more than thirty days with the fulfilment of at least two enforceable or recognized-in-writing monetary claims of at least two creditors, despite the fact that it has been called upon in writing to fulfil its obligations by one of these creditors. It is necessary to point out that the Act on Bankruptcy does not stipulate a specific provision on creditor's entitlement to petition for bankruptcy in the case of the excessive indebtedness of debtor. This is due to the fact that within the filing for initiation of bankruptcy proceeding, creditor has the burden of proof to document that overdue claim from at least two creditors is present. In case of indebtedness, creditor supposedly would not be able to bear the burden of proof.

345. In the petition for initiation of bankruptcy proceeding, creditor has to prove all the facts and circumstances, based on which one can reasonably presume that the debtor is insolvent. Apart from the general prerequisites, a creditor's petition for bankruptcy proceeding must contain the following documents, which prove:

(1) existence of outstanding claims;
(2) facts showing that those creditors whose claims have been proven by enforceable decisions or recognized by the debtor in writing have called upon the debtor in writing to settle the claims;
(3) petitioner has made advance payments to cover the remuneration and costs of a preliminary trustee (in case of natural person it is EUR 663.80 and in case of legal entity, EUR 1,659.70); and
(4) appointment of a service of process agent, in case a creditor does not have its seat in the Slovak Republic.

346. In case a creditor wrongfully petitioned for bankruptcy, it might be held liable for the damage incurred by it in connection with the effects of initiation of the bankruptcy proceeding, unless the creditor proves that in filing the petition for bankruptcy he/she acted with reasonable professional care. This liability is connected not only to the debtor but also to other third parties. The preconditions for liability are:

- filling a petition for bankruptcy by a creditor;
- discontinuance of the bankruptcy proceeding due to the debtor proving its solvency;
- occurrence of damage;
- casual relationship between the effects of the commencement of the bankruptcy proceeding and the occurred damages; and
- failure of the creditor to act with reasonable professional care.

III. Debtor's Petition for Bankruptcy (Voluntary Bankruptcy)

347. Most of the bankruptcy proceedings are initiated by debtors themselves, while under the Commercial Code and the Act on Bankruptcy a debtor must act within reasonable professional care and thus file a petition for bankruptcy proceeding within thirty days from the moment it knew or should have known with maintaining the due care that it is excessively indebted. The same duty applies for the statutory authority of debtor or its member/s, or for the liquidator of debtor or its legal representative. In case of failure to petition for bankruptcy, a debtor or its representative (a statutory body and its members) might be held also criminally liable for the failure to file for bankruptcy, with the sentence to a term of imprisonment of from six months up to five years.

348. If the petition for initiation of bankruptcy proceeding is filed by a debtor, besides the requirements stated in subsection II, a debtor is obliged to attach a list of its assets and liabilities together with the list of its related persons, who are under the Act on Bankruptcy directly or indirectly economically or factually connected to the debtor. Moreover, if a debtor keeps its accounts according to a specific regulation, the petition must contain the last annual individual financial statements together with the extraordinary individual financial statements if drawn later than the last annual individual financial statement. If the individual financial statement has been subject to verification by an auditor, the auditor's report shall be as well disclosed.

A. Liability of Debtor

349. A person who, during the four years prior to the bankruptcy proceedings, in the capacity of a statutory body or its member, liquidator or the legal representative of the debtors, has breached its duty to timely file a bankruptcy petition has the obligation, from the moment of declaration of bankruptcy, to pay EUR 12,500 to a company. Modification or elimination of this claim is forbidden (by ways of company waiving its right or by the company's Statute). This provision applies for limited liability companies and JSCs. The highest amount of the fine may be twice the minimum amount of a capital company. If more persons breached their duty, they are liable jointly and severally.

350. Only a person who proves that he/she did not breach its duty to timely file a bankruptcy petition or that he/she acted with due care will be released from this obligation. Furthermore, one, who is not authorized to act on behalf of the debtor alone, will be released from this obligation if he/she proves that he/she could not fulfil its obligation due to the lack of cooperation of those with whom he/she should have been acting together and from the moment he/she got to know or ought to have known of the breach of this obligation, he/she filed the deeds notice that the debtor is over-indebted.

IV. Commencement of Bankruptcy Proceeding and Bankruptcy Declaration

351. If the court finds that all the statutory requirements for the commencement of the bankruptcy proceeding have been met, within fifteen days after the delivery, the court shall decide on its acceptance. Otherwise, it will dismiss the petition within the same time period. All the incomplete petitions are not automatically disregarded, and according to the Code of Civil Procedure, the court instructs the petitioner at the latest fifteen days after the delivery of incomplete petition on the deficiencies, which shall be removed within ten days. If the petitioner fails to remedy the deficiencies, the court dismisses the petition in its entirety. Otherwise, the court initiates the bankruptcy proceeding.

352. Once the petition for the proceeding has been accepted, the court will within five days from the commencement of the proceeding call upon the debtor to comment on the petition and prove its financial solvency and provide the copies of the necessary documents. Furthermore, the court within five days determines the hearing date, where it summons the debtor and notifies all the creditors identified in the petition. Moreover, the court invites the debtor to express its views on the possibility of the court to declare the debtor bankrupt without a court hearing. If a debtor agrees, court cancels the hearing.

353. In the case, a debtor did not prove its solvency court declares the bankruptcy of the debtor. Otherwise, the court dismisses the case. In case, when the bankruptcy is declared, only a debtor has the right to appeal, while in case the petition is dismissed, both debtor and creditor are entitled to file for an appeal. The Court of Appeals shall render a decision within forty-five days after referral.

V. Effects of Bankruptcy

354. Before going to the effects of the bankruptcy, it needs to be clarified that the bankruptcy proceeding has two main stages when it comes to the start of the bankruptcy. The first one is the 'commencement' of the proceeding, which starts once the petitioner files its motion for commencement of the bankruptcy proceeding and the second part – 'bankruptcy resolution' – of the process starts by rendering a court resolution (*uznesenie*), which is then immediately published in the *Commercial Bulletin* (*Obchodný vestník*). By the publication, the bankruptcy proceeding begins. From this moment on, any new bankruptcy proceeding of the same debtor is precluded. If any new petition for initiation of the bankruptcy proceeding is delivered during this time, the court regards it as an application for accessing to the bankruptcy. The Bankruptcy Act enumerates list of effects, which begin either by the commencement of the bankruptcy proceeding and those, which begin with the rendering the bankruptcy declaration by a court and its subsequent publication.

355. The commencement of bankruptcy proceeding has the following effects:

(1) Debtor is obliged to limit its activities only to ordinary legal acts; in case the debtor breaches this obligation, the validity of the concerned legal acts may be contested.
(2) No enforcement proceedings may involve the assets and property of debtor; all already commenced enforcement proceedings shall be suspended.
(3) No security rights should be created over the assets of debtor and no enforcement of security rights shall be initiated and those, which have been initiated, shall be discontinued; this does not affect the performance of security rights over receivables in bank account, state bonds, convertible securities or voluntary auctions.
(4) Dissolution of a company without liquidation shall be suspended.

356. Further effects on a debtor come with the bankruptcy resolution, which has the following effects:

(1) Court appoints a trustee who dispenses with the bankruptcy assets instead of the debtor in order to wind up the business and liquidate the assets.
(2) All court and administrative proceedings are suspended, expect tax and custom proceedings.
(3) All claims against the debtor and all debtor's claims against creditors and third persons become immediately due.

VI. Lodging of Claims

357. Once, a bankruptcy proceeding has been commenced, all the creditors should promptly lodge their claims. According to the Act on Bankruptcy, there are two different applicable regimes, one under the Slovak law and one under EC Regulation 1346/2000. The proceeding under Slovak law is compulsory for all residents in the Slovak Republic and creditors outside of the EU. The creditors resident in other EU Member States are entitled to choose between the Act on Bankruptcy and the EU Regulation.

358. The method of lodging claims is two-folded. Claims are lodged not only in the court but also simultaneously with the trustee. The period when bankruptcy creditors may lodge their claims is a forty-five-day period starting from the declaration of bankruptcy. If the creditor delivers its claim after the determined period, its application is accepted; however the creditor may not exercise any voting rights and other rights related to the filed claim. The court is not obliged to invite creditor to supplement or correct an incomplete or incorrect application. The creditor is responsible for inaccuracy of the data stated in its application. If the trustee rejects the creditor's claim and the court states within the proceedings on determination of a rejected claim that the creditor was not entitled to the payment of the amount of the lodged claim, or that the creditor claimed an excessive amount (the real claim is less than 75%), the creditor may be obliged to pay a penalty in the amount determined by the court in favour of the affected party, unless the creditor proves that it proceeded in lodging its claims with due care.

359. If the claim is duly lodged, the trustee verifies whether it is well founded and if so, the trustee accepts the claim. Otherwise, it will reject the claim. Under the Act on Bankruptcy, the trustee only can reject the lodged claim within a period of thirty days after expiry of the period for lodging claims. If the claim is rejected, creditor may initiate a specific legal proceeding against the trustee before the court within thirty days. If then the court decides that the claim is well founded, the creditor may exercise its rights in the proceedings. Otherwise, if the claim is unfounded or that the amount claimed is excessive, the creditor may be significantly fined by the court.

VII. Realization of the Assets

360. Realization means converting all assets subject to bankruptcy into money value in Euro in order to satisfy the creditors. Realization also includes securing the debtor's cash, receiving performance from the debtor's monetary claims and disposal of the debtor's company or its part for valuable consideration. In order to satisfy the creditors from the debtor's assets and estate, the Act on Bankruptcy governs classification of the assets into so-called general estate (assets subject to bankruptcy which do not belong to any of the separate estates, i.e., assets from which unsecured receivables of the creditors are satisfied) or so-called separate estate, covering all the other types of assets.

361. Realization of assets subject to bankruptcy aims at maximizing the proceeds in the shortest possible time and at the lowest cost. When realizing assets subject to bankruptcy, the trustee should act with due professional care in order to best fulfil the aim of the realization, while observing the rules laid down for realization by the Act on Bankruptcy and other applicable rules. The trustee appointed upon the resolution of bankruptcy should, without delay, realize the assets that are imminently perishable, or likely to be destroyed or suffer other substantial deterioration; no instruction of the competent authority or a judicial decision is required.

362. The trustee keeps clear records of the realization of assets subject to bankruptcy; separate records should be kept for the general estate and for each individual estate. Following the realization of an estate inventory item, the trustee should allocate the proceeds to the inventory item that was realized. Where the trustee realizes several inventory items at the same time and it is not possible to determine the individual proceeds, he/she should proportionately divide the total proceeds among the items concerned according to their counter value; this calculation is based on the value indicated in the inventory.

363. The trustee should deposit the proceeds of the realization of the assets subject to bankruptcy in a newly opened bank account; the interest paid by the bank in respect of the balance in the account should be considered to be proceeds of the realization of assets subject to bankruptcy.

364. The Act on Bankruptcy defines several methods for realization of assets of a debtor. The trustee in order to realize the assets may:

- publish a public tender;
- entrust an auctioneer with the sale of the assets;
- entrust a securities trader with the sale of the assets;
- organize an auction, competitive bidding or any other competitive procedure aiming at the sale of the assets; and
- sell the assets using any other appropriate method.

365. Concerning the distribution of the liquidated assets, a secured claim of a secured creditor should be satisfied, to the extent established, from the proceeds of the realization of the assets constituting the separate, individual estate of the secured creditor that remained after the claims against the estate linked to the inventory items of the assets constituting the separate estate had been deducted. Where a secured claim of a secured creditor cannot be satisfied in full, the remaining part should be satisfied as an unsecured claim.

366. Unsecured claims should be satisfied, to the extent established, from the proceeds of the realization of the assets constituting the general estate that remained after the claims against the estate linked to the inventory items of the assets constituting the general estate had been deducted. Where unsecured claims cannot be satisfied in full, they should be satisfied proportionately.

367. Claims linked to an obligation of subordination pursuant to a specific legal provision ('subordinated claims') should be satisfied, to the extent established, from the proceeds of the realization of assets constituting the general estate that remained in the general estate after other unsecured claims had been satisfied in full. Where subordinated claims cannot be satisfied in full, they should be satisfied proportionately.

VIII. Closure

368. The court decides to cancel a bankruptcy proceeding owing to lack of assets, also without any motion, if it establishes that the bankrupt's assets are insufficient to satisfy claims against the estate; in its resolution, the court should decide on the remuneration and the costs of the trustee to be paid from the debtor's assets, on the advance of the remuneration and the costs of the temporary trustee or on the advance of the payment of the costs of the bankruptcy proceedings.

369. In the case the bankruptcy proceeding was successfully carried out by the trustee and the creditors were satisfied, the court decides, based on the trustee's motion, on the cancellation of the bankruptcy proceeding after the final distribution of the proceeds has been made.

370. On the date of cancellation of the bankruptcy proceeding, the trustee should close the books of account and draw up a separate financial statement pursuant to specific legal provisions. The trustee should also hand over to the debtor or, if appropriate, to the liquidator, all required documents and the remaining assets, and ensure that any further action related to the cancellation of the bankruptcy proceeding be taken. Once the action has been taken, the court should officially revoke the trustee from his office.

IX. Personal Bankruptcy (Small Bankruptcy)

371. Personal Bankruptcy is a fairly novel legal institute, which entitled also natural persons – non-entrepreneurs – to file for bankruptcy. This institute allows an individual to solve his/her bad financial situation and relinquish of his/her debts. The personal bankruptcy is also called small bankruptcy because it may be commenced also by other persons than the non-entrepreneurs, namely by natural persons – entrepreneurs – or legal persons, if:

(1) their assets probably do not exceed EUR 165,000; or
(2) turnover of the debtor in the last completed financial year prior to bankruptcy filing does not exceed EUR 333,000; or
(3) probably debtor does not have more than fifty creditors.

372. Concerning the personal/small bankruptcy, there are several differences with the classical bankruptcy proceeding. The legislator's aim was to simplify the proceeding and speed up the entire procedure while encouraging also the non-entrepreneurs to file for a bankruptcy if necessary. The value of the debtor's assets must at least reach EUR 1,659.70 in order for the court not to dismiss the proceeding. This amount is justified by the necessity to pay the advance payments and fees for the procedure and trustee. However, secondarily due to this, those non-entrepreneurs who otherwise would fulfil other requirements to not possess such amount and therefore the number of filings for personal bankruptcy is minimal.[45]

§2. Restructuring (Reštrukturalizácia)

373. Where the debtor is threatened with bankruptcy or where the debtor is insolvent, besides bankruptcy proceeding there is one more option for the debtor – to opt for either court (formal) restructuring or out-of-court (informal) restructuring. In case of restructuring, a debtor authorizes a trustee to produce a restructuring opinion in order to establish whether the requirements for the debtor's restructuring have been met. This is without prejudice to the debtor's obligation to file a petition for the initiation of bankruptcy in time.

I. Trustee's Opinion

374. The trustee's opinion has to be prepared by a trustee who is listed in the list of trustees. The trustee has to prepare the opinion impartially and apply his/her professional level of care. Debtor shall provide all necessary documents, information and explanation and cooperate during the entire time for proper preparation of the opinion. The creditors are also entitled to appoint a trustee and to file a petition for restructuring. However, in order to prepare the opinion, creditors need substantial access to the documents of debtor and therefore, unless the debtor agrees to the restructuring, a successful initiation of the restructuring is unlikely to occur in practice.

375. In the opinion, trustee recommends restructuring of the debtor only if the following conditions are met simultaneously:

(a) a debtor has not ceased to perform its business activity;
(b) a debtor is insolvent or insolvency is imminent;
(c) financial statements provide a trustworthy and true view of the circumstances concerning the bookkeeping and financial condition of a debtor;
(d) at least two years have passed since the last restructuring of a debtor or its legal predecessor;
(e) It is reasonable to expect maintaining at least a substantial part of the debtor's business; and
(f) in the case of restructuring authorization, it is reasonable to expect a greater range of creditors' satisfaction than in a case of bankruptcy proceeding.

---

45. *See* the Statistics provided by the Ministry of Justice of the Slovak Republic, available online at: http://www.justice.gov.sk/Stranky/Informacie/Statistika-konkurznych-konani.aspx/ (accessed 31 May 2013).

376. If the trustee does not recommend the restructuring despite the fact that during the time of preparation of the opinion the requirements were met, he/she is liable for caused damage to one for whom he/she prepared the opinion, unless trustee proves that he/she did not recommend the restructuring due to the lack of cooperation of the debtor.

377. Once a court ascertains that the petition formally complies with the statutory requirements and that it is fully supported by the trustee's opinion, the court must initiate restructuring proceedings within fifteen days of the receipt of the petition. Otherwise, it will dismiss the petition within the same time period. In case of incomplete petitions, the court does not instruct the petitioner to remove the deficiencies. The court resolution on the commencement must be then subsequently published in the *Commercial Bulletin* without delay. Formally, the restructuring proceedings effectively start at 12 noon the next day after the publication. From this moment on, debtor has to restrict all its activities only to ordinary legal acts.

378. After the restructuring proceeding has been commenced, the court must ascertain whether the preconditions for the restructuring have been satisfied. The court is bound by the recommendations of the trustee and unless there are clear deficiencies, the court is obliged to issue a restructuring resolution and appoint the trustee, who prepared the opinion, within thirty days after the commencement of restructuring proceeding.

379. Once the court approves the restructuring procedure, creditors may start to lodge their claims. Only those creditors will have the right to exercise their claims and become members of the creditors' committee, who have in a manner prescribed by the Act on Bankruptcy registered their claims. If they do not lodge their claims properly and timely, within thirty days from the approval of the restructuring, their rights to pursue those claims expire once the restructuring plan is approved. The lodging procedure is similar to one for bankruptcy proceeding described in §1, VII of this chapter.

II. Business Activities of Debtor During Restructuring

380. Despite the restructuring, debtor remains in possession of its business, though, under supervision of the trustee, court and its creditors. Within the court resolution, the court may specify and limit the scope of those legal acts of the debtor that require the approval of the trustee. The creditors' committee may extend this scope of legal acts at any time during the restructuring. Such decision becomes effective once published in the *Commercial Bulletin.*

381. The trustee during the restructuring proceeding has to supervise the business of the debtor. Trustee while carrying out its duties with a professional level of due care has to follow the development of the financial and business situation. In case that the situation dramatically changes and the successful completion of the restructuring cannot be reasonably expected, the trustee shall immediately petition the court to declare bankruptcy and thus start the bankruptcy proceeding. Furthermore, the trustee has to ensure that the debtor does not diminish the value of its assets or otherwise frustrates successful completion of the proceeding. If such situation would take place and the debtor repeatedly or seriously breached its legal obligations, the trustee must without any delay petition the court to declare bankruptcy.

382. Besides the creditors' committee, trustee it is also the court which oversees the activities of debtor together with the activities of the committee and trustee. The court is authorized to require trustee the explanations or reports on the progress of restructuring, which the trustee has to provide in specified period.

III. Restructuring Plan

383. The restructuring plan is the key document of the restructuring proceeding. The restructuring plan is a document providing for formation, modification or termination of the rights and obligations of the plan participants as well as for the scope and way of satisfying those participants of the plan, who lodged their claims with the trustee in time or are the shareholders of the debtor. After the court confirms the restructuring plan, all participants are bound by it. The plan is divided into descriptive part and binding part.

384. The measures and steps taken by the plan are flexible and in certain cases might be general. Giving an example, they may establish a restructuring of debts, converting debts into equity, converting into different legal form of business, transferring some of the assets of debtor to newly establish entity or even suggest a merger. The final draft of the restructuring plan must be submitted for a prior approval to the creditors' committee within ninety days of the authorization of restructuring. This time limit may be extended by additional sixty days, if reasonably requested. The extension of period together with the reasons is immediately delivered to the creditors' committee and subsequently published in the *Commercial Bulletin*. If the restructuring plan is not submitted within the period, the trustee shall immediately petition the court to declare bankruptcy.

385. After the final draft of the restructuring plan is delivered to the creditors' committee, the committee has fifteen days to decide. If the creditors' committee has any objections to the plan, it may request the person who submitted the plan, usually a debtor, to revise the draft within a period no longer than fifteen days. If the creditors' committee rejects the proposed draft or does not approve it within the limited period – fifteen days – the trustee immediately petitions the court to declare bankruptcy. Otherwise, once the creditors' committee approved the draft of restructuring plan, the committee without any delay requires the trustee to convene the approval meeting.

386. The voting during the approval meeting takes place in at least two groups, one consisted of secured creditors whose rights are affected and the second group of the other unsecured creditors. Where relevant, the shareholders of the debtor form the third group. The party submitting the plan may divide the groups into further separate groups, which would share identical economic interest. In order to approve the restructuring plan, the following requirements have to be met:

(1) In each group of secured creditors, more than two-thirds value majority approval.
(2) In each group of unsecured creditors, a simple value majority approval.
(3) In each group of shareholder, a simple value majority approval.
(4) In aggregate, a simple majority of votes by value of creditors attending the approval creditors' meeting.

387. The restructuring plan, which is approved by the creditors' committee, shall be delivered to the court within ten days after the meeting together with the minutes. Unless there are obvious reasons for a rejection of the restructuring plan, the court confirms the restructuring plan in fifteen days by a resolution, which is subsequently published in the *Commercial Bulletin*. The restructuring plan is, however, not published, unless a new loan agreement has been concluded. In such case, the relevant facts connected to the loan agreement become public. The parties and their representatives have the right to inspect the court file and to make excerpts and photocopies of the file.

388. Under the Act on Bankruptcy, the confirmed and published restructuring plan in the *Commercial Bulletin* is considered to be a legal act in the form and manner required by special regulation for the formation, modification and termination of the rights and obligations contained in the restructuring plan. If for the formation, modification and termination of the rights and obligations included in the plan, a decision of a competent authority is required by the Act on Bankruptcy, the right or obligation arises only from the decision of the competent authority. The competent authority may not refuse to issue a decision on the sole ground that the plan was not taken in a form or manner required by special regulation. Thus, once a court renders a resolution of restructuring plan, the legal fiction of perfection is linked to the restructuring plan.

389. The restructuring procedure ceases to exist by publishing the court's resolution on termination of the restructuring proceeding in the *Commercial Bulletin*, all the effects arising from the initiation of the proceeding cease and the suspended proceedings halt. If the binding part of the restructuring plan does not stipulate otherwise, the function of creditors' committee together with trustee ceases to exist.

Chapter 7. Negotiable Instruments

§1. Notion and Basic Features

390. The Slovak law uses the term 'securities' rather than 'negotiable instruments'. Under Act No. 566/2001 Coll. on securities and investment services (the Securities Act) as amended, a security means any instrument or record which is assessable in monetary terms, made in a form stipulated by law, carrying rights as defined in this Act and in special laws (e.g., Act on bonds, Act on bills of exchange and cheques, etc.), in particular the right to demand certain assets or exercise certain rights against persons specified by law.

§2. Different Kinds of Negotiable Instruments

391. Here are the following chosen instruments (securities) recognized by the Slovak law:

- *Share* is a security to which is attached the right of the shareholder to participate in the company's management, its profits and liquidation surplus if the company is dissolved. Shares can be issued as a bearer share (also a holder share), which may be issued in paper form or book-entry form and as a registered (*au nom*) share which may be issued only in book-entry form.
- *Interim certificate* is issued by the JSC before its entry into Commercial Register to the subscriber instead of all subscribed and not fully paid shares of one class.
- *Shares in investment funds* carry a fund shareholder's right to a corresponding share in an open-end fund's assets and a right to a proportion of the income from these assets. A fund share may correspond to one or more shares in an open-end fund's assets.
- *Bonds* is connected to the right of the holder to require repayment of a sum owed in a nominal amount (the par value) and payment of yields on it at a certain date and the duty of the person authorized to issue the bonds (the issuer) to fulfil these obligations.
- *Coupon* is issued for exercising the right to income from shares, interim certificates, bonds or shares in investment funds. Coupons may be issued as registered paper securities or order securities. Coupons are issued in the form of coupon sheets. A coupon sheet may include a talon, which entitles the holder to receive a coupon sheet. The talon is not a security.
- *Bill of exchange/promissory note* is a certificated (paper) security in which a drawer either promises to pay to a certain person certain financial sum (promissory note) or orders to a drawee to pay (bill of exchange). It can be issued upon order (preferably); on the basis of a special statement written by a drawer it can be issued upon name and is transferable by cession.
- *Cheque* is similar to a bill of exchange – the drawer orders to the third person, usually to a bank, with which the drawer has an open account, to pay a certain financial amount. Cheque may be issued only as a certificated security and can be issued upon bearer, holder and upon name as well.

- *Travel cheque* gives to the stated person or to the bearer the right to obtain certain financial sum upon its presentation for payment according to the terms determined by the cheque drawer. Provisions concerning bill of exchange, promissory note and cheque do not apply to travel cheques.
- *A bill of lading* is stipulated in the Commercial Code in connection with contract on the carriage of things. A bill of lading incorporates the right to demand delivery of the goods from the carrier in accordance with the content of this document. The carrier is required to deliver the goods to the person entitled under the bill of lading, if the person shows him/her the bill of lading and confirm receipt on it.
- *Investment certificate* is a security which value is based on the indices, interest rates, equities, debt securities, foreign exchange rates, commodities or other underlying assets, or a combination thereof. The interest certificate represents a right to compensation: (a) through an acquisition of financial instruments or gold that represent the underlying asset of the investment certificate; (b) in liquid assets or (c) in a combination of the methods under (a) and (b).

Similar applies to *warehouse certificate* incorporating the right to demand for handing over of the stored thing. It can be issued upon bearer, holder and upon name as well.

§3. Bills of Exchange and Promissory Notes

392. Regulation of Bills of Exchange and Promissory Notes (together with Cheques) is governed by Bill of Exchange and Cheque Act No. 191/1950 Coll. as amended. In the following text, no difference will be made between a bill of exchange and a promissory note. Speaking about a bill of exchange, we mean also promissory note, unless otherwise is stated or arises from the context. The Slovak law uses for a bill of exchange and a promissory note only one expression (*zmenka*).

I. Introduction

A. Notion

393. Promissory note (*vlastná zmenka*) in its substance is a promise of a drawer (issuer) to pay to a creditor (payee) certain financial sum. As a rule, a promissory note therefore contains characteristic expression 'I will pay to Creditor … EUR (Signed) Issuer'. In its basic form it has only two participants – drawer and creditor (payee). The drawer of a promissory note is a direct debtor obliged by his/her sign to pay at the due date.

394. Different situation comes with a bill of exchange. The bill of exchange (*cudzia zmenka*) is distinguished from the promissory note *inter alia* by the fact that, in its basic form, it includes more than two participants. There are drawer and payee again, but together with another participant – drawee. Substance of a bill of exchange is in payment order of a drawer to a drawee to pay certain financial sum to a payee. A bill of exchange therefore contains characteristic expression 'Pay to Creditor … EUR – Mr Drawee in Bratislava; (Signed) Issuer'.

395. A bill of exchange is a security on request (*ordre* paper). When applying rights from the bill of exchange it is always necessary to present the bill or to hand it over to obliged person. Therefore, the bill is a presentation security. Usually, the bill is a circulation security, which can be transferred by endorsement. However, the transferability may be excluded by negative clause for request and the paper is called a *rekta* bill. A bill cannot be issued as bearer bill since the bill cannot be *au porteur*. First entitled person has to be always written on the bill.

396. A bill is legal subject (object). Acquiring a bill means purchase of claims incorporated in the bill. A bill is eligible subject of disposition, ownership and lien right. Using bills is characterized by so-called bill stringency (*rigor cambialis*). In substantive legal regulation, the bill stringency means in particular obligatory legal regulation of bill elements, formal validity of a bill (signatures or other statutory elements may not be real or based on material truth) as well as strict conditions of performing and maintaining rights connected with short statues of limitations.

397. The Act allows that number of participants can be reduced, since drawer, drawee and creditor do not have to be three different persons. The Act enables a bill of exchange drawn on the drawer himself/herself and a bill of exchange payable to his/her order. The bill of exchange with only one participant is not valid. Bill of exchange drawn on the drawer himself/herself is a bill of exchange, where drawer declares himself/herself as a creditor (by words 'to my own order'). Drawer and payee is the same person in this case.

398. Bill of exchange payable to drawer's order is a bill of exchange where the drawer orders to himself/herself to pay to a payee. Drawer and drawee is the same person here. To get a direct debtor, the bill of exchange has to bear an acceptation by the drawee.

B. Participants

399. Person becomes liable on a bill only after its signature is put on it. Debtors (drawers) may sign the bill of exchange in the position of direct or indirect (regress) debtor. Direct debtor is the one against whom it is possible to claim directly and without so-called preserving (maintaining) acts (presentation and protest). Putting forward the claim is in fact not bound with other presumptions than due presentation of a bill of exchange.

400. On the other side, regress debtor is a secondary debtor. He plays a role of a certain security against which is usually proceeded only in case when requested procedure is not kept. It includes cases when bill of exchange was not accepted, or although it was accepted, at the due date it was not paid. Therefore, rights against regress debtors can be exercised within so-called protest only after executing certain maintaining acts (typically presentation of the bill of exchange for acceptation or payment and execution of a protest for non-acceptance or non-payment, unless the holder was from this duty liberated in special cases).

401. Drawer (Issuer): The Slovak law does not make a difference in terminology between a drawer of a promissory note (issuer) and drawer of a bill of exchange. Issuer as an author of promise or order to pay is a key person of bill relations. Without his/her signature the bill is not valid. Issuer is a bill debtor; key question for his/her position in hierarchy of bill debtors is whether he drew a bill of exchange or a promissory note. It is essential to distinguish both two issuers. The difference is in extent of creditor's rights against them.

As was mentioned above, issuer of a promissory note obliges himself/herself to pay at the due date. So he is the direct debtor.

Unlike issuer, drawer of a bill of exchange is in a position of indirect, regress debtor. The drawer guarantees both acceptance and payment. Drawer can be liable for the payment after the bill of exchange was not accepted or paid. Drawer may exclude himself/herself from guaranteeing acceptance with special stipulation 'without recourse for acceptance'.

402. Creditor (Payee): The payee is the person named on the face of the bill of exchange or a promissory note to receive payment. Payee is the first beneficiary of a bill. Usually, he is named in words 'Pay to the order of Jozef Novak (payee)'. The drawer and the payee in case of bills of exchange drawn 'to the order' may be the same person, as was already mentioned above.

403. Drawee: Drawee is an addressee of payment promise of the drawer. For the moment he is not obliged, but absolutely necessary participant – statement of his/her name is one of the requirements of a bill of exchange. He becomes a real debtor only by the acceptance.

404. Acceptor: Drawee is obliged only by the written acceptance of a drawer's order. On the spot acceptance of the bill prevails. From the payee's point of view, such an acceptance is comfortable: before passing on the bill to the creditor, the drawer ensures acceptance by the drawee and accepted bill is passed on to the creditor. Only the person stated as a drawee can accept the bill. Acceptor is then – similarly to issuer of a promissory note – obliged in a position of direct bill debtor. If he pays the bill, he has no other option to recourse further bill debtors.

405. Avalist: The Act stipulates a special guarantee for payment of a bill – so-called *aval*. The avalist is a person giving an aval guarantee. The avalist is usually not obliged yet. A person who has signed the bill as well may give this guarantee. The avalist is bound in the same manner as the person for whom he has become a guarantor.

406. Endorser and Endorsee: In most case, the bill, even if not expressly drawn to order, may be transferred by the means of endorsement. Parties of endorsement are endorser who by the means of endorsement endorses rights arising from the bill to the other party, the endorsee. The first endorser is the payee. Endorser is an indirect (regress) debtor. Under the Act he guarantees payment of the bill unless he excluded himself from the guarantee by a special stipulation.

407. Domicile: A bill of exchange may be payable at the domicile of a third person either in the place where the drawee has his/her domicile or in another place. The person stated as a domicile is neither bounded nor beneficiary, he is only a mediator through whom the bill should be paid. Usually a bank is the domicile.

C. Forms

408. The bill of exchange or promissory note must be in writing. An oral bill or note is not allowed. Writing includes handwriting, typing or printing. The bill cannot be entered in a book like shares or bonds. Actually, it can be written on whatever substratum, which is capable in a relatively stable form to keep the text and to enable to distinguish reverse and obverse side and to join the allonge as well. Usually, paper serves as the substratum. If there is no place for other statements, a copy of the paper or allonge can be used.

409. The drawer or issuer must sign the bill of exchange or promissory note. The signature may be made only by handwriting by pen or pencil, not by typewriter, by print or only by stamp. Text of the paper is usually a result of filling in and signing of blank forms.

410. Blank bill of exchange: Blank bill can be defined as a bill, which its signatory intentionally issued as an incomplete one on the condition that the bill completion right was agreed. The bill completion right agreement usually concerns bill sum and date of due date.

D. Principle of Independence of Bill Statements

411. The Act states that if a bill of exchange bears signatures of persons incapable of binding themselves by a bill of exchange, or forged signatures, or signatures of fictitious persons, or signatures which for any other reason cannot bind the person who signed the bill of exchange or on whose behalf it was signed, the validity of obligations of the other persons who have signed is not prejudiced. This expresses one of the key principles of the bill law – principle of independence of bill statements, as part of bill stringency concept mentioned above. Effects of a particular signature thus do not depend on the fact that whether a statement of particular debtor is binding, or not, or whether even undersigned presumed debtor exists.

E. Transfer

412. As regards the way of transfer, bill of exchange can be drawn only upon order or upon name. A bill of exchange drawn to a holder is not allowed since the name of the first payee is a requirement of bill. It distinguishes a bill from cheque.

413. Bill may be generally transferred in three ways (1) by endorsement, (2) by a written contract (assignment of a debt) or (3) by passing over on the basis of an informal agreement. The primary and usual method is endorsement. Differently from some other securities, it is not necessary to write a statement that a bill is drawn 'to order'. The other two ways of transfer – by assignment of a debt and by merely passing the rights over – are possible only provided that all preconditions set by the Act are met. The Act states clearly that every bill of exchange, even if not expressly drawn to order, may be transferred by the endorsement. When the drawer has inserted in a bill of exchange the words 'not to order' or an equivalent expression, the instrument can only be transferred according to the form, and with the effects, of an ordinary assignment. Bills of exchange with such a clause of the drawer are called restrictive bills of exchange.

414. An endorsement must be unconditional. A partial endorsement is null and void. An endorsement to bearer is not allowed and is deemed to be a blank endorsement.

415. The bill of exchange may also be only passed over. This is the most informal and fastest way of transfer of rights relating to bills of exchange called also 'blanket tradition'. Blanket tradition is admissible with bills of exchange where the line of endorsements is completed with a blanket endorsement (the endorsement may consist simply of the signature of the endorser and the endorsee need not be specified). The possessor may then decide to pass the bill over to third person without writing anything on it.

F. Requirements of Promissory Note

416. According to the Act a promissory note must contain:

(1) designation 'promissory note' embodied in the paper and expressed in the language in which the paper is executed;
(2) unconditional promise to pay a determinate sum of money;
(3) statement of the time of payment;
(4) statement of the place where payment is to be made;
(5) name of the person to whom or to whose order payment is to be made;
(6) statement of the date and of the place where the promissory note is issued;
(7) signature of the issuer.

417. As requirements for the clause, the time of payment, the name of the payee and the signature of the drawer are regulated in the same way like the bill of exchange, please *see* below.

418. A paper in which any of the requirements mentioned above are absent is invalid as a promissory note except in the following cases foreseen by the Act. A promissory note in which the time of payment is not specified is deemed to be payable at sight. In default of special mention, the place where the instrument is made is deemed to be the place of the domicile of the issuer. A promissory note, which does not mention the place of its issuance, is deemed to have been made in the place mentioned beside the name of the issuer.

G. Requirements of Bills of Exchange

419. According to the Act bills of exchange contains:

(1) term 'bill of exchange' embodied in the paper and expressed in the language in which the paper is executed;
(2) unconditional order to pay a certain sum of money;
(3) name of the person who has the obligation to pay;
(4) due date;
(5) place of payment;
(6) name of the person to whom or to whose order payment is to be made;
(7) date of the drawing of the bill of exchange.
(8) signature of the drawer.

420. The due date need not be stated at all in the bill of exchange. A bill of exchange in which the time of payment is not specified is deemed to be payable at sight. The place of payment and the place of the drawing of the bill of exchange need not result from the bill directly, but they may be indirectly deduced from other pieces of information in the bill.

Here are details on the above-mentioned essential elements of the bill of exchange.

421. Stipulation relating to bills of exchange: A bill of exchange must primarily include a designation that it is a bill of exchange. This stipulation has to meet two cumulative preconditions. First, the designation must be inserted directly in the text of the bill. The second precondition is that the designation of bill of exchange must be written in the language in which the whole document is written. The bill should be drawn only in one language. The bill may be written in any language and the parties are not restricted in this way.

422. Unconditional payment order: The core of the bill of exchange is a payment order of the drawer addressed to the drawee. The use of a certain form for this order is not prescribed but it must be clear from the text of the bill. Usually, a simple imperative 'Pay' is used. This order must be unconditional and must be expressed in a certain sum of money.

The money relating to bills of exchange must be expressed in words or figures, or in both ways (it is actually required by all bill forms for security reasons). If the sum of money relating to bills of exchange is expressed differently in figures and words, the bill of exchange is not invalid for ambiguity. The Act foreseen such cases and states that when the sum payable by bill of exchange is expressed in words and also in figures and there is a discrepancy between the two, the sum denoted by the words is the amount payable. When the sum payable by bill of exchange is expressed more than once in words or more than once in figures, and there is a discrepancy, the smaller sum is the sum payable.

The statement of currency also requires the certainty of the sum of money relating to bills of exchange. It is not possible to pay interest on the sum of money relating to bills of exchange except for sight bills. When a bill of exchange is payable at sight, or at a fixed period after sight, the drawer may stipulate the sum payable will bear interest. In the case of any other bill of exchange, this stipulation is deemed not to be written. The rate of interest must be specified in the bill of exchange; in default of such specification, the stipulation is deemed not to be written. Interest runs from the date of the bill of exchange, unless some other date is specified.

423. Name of the drawee: Following the above-mentioned, the drawee is an addressee of the payment order of the drawer. An obligation arises for him/her only based on his/her acceptance. The drawer may designate himself/herself as the drawee. To state the name (designation, trade name) of the drawer should be sufficient. Other data (residence, company registration number, seat, etc.) are only appropriate but the Act does not require them for validity of the bill of exchange.

424. Indication of due date: The due date need not be expressly written in the bill of Exchange. In such case the Act states that the bill is payable at sight. The bill of exchange may be payable at sight, at a fixed period after sight, at a fixed period after the date of drawing and on a fixed day. Bills of exchange with another type of due date are invalid. Bills of exchange payable by instalments are also null and void.

425. Place of payment: There are two ways of stating the place of payment. First, the drawer may determine it expressly. However, if the drawer omits to state the place in the bill it does not result in invalidity of the bill. In such a case, the Act states that the place of payment is the place stated with the name of the drawer. But if there is no place written in the bill, such bill of Exchange is considered invalid. The place of payment may be stated in the bill also through the domicile, e.g. 'Payable at the City Bank, Bratislava'.

426. Designation of the payee: The bill must always include the name of its first acquirer – creditor (payee). The drawer and the payee may be identical (draft to one's own order).

427. Day and place of drawing: The bill of exchange must include the day and the place of drawing. The day must exist and must be sufficiently clear (day, month, year). The date of drawing must always precede the date of payment. A bill of exchange, which does not mention the place of its issue, is deemed to have been drawn in the place mentioned beside the name of the drawer. If no place is stated, the bill is considered invalid.

428. Signature of the drawer: The last essential element of bill of exchange stated by the Act is the own-handed signature of the drawer.

H. Acceptance of the Bill of Exchange

429. By the bill of exchange the drawer orders the drawee to pay a certain sum of money to the payee. Until the drawee learns the content of the bill (by acceptance), he is still only a potential debtor. Acceptance makes the drawee a direct debtor from the bill of exchange who has a duty to pay at due date. Obviously, acceptance is relevant only to the bill of exchange and not the promissory note. It is expressed by the word 'accepted' or any other equivalent term. A bill is signed by the drawee. If the drawee crosses his/her acceptance written on the bill, before he returned it, the acceptance is refused. Until proven otherwise, it is assumed that crossing happened before returning the bill.

I. Aval

430. Payment of a bill of exchange may be guaranteed by an aval wholly or partially. This guarantee may be given by a third person or even by a person who has signed as a party to the bill. The avalist is usually a person who is not bound by any bill of exchange yet. The person for whom the avalist has guaranteed is called the debtor under aval. If the debtor under aval is not specified in the aval then it is presumed that it is the drawer. Therefore, the obligation of the debtor under aval must be clear from the bill at least formally. The formal principle holds that without the debtor under aval there is no avalist.

431. One avalist may be the avalist for several persons and several persons may also be avalists for one debtor.

432. The avalist's obligation may arise and be valid only if first the bill of exchange and the written form of the aval are valid. The aval is given either on the bill itself or on an allonge. It is expressed by the words 'as aval' or by any other equivalent formula and signed by the avalist. It is deemed to be constituted by the mere signature of the avalist placed on the face of the bill, except in the case of the signature of the drawee or the drawer or issuer.

433. Obligation of the avalist is valid even when the obligation which he has guaranteed is invalid for any reason other than defect of form. When the avalist pays a bill of exchange, the rights arising out of the bill of exchange against the person guaranteed and against those who are liable to the latter on the bill of exchange pass to the avalist.

J. Payment for the Bill of Exchange

434. A bill of exchange payable at sight is payable on presentment. It must be presented for payment within a year of its date. The drawer may reduce or extend this period. The endorsers may reduce these periods.

435. The holder of a bill of exchange payable on a fixed day or at a fixed period after date or after sight must present the bill for payment either on the day on which it is payable or on one of the two business days which follows. The drawee that pays a bill of exchange may require confirmation of receipt by the holder. The holder may not refuse partial payment. In case of partial payment the drawee may require this payment to be made on the bill and a confirmation of receipt. The holder of a bill of exchange cannot be compelled to receive payment before the due date.

436. The bill of exchange is a circulating security, which may be transferred many times. The debtor may usually only guess who will present him/her the bill at the time of its due date. Neither the original assignee nor the new ones have the duty to notify him/her about transfers. The debt from the bill is therefore constructed in such a way that the possessor exercises the right to payment by presenting the bill for payment to the direct debtor.

437. The possessor has the right to payment against direct debtors in the first place. It is either the acceptant or the drawer. Presenting the bill for payment to these persons within prescribed periods is a right and at the same time an important duty of the possessor since its failure is sanctioned by the Act.

K. Protesting the Bill of Exchange

438. Default of acceptance or of payment must be evidenced by a public act (protest for non-acceptance or non-payment). Protest for non-acceptance must be made within the limit of time fixed for presentment for acceptance.

439. Protest for non-payment of a bill payable on a fixed day or at a fixed period after date or sight must be made on one of the two working days following the day on which the bill is payable. In the case of a bill payable at sight, the protest must be drawn up under the conditions specified in the foregoing subsection for the drawing up of a protest for non-acceptance. The possessor may be relieved from the duty of protest by including the clause 'without protest' in the bill or by a clause of a similar meaning.

440. The protest is a written qualified certificate that a certain participant of the bill relationships (e.g., debtor) was asked to fulfil his/her obligations (to pay the bill) but he/she failed to do so. The law determines the content of the certificate and the bodies that may issue such an instrument. A court, a notary public or a municipality office must issue protest.

441. Protest must contain:

(1) names of the persons for whom and against whom it is being made;
(2) information that the person against whom the protest is being made has been, without any result, requested to act on the bill of exchange, or that the person could not be contacted, or that neither the premises where he does business nor his/her apartment could be located;
(3) information about the place and time when the request or the failed attempt at such a request has been made;
(4) note, in cases of acceptance or payment for honour, from whom, for whom and how the acceptance or the payment for honour was offered or made;
(5) in the event that the drawee to whom the bill of exchange was presented for acceptance requests that it be presented to him/her again on the following day, a note about this fact;
(6) literal copy of the bill of exchange (copy) with all endorsements and notes;
(7) signature of the protesting body and the official seal or the official stamp.

442. In addition to evidentiary purposes, the protest has the effect of the second preserving act (the first one being presentment). If the possessor does not have this certificate issued, it can even lead to cancellation of bill rights. After the expiration of the limits of time fixed for the presentment of a bill of exchange, the holder loses rights of recourse against the endorsers, against the drawer and against the other parties liable, with the exception of the acceptor.

L. Bill Notification

443. If the bill was not accepted or paid for, the possessor may exercise his/her rights of recourse against indirect debtors after accomplishing preserving acts (i.e., after presenting the bill, or after properly protesting the bill).

M. Statute of Limitations

444. Limitation periods mentioned in the Act are slightly different from the general limitation periods pursuant to Civil Code or Commercial Code. All bill claims arising out of a bill of exchange against the acceptor are barred after three years from the due date. Claims of the holder against the endorsers and against the drawer are barred after one year from the date of a protest, or from the due date where there is a stipulation 'without costs'. Actions by endorsers against each other and against the drawer are barred after six months from the day when the endorser paid the bill or from the day when he was sued for the claim.

§4. Cheques

445. The second and third article of the Act governs cheques. Regulation of cheques is similar to bill of exchange regulation – the drawer orders to the third person, usually to a bank, with which the drawer has an open account, to pay a certain financial amount.

I. Notion

446. Cheque can be defined as a precise instrument. It belongs to securities with the specific claim, and thus it is a payment security. When applying the cheque claim, the cheque has to be presented to the drawee or cheque debtor and handed over against the payment of money.

447. Cheque payment is essentially an order to the issuer (account owner, debtor) to pay a certain amount in favour of the entitled owner (holder) of the cheque to the drawee (monetary institute) to debit his/her account.

II. Participants

448. Issuer: Issuer is an indirect debtor. He/she is liable always for payment of a cheque and he/she cannot exclude his/her responsibility for payment of the cheque. Any clause excluding the liability of issuer is legally declared unwritten, so it is not taken into account and the validity cheque is not affected.

*449. Owner: O*wner is a cheque creditor and his/her name does not need to appear on the cheque. Unlike a bill of exchange, where a form a bearer security is not allowed, the cheque may be issued as bearer (to owner). Designation of the entitled person is not an obligatory element of a cheque. However, it usually belongs to regular elements.

450. Drawee: A valid cheque contains the name of the drawee. Drawee is the person who mediates the payment of the cheque. In essence, it is a participant of cheque relationship, whom the order is addressed by the cheque issuer to pay the cheque owner (the creditor) the amount specified on the cheque. The name of the drawee is not usually part of a base text of cheque, the core of which is the payment order. Designation of the drawee is usually outside the continuous text of the cheque and is usually made in the upper left corner of the cheque. Drawee is basically the addressee of the issuer's command.

III. Forms

451. Bearer cheque (au porteur cheque): Due to the fact that the cheque is in terms of entitled person completely anonymous the cheque contains no specific designation of owner, it can automatically be considered as a bearer cheque. Alternative *au porteur* clause is that the cheque is issued in the benefit of the individual person mentioned in the cheque with the clause 'or to owner' or 'or to the bearer'.

452. Cheque to the order (order cheque): The nature of such a cheque is the fact that the cheque contains the name of the person in whose favour it is issued, i.e., the name of the owner. If there is no other clause in a cheque next to the owner, based on the Act this cheque is considered as an order cheque. It is also called statutory order cheque. The clause 'to order' need not to be connected to the name of the owner. In case of an order cheque, the owner has to show his/her entitlement not only by detention or control of cheque but also by the cheque itself.

453. Cheque to the name (recta cheque): This type of cheque is not widespread and is rather an exception. This form of cheque must include the name of the owner with rekta clause. It reads 'not to order' or other clauses of the same importance. The owner has to show his/her entitlement by detention or control of cheque, and also by the cheque itself, and any other (next) must show an agreement on assignment of claim. In these agreements, the owner has to be designated as the assignee. Rekta cheques are transferable only by and with effects of an ordinary assignment under the Civil Code.

IV. Requirements of Cheque

454. According to the Act, bills of exchange contain:

(1) term 'cheque' embodied in the paper and expressed in the language in which the paper is executed;
(2) unconditional order to pay a certain sum of money;
(3) name of the person who has the obligation to pay;
(4) place of payment;
(5) date of drawing of the cheques;
(6) signature of the drawer.

455. The due date need not be stated at all in the cheque. A cheque in which the time of payment is not specified is deemed to be payable at sight. The place of payment and the place of the drawing of the cheque need not result from the cheque directly but they may be indirectly deduced from other information in the cheque.

V. Transfer

456. Transfers of cheques can be divided according to the benefit of whom the cheque was issued. In other words, according to the form of the cheque – order, name, or bearer.

Chapter 8. Organization of Financial Markets

§1. Introduction

457. From 1 January 2006, the entire supervision of financial market is carried out by the National Bank of Slovakia (NBS) (*Národná Banka Slovenska*), thus overseeing banking, capital market, insurance and pension saving. The objective of the integrated financial market supervision is to provide the stability of the entire financial market, as well as to the secure and sound operation of the financial market in the interest of maintaining the credibility of the financial market, protecting clients, and respecting the competition rules.

458. Basic activities of the integrated financial market supervision include not only on-site and off-site supervision over supervised entities of the financial market but also acting and deciding on supervision issues (e.g., grant permissions, licence consents, sanctioning), preparing the draft regulations and implementing the EU and national legislation. Therefore, in addition to its other activities, the tasks of the NBS since the beginning of 2006 have included the granting of the permissions, approvals, consents, prior consents and other decisions concerning the financial market, which were the responsibility of the Financial Market Authority until the end of 2005. Legal effects of acts taken before 2006 remain the same.

I. General Structure

459. Generally, we could divide the financial market in the Slovak Republic into four basic areas:

- Banking.
- Insurance.
- Securities Market.
- Pension Savings.

460. This structure is derived from the general structure applied by the EU and a majority of its Member States. The national legislators transpose the legislation of the EU and adopt amendments to the existing law in order to provide for the integrated financial system. The sole supervisory and enforcement body on the financial market is the NBS. The Slovak Republic exercises the options and national discretions available under the EU legislation and the general criteria and methodologies used by the NBS in the Supervisory Review and Evaluation Process.[46]

46. For more on the supervisory disclosure *see* the European System of Financial Supervision, available online at: http://eba.europa.eu/supervisory-disclosure.aspx/ (accessed 31 May 2013).

II. Oversight

461. The Financial Market Supervision Unit of the NBS (FMS Unit) performs methodological, regulatory, analytical and supervisory activities on the financial market in Slovakia. Furthermore, the FMS Unit is responsible for identifying possible risk arising out of the activities carried out by the participant on the financial market. Each market participant that falls under FMS Unit supervision is assessed as to its exposure to risk with regard to its individual activity as well as to its influence on the entire system.

A. Banking, Payment Services, Electronic Money & Foreign Exchange Sectors Oversight

462. As of 1 May 2019, there were twelve banks and fifteen branches of foreign banks operating in the banking sector in the Slovak Republic, together with 335 providers of free cross-border banking services.

463. The supervision activities in the banking sector, i.e., over banks and branches of foreign banks, are exercised on the basis of annual supervision programme as to evaluate risk profiles of the entities under supervision plus calculation of capital adequacy requirements for all bank institutions. Given the fact that the EU is assessing Basel III and it is its intention of applying the Basel III requirements on the European banks, the NBS is also preparing its materials concerning the application of the Basel III in the Slovak Republic. NBS stated that it was its top priority to monitor credit and market risks of banks, their capital adequacy and liquidity, and to assess the internal credit and market risk models of banks and the changes made in these models.[47]

464. The FMS Unit analyses monthly the statements and reports supplied regularly by banks and branches of foreign banks, quarterly the risk profiles of individual banks and annually prepares comprehensive reports on banks, including a detailed evaluation of their financial indicators, in addition, assesses the risk of those banks that are subsidiaries of banks based in another Member State of the EU in order to prepare detailed risk profile reports. Moreover, the NBS in particular examines and evaluates the management organization, division of responsibilities, adopted strategies, systems and procedures introduced within the performance of licensed banking activities and information flows of a bank or branch of a foreign bank.

465. Under the Act on Banks, a banking supervisory authority of a foreign state may generally exercise its supervision in the territory of the Slovak Republic over operations of a branch of a foreign bank and over a bank subsidiary of a foreign bank, solely on the basis of an agreement concluded between the NBS and the supervisory authority of the foreign state. The banking supervisory authority of

47. *See* NBS Annual Report 2012, 29.

another country shall notify the NBS before its activities. The personnel of the supervisory authority of the foreign state have the same rights, duties and responsibilities as the personnel of the NBS authorized to carry out the on-site inspections. However, they are not obliged to prepare a written protocol of the inspection or to determine or notify the supervised entity in writing. The same applies to the NBS in connection with the branches of Slovak banks in third countries.

466. In the area of payment services and electronic money issuance, the focus of the NBS and the FMS Unit is to evaluate the character of activities performed by these entities and their overall risk profile. The assessment consists of verification of the system payment services, selected risk and the risk management system, a compliance with the business conditions and the binding legal regulation. Usually, every institution is evaluated each year.

467. Concerning the foreign exchange sector, the FMS Unit checks the compliance with Foreign Exchange Act No. 202/1995 Coll., focusing on the area of trade in foreign exchange assets in the range of currency exchange activity, consisting of purchase and/or sale of foreign currency together with the compliance with the foreign exchange reporting obligation by entrepreneurs.

B. Insurance, Pension Savings, Financial Intermediation Oversight

468. The FMS Unit in insurance system verifies the reports, ad hoc reports from Slovak insurance entities as well as from branches of insurers from other Member States, which are active in the territory of the Slovak Republic. Furthermore, it verifies compliance with Insurance Act No. 8/2008 Coll., related laws and generally binding legal regulations implementing these laws, together with the terms and conditions laid down in licences issued under the Insurance Act.

469. The Slovak Republic undertook a major pension reform in 2005, where, besides the public pension, the Government introduced mandatory second and voluntary third pension pillar. The first pillar represented the mandatory public pillar, the second pillar, the mandatory private funded scheme, while the third pillar, the voluntary private funded scheme. However, in 2015, the Government substantially amended the system and transformed the second mandatory pillar into voluntary for people under 35 years of age. As a result of the regulatory change, new intermediaries were formed, which provide services in connection with the second and third pillar. In the light of regulatory amendments to the Insurance Act, enforceable from 1 January 2015, the Social Insurance Agency shall establish and maintain a Central Information Bidding System (*Centrálny informačný ponukový systém*) that will serve to interface relevant offers for pension savers as to the existing banking and asset management institutions. This system shall ensure transparency of the system and reduce the administrative burden of pension savers. The FMS Unit also carries out its supervisory activities with regard to the pension saving entities. Moreover, in connection with the voluntary pension saving entities, the FMS Unit focuses on checking, analysing and evaluating the reports and statements of four banking institutions and four supplementary pension asset management companies, which manage fifteen supplementary pension funds under Supplementary Pension Savings Act No. 650/2004 Coll.

470. In the area of financial intermediation and financial counselling, the NBS together with FMS Unit verify the intermediaries falling under the supervision for compliance with the obligations under Financial Intermediation and Financial Counselling Act No. 186/2009 Coll. The NBS generally verifies the compliance with statutory reporting requirement, and with regard to the EU MiFID, MiFID II, MiFIR or Market Abuse Regulation, the intermediaries shall carry out their business with professional competence, which shall be supervised by the national supervisory bodies, mainly on the conduct of professional examinations.

C. Securities Market Oversight

471. As at 31 December 2014, there were three issuers of securities admitted to trading on the main market, four issuers admitted to parallel market and fifty-four issuers admitted to the free market. All of these issuers are subject to disclosure requirement under Stock Exchange Act No. 429/2002 Coll. The NBS verifies their annual reports, semi-annual reports together with preliminary statements and other documents, which they are obliged to disclose. Additionally, the NBS supervises fifteen domestic investment firms, which are non-bank entities and ten foreign investment firms, which are pursuing activities under Securities Act No. 566/2001 Coll. (Securities Act). Moreover, the collective investment sector is currently comprised of seven domestic asset management companies, two foreign asset management companies compliant with Collective Investment Act No. 203/2011 Coll.

472. Generally, the NBS has to verify the compliance of these intermediaries with the relevant statutory provisions, which are applicable to them. Majority of these regulations is directly influenced by the EU regulations. Specific duty under these acts is the disclosure obligation, which can be regarded quite extensive. The intermediaries are assessed on a regular basis not only as to the information they provide to the NBS but also as to what kind of information they disclose to the public, which is under close supervision of the NBS and the FMS Unit.

§2. Banking

473. Although the financial crisis hit the Slovak Republic quite extensively, the recovery has been satisfactory. Given the general economic indicators, as to the profitability of the banking sector in the Slovak Republic in 2019, it may be said that the Slovak Republic is a small country with around 3 million households, which means that the number of customers for fifteen banks is relatively small.

Thus, there is a high concentration of banking services. The aggregate market share of the ten largest Slovak banks is 85.2% indicating the dominance of the largest banks in the sector, where the three biggest banks have a share of fifteen. The concentration of the banks in the Slovak Republic is the second largest concentration level in the Central European Region.[48]

474. Banking regulation in the Slovak Republic comprises several acts, namely Act No. 483/2001 Coll. on Banks and on amendments and supplements to certain laws (Act on Banks), Act No. 276/2009 Coll. on measures to mitigate the effects of the global financial crisis on banking sector and on amendments and supplements to certain laws and NBS Act No. 566/1992 Coll. (National Bank Act) and other implementing regulations.

475. Since 2012, Slovak Government introduced the banking tax, where the Government collects tax revenues from banks via a new tax on its indigenous banks and the branches of foreign banks operating in the Slovak Republic. By using this tax, the Government creates a fund, which may be used in case of future crisis to address potential problems in the banking sector.

I. Obligation to Register

476. Under the Act on Banks, a bank is defined as a legal entity with its registered office in the territory of the Slovak Republic, founded as a JSC, which (a) accepts deposits and (b) provides loans. For these activities a bank has to hold a banking licence. Each bank has to be formed as a JSC; any other legal form of a bank is prohibited. In addition to the basic two activities a bank may carry out any of the following activities:

(1) Provide payment services and settlement.
(2) Provide investment services, investment activities and ancillary services in accordance with a separate law and investment in securities for own account.
(3) Trade for the bank's own account:
   (a) in financial instruments of the money market in Euro and foreign currencies, including exchange services;
   (b) in financial instrument of the capital market in Euro and foreign currencies;
   (c) in precious metal coins, commemorative banknotes and coins, sheets of banknotes and sets of circulation coinage.
(4) Manage receivables for the client's account, including advisory services.
(5) Financial leasing.
(6) Provide guarantees, open and endorse letters of credit.
(7) Business advisory services.
(8) Issue securities, participate in securities issuing and provide related services.
(9) Financial intermediation.

48. Deloitte, The Banking Sector in Central Europe, Performance Overview: Slovakia, p. 17.

(10) Provide safe custody of assets.
(11) Rent safe deposit boxes.
(12) Provide banking information.
(13) Engage in special mortgage transactions.
(14) Perform functions of a depository pursuant to special regulation.
(15) Process banknotes, coins, commemorative banknotes and coins.

477. A banking licence is a licence to establish a bank or a branch of a foreign bank and to perform banking operations and activities by this bank or branch of a foreign bank in the extent specified by this licence and according to the conditions established by the Act on Banks and other special regulation. If there is a special permit for some of the activities listed above, a banking licence to perform these activities may only be issued after the special permit comes into force (e.g., activities connected to collective investments). This, however, is not applicable to foreign EU banks, which hold a passport, issued by other Member States for those activities.

II. Banking Licence

478. Under the Act on Banks, there are two types of banking licences: one, a banking licence granted under Slovak National Council Act No. 310/1992 Coll. on home savings, issued by the NBS; and, second, a licence to provide mortgage transactions granted by the NBS following an agreement with the Ministry of Finance of the Slovak Republic.

479. All applications shall be submitted to the NBS. In order to obtain a banking licence, all of the following conditions and requirements have to be met:

(a) Minimum monetary deposit towards a bank's registered capital of EUR 16,000,000 and a minimum monetary deposit towards the registered capital of a bank performing mortgage transactions of EUR 33,200,000.
(b) Transparent and trustworthy origin of registered capital and other financial resources of the bank according to Act No. 297/2008 Coll. on the prevention of money laundering and terrorist financing.
(c) Eligibility and suitability of persons who would become shareholders with qualified interest in the bank, and transparency of their relations with other persons, above all transparency of their interests in registered capital and voting rights.
(d) Proposal of members of the statutory body of the bank.
(e) Professional competence and integrity of persons nominated as members of the statutory body, as an authorized agent (*prokurista*), as members of the Supervisory Board, officers, as the head of the internal control department and the head of the internal audit department.
(f) Draft of Articles of Association.
(g) Business plan with a proposed strategy for the bank's operations supported by realistic economic calculations.

(h) Transparency of a closely connected group which includes the bank's qualified shareholder/s.
(i) Close links within the group according to (h) do not obstruct supervision.
(j) Legal system and its application in the state in which territory the group according to (h) has close links, do not obstruct supervision.
(k) Registered office, head office and principal banking activities of the future bank must be located or carried out in the territory of the Slovak Republic; the bank may conduct banking activities also outside the territory of the Slovak Republic through its branch or without establishing a branch according to the conditions established by the Act on Banks.
(l) Document the ability of shareholders establishing the bank to overcome a potentially difficult financial situation of the bank.
(m) Conditions, equivalent to those for the issuance of an investment services licence, are met, as appropriate, in relation to the requested scope of investment services, investment activities and ancillary services.
(n) Conditions, equivalent to those for the issuance of a licence for providing payment services, are met in relation to the requested range of payment services.
(o) Conditions, equivalent to those for the issuance of electronic money, are met in relation to the requested issuance of electronic money.
(p) Appropriate and adequate technical systems, resources and procedures for the proper performance of banking activities and material-technical support for the performance of banking activities.
(q) Appropriate and adequate organizational and personnel conditions for the exercise of banking activities, operational management and control system including the internal control and internal audit system, risk management and prudential rules.

480. Furthermore, before commencing the licensed banking activities, a bank must demonstrate the following:

(1) Registered capital has been fully paid up.
(2) Technical, organizational and personnel readiness to conduct licensed banking activities of the bank, the existence of a management and control system of a bank, including an internal control department, an internal audit department, and a system of risk management.
(3) Regulation of legal relations with a member of the statutory body, and a branch of a foreign bank with the head of the branch of a foreign bank, by a written contract.

481. Once a bank obtains the written notification from the NBS, it may commence with its activities. The banking licence is granted for an indefinite period of time and is not transferable to another person or to the bank's legal successor.

482. A foreign bank when establishing a branch in the Slovak Republic has to submit together with an application a binding written statement from the banking supervisory authority of the country, where it has a registered seat, as well as a written commitment by the foreign banking supervisory authority that it will inform in writing the NBS in time of any changes in the maintenance of own resources in respect to the requirements and liquidity and on other facts that could adversely affect the ability of the foreign bank to meet its obligation in the Slovak Republic.

483. A foreign bank registered in a Member State of the EU may conduct, through its branch, banking activities listed above, except (1) providing banking information and (2) engage in special mortgage transactions, without a banking licence from the NBS, if a licence to perform these activities has been granted by a Member State, subject to a written statement from the supervisory authorities of the concerned Member State delivered to the NBS. In addition, foreign banks with registered offices in a Member State may freely advertise banking activities in the Slovak Republic in accordance with the law of the Slovak Republic. The Act on Banks further stipulates some additional risk-mitigation measures for the branches of the foreign banks, given the fact that the foreign law together with foreign supervisory authority primarily regulates them.

III. Corrective Measures and Sanctions

484. If the NBS finds any shortcomings in the operations of a bank or branch of a foreign bank consisting in a failure to comply with the terms specified in its bank licence or a decision on a prior approval, or the requirement and obligations specified in other decision of the NBS imposed on a bank or branch of a foreign bank or for a violation or circumvention of other provisions of the Act on Banks, Acts of the EU pertaining to banking activities, separate regulations or generally binding regulations governing the conduct of banking operations, the NBS may, depending on the scope, seriousness, duration, consequences and nature of the shortcomings:

(a) order a bank or branch of a foreign bank to adopt recovery measures;
(b) order a bank or branch of a foreign bank to submit special reports and statements;
(c) order a bank or branch of a foreign bank that the unauthorized activity be terminated;
(d) impose on a bank or branch of a foreign bank a penalty from EUR 3,000 to EUR 332,000 and in case of a reoccurrence or grave violation up to EUR 664,000;
(e) limit or suspend the conduct of certain banking activities of a bank or branch of a foreign bank of the exercise of certain types of transactions;
(f) revoke the banking licence for certain banking activities or revoke the entire banking licence;
(g) order correction of accounting books or other records on the basis of findings of the NBS or an auditor;
(h) order the publication of the corrections of incomplete, incorrect or untrue information that a bank or branch of a foreign bank published according to a disclosure obligation stipulated by law;
(i) order the settlement of a loss from business operations using registered capital, after using retained earnings, and funds created from profit, and capital funds to cover the loss;

(j) in special circumstances introduce forced administration over a bank;
(k) withdraw the banking licence of a bank or branch of a foreign bank for specifically stated reasons;[49]
(l) order a bank or branch of a foreign bank to adopt measures to improve its risk management;
(m) require a bank to maintain its own funds in an amount exceeding the capital requirements;
(n) require a bank, for the purpose of the maintenance of own resources of the bank in respect to values corresponding to the requirements, to apply special procedures taking into account the impairment of its assets, and expected losses on its off-balance sheet items calculated by the bank do not correspond to the objective facts;
(o) require a bank or branch of a foreign bank to reduce significant risks undertaken during the course of its activities;
(p) impose on a bank or branch of a foreign bank to maintain the set scope of assets of a bank or branch of a foreign bank in the prescribed amount;
(q) require a bank to restrict the provision of variable components of the total remuneration of persons[50] by determining the percentage of the total remuneration paid to these persons within at least one of the previous calendar years, in order to maintain the bank's capital;
(r) order a bank to use its profits to maintain the amount of its own funds in excess of the value of capital requirements;
(s) order a bank to take action specified in the recovery plan of the bank in order to achieve the remedy within the times set determined by the NBS;
(t) order a bank to update its recovery plan;
(u) order a bank to convene a general meeting of the bank and determine the programme of this general meeting; If a bank fails to meet this obligation, the NBS convenes a general meeting of the bank and determines its programme;
(v) order a bank to withdraw within a specified time a member of its board of directors, Supervisory Board, procurator or the manager of a bank;
(w) order a bank to develop a plan on restructuring negotiation with its creditors;
(x) order a bank to carry out changes in its business strategy;
(y) order a bank to carry out changes in its organizational structure and in the execution of its activities;
(z) order a bank to submit all information to the Resolution Council in order to update the plan for crisis resolution or to the preparation of the resolution plan for the evaluation of assets and liabilities.

485. Furthermore, the NBS may impose a fine on a member of the statutory body or Supervisory Board of a bank, a chief executive officer of a branch of a foreign bank, or authorized agent or a senior officer of a financial holding company for

49. *See* s. 63 of the Act on Banks.
50. These persons include the members of the statutory body, bank managers responsible for risk management, managers responsible for bank transactions, or the employees responsible for risk management, including bank employees entitled to determine the limits or the limits of the bank risk management. *See* s. 23a of the Act on Banks.

any violation of the provisions of the Act on Banks, separate laws and generally binding regulations governing the conduct of banking activities on an individual basis.

486. Moreover, the NBS may impose a fine on a legal person that is part of a consolidated group over which it performs supervision on a consolidated basis, according to the scope, seriousness, duration and nature of the violations, in the amount from EUR 3,300 to EUR 664,000 if the legal person:

(1) does not allow an on-site inspection;
(2) fails to supply the requested returns, reports, and other statements for the purposes of supervision on a consolidated basis;
(3) provides incorrect, untrue or incomplete returns, reports and other statements or fails to observe the deadlines set for their delivery; or
(4) fails to observe the duties stipulated by the agreed conditions for the exercise of supervision on a consolidated basis and the method of information exchange in a written agreement concluded between the consolidated group and the competent supervisory authority of other Member State.

The Act on Banks further stipulates details of the stated measures, their applications, scope and limitations.

§3. Insurance

487. The insurance industry is a sector of financial services, which comprises legal entities assuming the insurance risk of other business entities, i.e., insurance and reinsurance business. The majority of the insurance and reinsurance entities providing insurance services are licensed in the Slovak Republic, while others are the insurance and reinsurance companies from other Member States of the EU or the European Economic Area.

488. The Slovak law governing the area of insurance is until 31 December 2015 Act No. 8/2008 Coll. on Insurance (Act on Insurance), which stipulated the requirements in order to obtain the insurance licence, the terms and conditions for pursuing the insurance and reinsurance activities and others. Since 1 January 2016, a new Act No. 39/2015 is applicable (New Act on Insurance). Given that the old law is applicable until the end of 2015.

489. Under the recent Act on Insurance, an insurance company is a legal entity in the form of a JSC or a European Company with its registered office in the territory of the Slovak Republic that pursues insurance activities upon the authorization to pursue insurance activities granted by the NBS within the proceedings under a special regulation. An insurance company from another Member State of the EU is a legal entity with its registered office in the territory of another Member State having a licence to pursue insurance activities granted to it in its home Member State. A branch of an insurance company from another Member State is a structural component of an insurance company from another Member State located in the territory of the Slovak Republic. A reinsurance company is a JSC or a European Company with its registered office in the territory of the Slovak Republic performing reinsurance activities upon the authorization granted by the NBS within the proceedings under a special regulation. Other entities than the insurance and reinsurance undertakings are not allowed to perform insurance and reinsurance business, unless otherwise stipulated by the Act on Insurance or other special act. A foreign insurance company (not from EU Member State) can only pursue insurance activities in the territory of the Slovak Republic through its branch and only if it has been granted an authorization to pursue insurance activities.

I. Authorization for Companies with Registered Seat in the Slovak Republic

490. The NBS grants the authorization to pursue insurance activities for the following insurance types:

(1) Life insurance according to the individual insurance classes.
(2) Non-life insurance according to the individual classes or group of insurance classes defined by the Act on Insurance.

491. Concerning reinsurance, the NBS grants the authorization to pursue reinsurance activities for the following insurance types:

(1) Life insurance.
(2) Non-life insurance.
(3) Life insurance and non-life insurance.

492. In order for an insurance or reinsurance company to obtain an authorization for the insurance licence, the following conditions have to be met:

(1) Paid minimum registered capital that is calculated based on the rules stipulated in the Act on Insurance.
(2) Transparent and trustworthy origin of the registered capital and other financial resources of the insurance company.
(3) Suitability of persons with qualified holding in the insurance company and transparency of relationships of these persons with other persons, especially transparency of holdings in the registered capital and in the voting rights.
(4) Professional qualification and trustworthiness of persons which are proposed for a member of the Board of Directors, authorized agents, chief executives of the insurance company in direct managing competence of the Board of Directors, for a responsible actuary and for a chief executive managing the department of internal audit.
(5) Transparency of the group with close links, which also includes a shareholder with a qualified holding in the insurance company.

(6) Exercise of supervision is not obstructed by close links within a group with close links.
(7) Exercise of supervision is not obstructed by the legal order and the manner in which it is exercised in the state in whose territory a group with close links has the close links.
(8) Insurance company must have its registered office and head office in the territory of the Slovak Republic.
(9) Technological and organizational readiness for pursuing the insurance activities, existence of managing and control system of internal control, including the department of internal audit and existence of risk management system.

493. The following principles shall apply for the calculation of the Minimum Capital Requirements for insurance and reinsurance undertakings:

(1) Calculation must be transparent and understandable to be audited in the future.
(2) The minimum capital requirement is the amount of eligible basic own funds of an insurance or reinsurance undertaking, whose fall below this threshold would expose the policyholders and the beneficiaries to an unacceptable level of risk if the insurance or reinsurance undertaking continued to operate.
(3) The linear function stipulated in section 5 below, applied for calculating the minimum capital requirement, corresponds to the value at risk of basic own funds of an insurance and reinsurance undertaking with a confidence level of 85% over a one-year period.
(4) The absolute lowest limit for the minimum capital requirement of an insurance or reinsurance undertaking, a branch of a foreign insurance or reinsurance undertaking shall be determined by the NBS by a legislative measure announced in the Collection of Laws.
(5) The minimum capital requirement is calculated as a linear function on the basis of these variables, subtracted by reinsurance ratio:
    (a) Technical reserves.
    (b) Premiums written.
    (c) Risk capital.
    (d) Deferred taxes.
    (e) Administrative costs.

494. The authorization to pursue insurance/reinsurance activities is granted for an indefinite period and cannot be transferred to another person or to a successor. The authorization to pursue insurance activities granted to an insurance/reinsurance company is valid for all Member States of the EU and entitles the insurance/reinsurance company to pursue insurance/reinsurance activities in the territory of another Member State through a branch established in another Member State on the basis of the right of the freedom of services.

II. Authorization for Companies with Registered Seat Outside the Slovak Republic and EU

495. The NBS decides on the granting of an authorization to pursue insurance activities to a foreign insurance or reinsurance company through its branch in the territory of the Slovak Republic. In order to grant the authorization, the following conditions have to be met:

(1) Assets in the territory of the Slovak Republic cannot be less than one-half of the guarantee fund and financial means in the amount of one-quarter must be deposited on a separate account in a bank throughout the entire period of operation of the branch of the foreign insurance company.
(2) Actual solvency margin resulting from the scope of the insurance activities pursued in the territory of the Slovak Republic shall be in accordance with Article 34.
(3) Credibility of the foreign insurance/reinsurance company and its financial capacity adequate to the scope of the insurance activities pursued through its branch.
(4) Professional applications and credibility of the persons proposed by the foreign insurance/reinsurance company to manage its branch, for an authorized agent and for a responsible actuary.
(5) Transparency of the group with close links, which includes the foreign insurance/reinsurance company.
(6) Exercise of supervision is not obstructed by close links within a group with close links.
(7) Exercise of supervision is not obstructed by the legal order and the manner in which it is exercised in the state in whose territory a group with close links has the close links.
(8) Foreign insurance/reinsurance company that has decided to pursue insurance/reinsurance company through its branch pursues a significant part of insurance activities in the state of its registered office.

III. Termination of the Authorization

496. The authorization to pursue insurance or reinsurance activities terminates in the following circumstances:

(1) On the date of the dissolution of an insurance/reinsurance company (including the foreign) for other reason than withdrawal of the authorization.
(2) On the date on which the property of an insurance/reinsurance company (including the foreign) was assigned for bankruptcy under special legislation.
(3) On the effective date of the decision of the NBS on granting prior approval.
(4) On the day following the expiry of the period during which an insurance/reinsurance company had to submit a motion to enter a record in the Commercial Register.

(5) On the date of the sale of the undertaking of an insurance/reinsurance company (including the foreign).
(6) On the date of termination of the activities of a foreign insurance/reinsurance company.

Unless it is the decision of the NBS the insurance/reinsurance companies have the obligation to notify the NBS in writing of the facts causing the termination of the authorization or termination of their activities without undue delay after their occurrence.

IV. Corrective Measures and Sanctions

497. If the NBS finds any deficiencies in the activities of an insurance company, reinsurance company, branch of a foreign insurance company or reinsurance company consisting in a failure to comply with the terms specified in its authorization or a decision on a prior approval, or the requirement and obligations specified in other decisions of the NBS imposed on an insurance company, reinsurance company, branch of a foreign insurance company or reinsurance company or for a violation or circumvention of other provisions of the Act on Insurance, Acts of the EU pertaining to insurance and reinsurance activities, separate regulations or generally binding regulations governing the conduct of insurance and reinsurance operations, the NBS may, depending on the scope, seriousness, duration, consequences and nature of the shortcomings:

(1) order an insurance company, reinsurance company, branch of a foreign insurance company or reinsurance company to adopt recovery measures in order to remove and eliminate the ascertained deficiencies;
(2) impose on an insurance company, reinsurance company, branch of a foreign insurance company or reinsurance company an obligation to draft a recovery plan;
(3) order an insurance company, reinsurance company, branch of a foreign insurance company or reinsurance company to submit special reports and statements;
(4) order an insurance company, reinsurance company, branch of a foreign insurance company or reinsurance company that the unauthorized activity be terminated;
(5) impose on an insurance company, reinsurance company, branch of a foreign insurance company or reinsurance company a penalty from EUR 3,000 to EUR 332,000;
(6) limit or suspend to an insurance company, reinsurance company, branch of a foreign insurance company or reinsurance company the authorization to conclude insurance or reinsurance contracts and to extend its obligations;
(7) order an insurance company, reinsurance company, branch of a foreign insurance company or reinsurance company to transfer the insurance portfolio or its part to other insurance company or branch of a foreign insurance company, or order the reinsurance company or branch of a foreign reinsurance company

to transfer the reinsurance portfolio or its part to other reinsurance company or branch of a foreign reinsurance company;

(8) restrict to an insurance company, reinsurance company, branch of a foreign insurance company or reinsurance company the free disposal of assets;
(9) withdraw from an insurance company, reinsurance company, branch of a foreign insurance company or reinsurance company the authorization fully or in a limited scope;
(10) order correction of accounting books or other records on the basis of findings of the NBS or an auditor;
(11) order the publication of the corrections of incomplete, incorrect or untrue information that a bank or branch of a foreign bank published according to a disclosure obligation stipulated by law;
(12) order an insurance company, reinsurance company, branch of a foreign insurance company or reinsurance company to carry to account the losses from operations with the registered capital after having carried to account the losses with retained profit from past years and with funds created from the profit;
(13) order compulsory receivership on an insurance company, reinsurance company, and branch of a foreign insurance company or reinsurance company.

The corrective measures and sanctions may be imposed separately or concurrently and repeatedly. Upon request by the competent supervisory authority of other Member States of the EU, the NBS is obliged to restrict or prohibit free disposal of the property of an insurance/reinsurance company from other Member States pursuing insurance/reinsurance activities in the territory of the Slovak Republic.

V. The Recent Act on Insurance

498. The recent Act on Insurance comprehensively regulates the rights and obligations of insurance companies and their supervision in accordance with Solvency II, which was adopted in the aftermath of the financial crisis. The aim of the Solvency II Directive is to ensure better protection of insurers and beneficiaries, enhance the competitiveness of the insurers in the EU, achieve deeper integration of the insurance market of the EU and to ensure a better distribution of capital resources. The new act also reinforces the supervisions of insurers and reinsurers through greater access to the solvency of supervised entities. The new enforcement system not only will control the quantitative indicators but also will include monitoring of the quality aspects. The most important changes could be divided into three areas, namely:

(1) system of governance;
(2) recognition of supervisory purposes and disclosure; and
(3) higher financial requirements.

§4. SECURITIES MARKET

499. The NBS, as it is the case for banking, insurance and as well the pension savings, is the responsible supervisory body in the area of securities market. The NBS supervises among others mainly the activities of stock exchange, central depository of securities, issuers of securities, collective investment schemes, investment firms and others. In the Slovak Republic, there is one stock exchange, the Bratislava Stock Exchange (BSE) founded on 15 March 1991. Clearing and settlement of securities is performed by the Central Securities Depository (CSD), which started its operations in 2004. Both the BSE and CSD are self-regulatory bodies. Generally, the Slovak capital market is as to its size and liquidity fairly limited. There are only several small institutional investors; as to 15 February 2013, there were fifteen investment firms and ten banks carrying out the investment activities. Trades in listed and unlisted securities are executed through BSE. Over-the-counter trades are negotiated with counterparties outside the BSE; however, all Over the Counter trades in listed securities must be settled via BSE.

500. The EU directives and regulations extensively influence the Slovak legal framework of the securities market.

I. Investment Firms

501. The activities of investment firms are governed by Act No. 566/2001 Coll. on Securities and Investment Services (the Securities Act). The Securities Act regulates securities investment services, some contractual relations involving securities, some relations associated with the activities of persons providing investment services, the business of the CSD, some relations associated with the activities of other entities in the financial market.

502. According to the Securities Act, an investment firm is a JSC, which has its registered office in the territory of the Slovak Republic and whose scope of business comprises providing of one or more investment services to clients or the performance of one or more investment activities on the basis of an investment services licence issued by NBS. The licence to provide investment services allows a person to establish an investment firm or a branch of a foreign investment firm in the Slovak Republic and carry out the business in the extent and under the terms and conditions defined in the licence. The share capital of an investment firm has to be at least EUR 730,000.

503. The licence to provide investment services is issued by NBS based on the submitted application. The fulfilment of the following conditions has to be proven by the investment firm:

(1) Paid-up share capital of the investment firm.

(2) Transparent and trustworthy origin of registered capital and other financial resources of the investment company according to Act No. 297/2008 Coll. on the prevention of money laundering and terrorist financing.
(3) Suitability of persons with qualified interest in the stock brokerage firm and transparency of relations between these persons, in particular transparency of their interest in share capital and voting rights.
(4) Professional competence and integrity of persons nominated as members of the Board of Directors or managerial employees (senior management), persons responsible for the compliance function, risk management function or internal audit function.
(5) Transparency of a group with close links of which a shareholder with qualified interest in the investment firm is a member.
(6) Close links within the group with close links do not prevent effective supervision.
(7) Law and its application in the country where a group with close links has close links do not prevent effective supervision.
(8) The investment firm shall have its registered office and head office in the territory of the Slovak Republic; ‘head office’ means the place from where the operation of the investment firm is managed or the place where the stock brokerage firm keeps the documents of its operation that are required for the exercise of supervision.
(9) Professional competence and trustworthiness of natural persons who are members of the statutory body of the financial holding company or mixed financial holding company, and the suitability of shareholders controlling the financial holding company or the mixed financial holding company, where the grantee of the licence is the investment firm, which becomes part of the consolidated group of the financial holding company.

504. An investment firm may use independent financial agents and bound financial agents for financial intermediation, provided that the independent financial agent and the bound financial agent are registered in the Register of Financial Agents, Financial Advisers, Financial Intermediaries from another Member State within the Insurance or Reinsurance Sector and Bound Investment Agents. An investment firm may use bound investment agents for the promotion of the investment services and secondary services for receiving and delegation of instructions from clients or prospective clients, placement of financial instruments and provision of investment advising in relation to such financial instruments and investment services and secondary services offered by the said persons only provided that the bound investment agent is registered in the Register of Financial Agents, Financial Advisers, Financial Intermediaries from another Member State within the Insurance or Reinsurance Sector and Bound Investment Agents or in a similar register kept in another Member State. An investment firm is obliged to ensure that a bound investment agent provides the information to the client in what position it is and which person it represents prior to the discussion with the client or a prospective client.

II. Collective Investment

505. The rules governing collective investment, the activities and operation of management companies and foreign management companies in the territory of the Slovak Republic, the establishment and management of common funds, the activities of depositories, the cross-border distribution of the unit certificates in common funds and securities of foreign collective investment undertakings, the protection of investors in collective investment schemes, the activities of other entities involved in collective investment schemes, and supervision in the field of collective investment are laid down in Act No 203/2011 Coll. on collective investment (Act on Collective Investment).

506. Collective investment represents a business activity, the main purpose of which is to raise funds from investors in order to invest them in accordance with a predetermined investment policy, based on the principle of risk spreading and risk limitation, for the benefit of the investors.

507. A management company is a JSC, registered in the Commercial Register established in the territory of the Slovak Republic for the purpose of establishing and managing common funds or European funds under a licence granted by the NBS.

508. Management of common funds is understood to mean managing investments in the common funds, administering the common funds, distributing unit certificates of the common funds, and promoting the common funds. Apart from establishing common funds and performing the activities mentioned in section 27(2) of the Act on Collective Investment, a management company may perform the following services provided that they are included in its licence:

(1) Financial instrument portfolio management or investment management for funds established under a separate regulation.
(2) Investment consultancy.
(3) Custody and management of unit certificates issued by management companies and securities issued by foreign collective investment undertakings, including holder's management, consisting of a minimum of the management of cash and financial collaterals.

509. A management company may not perform activities other than those permitted under the Act on Collective Investment. Management company licence is granted by NBS. The licence is granted for an unlimited period of time and may not be transferred to another entity, nor passed on to the legal successor of the management company. A management company may issue shares only in the form of registered book-entry common shares. The business name of a management company must include the designation '*správcovská spoločnost', akciová spoločnost*' or the abbreviation *'správ. spol., a.s.'*. A management company may commence the activities stated in the licence only after the licensed activities have been registered in the Commercial Register and after the conditions stated in the Act on Collective Investment.

510. A common fund is a fund consisting of common assets (held by fund unit holders), which a management company has raised through the issuance of unit certificates and their investments. The unit certificates represent the equity rights of fund unit holders. A common fund is a collective investment undertaking which is not a legal entity and which a management company manages. Management companies establish common funds by issuing unit certificates. The assets of a common fund comprise the common assets of its fund unit holders. A common fund's assets are not included in the assets of the management company. Each fund unit holder may independently exercise his/her rights towards the management company. A common fund may be established only on the basis of a licence granted in accordance with the Act on Collective Investment. A licence for the establishment of a common fund may only be granted after the management company has been established.

511. There are two basic types of common funds:

(1) open-ended common fund; and
(2) closed-ended common fund.

512. An open-ended common fund is a common fund in which the fund unit holders may redeem their unit certificates on request; it may be established for a definite or indefinite period, while a closed-ended common fund is a common fund in which the fund unit holders may not redeem their unit certificates on request; it is established for a definite period not exceeding ten years.

513. In addition, the Act on Collective Investment differentiates between a standard common fund and a special common fund. A standard common fund is a common fund in which money raised from investors (fund unit holders) on the basis of a public offering is invested in transferable securities and other liquid financial assets. All standard common funds are open-ended common funds. A standard common fund that meets the conditions of the Act on Collective Investment is deemed to be a fund that meets the conditions of the EU's legally binding act governing collective investment. A special common fund is a common fund which is not a standard common fund and in which money raised on the basis of a public or private offering is invested in assets specified in the Act on Collective Investment or in the rules of the special common fund. Special common funds are either open-ended common funds or closed-ended common funds.

514. A common fund may comprise two or more sub-funds, and in that case it is called an 'umbrella fund'. A sub-fund comprises a part of the assets and liabilities of the umbrella fund, which for the purposes of accounting is separate from the rest.

Each sub-fund must differ from other sub-funds of the same umbrella fund in one or more of the ways specified in the fund rules of the umbrella fund.

515. A unit certificate is a security that carries a fund unit holder's right to a corresponding share in the assets of a common fund, and a right to a proportion of the returns on these assets. Unit certificates are issued for one or more units.

516. A foreign management company is a legal entity, which has its registered office in a country other than the Slovak Republic and which is licensed in that country to establish and manage collective investment undertakings. The branch of a foreign management company is an organizational unit of a foreign management company, which is situated in the territory of the Slovak Republic; all the branches that a foreign management company based in an EU Member State establishes in the Slovak Republic are treated as a single branch in regard to their authorization to conduct activities in the Slovak Republic.

517. A foreign collective investment undertaking may be either:

(1) foreign common fund; or
(2) foreign investment company.

518. A foreign common fund is a collective investment undertaking, which is not a legal entity, and which is established and managed by a foreign management company or by a management company in accordance with the law of the country in which the foreign common fund is established. A foreign investment company is a foreign legal entity that is a collective investment undertaking according to the law of the country in which it has its registered office. A foreign investment company may be managed by a foreign management company or by a management company.

§5. Pension Savings

519. Act No. 43/2004 Coll. on Retirement Pension Saving (Act on Retirement Pension) governs the pension saving system, its scope, organization, funding, the legal relations under which retirement pension saving is conducted and supervision is governed by the NBS. Since 2005, pension assets have been managed by pension funds management companies established specifically for this purpose.

520. The contributions are paid to the Social Insurance Agency, which was founded on 1 November 1994 by Act No. 274/1994 Coll. as a statutory institution to administer the sickness insurance and the pension security substituting thus its ancestor the National Insurance Institution. As of 1 January 2004, the Slovak Insurance Agency administers social insurance: that means the sickness insurance, the pension insurance – old-age and invalidity insurance – the accident insurance, the guarantee insurance and the unemployment insurance. From 1 January 2005, the

Slovak Insurance Agency is responsible also for approval and acceptance of contracts with Pension Fund Management Companies (PFMCs), which administer the second pillar of the pension system – mandatory private funded scheme. The Slovak Insurance Agency collects contributions for the second pillar and sends it to PFMCs, which then according to the Act on Retirement Pension manage these assets.

521. Each PFMC is obliged to establish and manage four pension funds – a bond pension fund, mixed pension fund, equity pension fund, and indexed pension fund. In the contract on retirement pension saving, the saver may choose to have two personal pension accounts and therefore pay contributions to two pension funds. Pension funds are differentiated by their defined investment policy and the degree of risk that it includes. Higher risk, i.e., a higher probability of lower or negative returns, is associated with investment in equity and indexed funds. Such investments are for savers who want to earn higher returns. If a saver decides to split his contributions between two pension funds, then by law one of the funds must be a bond pension fund, the only fund in which the fund assets are guaranteed against a decline in the value of the pension unit. When a saver reaches the age of 50, the PFMC is required to begin gradually shifting his assets into the guaranteed bond pension fund.

522. In addition to the second pillar, there is the third pillar – voluntary private funded scheme governed by Act No. 650/2004 Coll. on Supplementary Pension Saving (Act on Supplementary Pension). The purpose of the supplementary pension saving system is to provide participants with an additional income in old age. In this system, most participants make contributions on a voluntary basis, with their employer making a proportion of the contributions on the basis of an agreement. The group of employees on whose behalf an employer is required to make contributions is defined in the Act.

523. In 2005 and 2006, the supplementary pension insurance companies that had been active in the supplementary pension sector since 1996 were transformed into Supplementary Pension Management Companies (SPMCs). At present there are four SPMCs operating in Slovakia. These companies establish and manage contributory supplementary pension funds that are differentiated by their investment policy. Participants use the contributory funds during the accumulation phase. SPMCs also manage payout supplementary pension funds, which are used solely to pay out supplementary pensions for a temporary period. A participant who wishes to have an annuity supplementary pension must transfer his supplementary pension savings to an insurance company and purchase a life annuity.

§6. Takeover Regulation

524. Takeover law forms a part of the Securities Act and applies to those companies whose shares carry voting rights and are listed on a regulated market in the

Slovak Republic or another Member State of the EU. The EU Takeover Directive[51] has influenced this part of the Securities Act. It can be characterized by transparency rules, a mandatory takeover bid rule, and at least a principle to adhere to the neutrality rule.

I. Takeover Bid

525. According to the Securities Act, a takeover bid is a public offer to conclude a contract for the purchase of all or part of the share of the offeree company or the exchange of all or part of these shares for other securities stipulated by a shareholder of that company, which is made either on a mandatory basis under the Securities Act or on a voluntary basis and which follows or has as its objective the acquisition of control of the offeree company. The control means holding of at least 33% of the voting rights attached to the shares of a single offeree company. In the case of mandatory takeover bid, the offeror is required to launch a takeover bid as a result of having acquired controlling stake in the offeree and voluntary takeover bid is where the offeror chooses to launch the takeover bid in order to acquire a controlling stake in the offeree company.

526. For the purpose of a takeover bid, 'shares' mean shares, interim certificates and other transferable securities, which carry voting rights and are admitted to trading on a regulated market in the Slovak Republic or in another Member State.

527. In case of mandatory takeover bids, an offeror has to announce its intention to make a takeover bid if:

- management of the offeror decides to make a bid; or
- events occur that oblige the offeror to make a mandatory bid (e.g., offeror acquires a controlling stake in the offeree); or
- the general meeting of a listed issuer decides that the shares will be delisted, in which special case the issuers are obliged to launch a mandatory bid to purchase all shared from its shareholders who either: (i) did not vote for the decision to delist their shares or (ii) did not attend the general meeting.

528. The offeror has to inform both the offeree's management board and the NBS of its intention to announce a takeover bid. In the case of mandatory takeover bids, the offeror has to inform the offeree and the NBS about the circumstances when and how the obligation arose. In the announcement sent to the NBS, the offeror has to enclose either an application for the appointment of an expert or an expert's report prepared in accordance with the provisions of the Securities Act concerning mandatory takeovers. Further, the offeror must publish the announcement in a daily national newspaper in the Slovak Republic or in a daily newspaper that has sufficient coverage in the Slovak Republic and in other EU Member States

51. Directive 2004/25/EC of the European Parliament and of the Council of 21 Apr. 2004 on Takeover Bids.

where the offeree's shares are traded on a regulated market. An offeror is obliged to submit a written proposal for the takeover bid to the NBS within ten business days after the publication in the newspapers.

529. Once informed, the offeree has to keep the information of takeover bid confidential. The management of the offeree must, without undue delay following the announcement of an intention to make a takeover bid, inform its Supervisory Board and the employees' representatives about the content of the takeover bid.

530. The NBS rejects a draft bid, which is not compliance with the Securities Act within ten business days from its submission. The NBS may ask the offeror for additional information or for correction of the submitted information in the draft within five business days from the submission. In such case, NBS gives the offeror no more than fifteen days to complete and resubmits its bid. After a draft bit is resubmitted, the NBS has a period of five business days to issue its decision.

531. The takeover bid shall include the following terms:

(1) Purchase Price.
(2) Bid Term (thirty days – seventy days from publication).
(3) Conditions.
(4) Withdrawal (in case of voluntary bid).
(5) Amendments.

532. The purchase price may be paid in either cash or shared or in a combination of the two. If the offeror offers any portion of the payment in shares, it must also offer a cash alternative. The bid price for shares in a mandatory bit must be adequate as to the value of the shares of the offeree. The adequacy of the offered prize is supported by an expert appraisal. Under the Securities Act, if the bid price is lower than the highest price paid by the offeror during the twelve months preceding the announcement of the takeover bid but is not lower than the price determined by the expert appraisal and not lower than the net asset value of the offeree share according to the most recent audited financial statements, such price shall be considered adequate. Nevertheless, the price may be not lower than the average price paid by the bidder for the offeree's shares acquired on the regulated market within twelve months preceding the announcement of the takeover bid. Moreover, the price offered for the same class of shares has to be the same for all shareholders.

533. Concerning the conditions of a voluntary bid, the offeror may stipulate that a certain minimum threshold of shares must be acquired in the course of a takeover in order for the bid to be deemed successful and binding.

534. With reference to the amendments of a bid, the offeror has to expressly provide in the bid that he/she can amend its bid in case of certain circumstances caused by persons other than the offeror or entities acting in cooperation with the offeror. The amendments have to be published and approved by the NBS.

535. Once a takeover bid has been announced and until its acceptance:

(a) offeror may not purchase shares of the offeree in other forms than through the takeover bid;
(b) offeree may not without a resolution of its general meeting:
  - decide to increase its share capital;
  - issue bonds combined with a pre-emptive right to subscribe new shares of the offeree or shares that are convertible into shares of the offeree;
  - buy back its own shares;
  - enter into commitment without receiving appropriate counter value;
  - take legal actions, which would result in a significant change in the assets of the offeree.
(c) management of the offeree may not perform any acts or take any measures that could hinder the ability of the target's shareholders from making a free informed decision with respect to the acceptance of the bid.

536. Besides NBS, which is empowered to issue the approval of the takeover bid or dismiss it and which supervises the entire takeover procedure, in case of a takeover, which would represent the concentration of the market according to special laws, the Slovak Antimonopoly Office has to be noticed.

A. Squeeze Out

537. With the transposition of the EU Takeover Directive, the squeeze out has been introduced for the first time in the legislative history of the Slovak Republic. The purpose of the squeeze out is that the majority shareholder of the company could pay off the minority shareholders in order to acquire 100% of the shares and thus freely facilitate the management, organization and business of the company.

538. Squeeze outs are possible under the Slovak law only for companies with listed shares on the regulated market, and only if:

(1) majority shareholder has carried out a mandatory or voluntary takeover bid announced after 1 January 2007 and this bid was not a partial bid and was unconditional; and
(2) majority shareholder holds at least 95% of the shares and has at least 95% of the voting rights.

539. Thus, in order to proceed with the squeeze out procedure, the majority shareholder has to launch the takeover bid at first. This takeover bid has to be executed via a stock exchange and adequate price has to be offered, as described in the above-stated Part A. Afterwards, the majority shareholder shall submit its squeeze out proposal to the NBS.

540. The right of squeeze out may be used not later than three months after the last takeover bid has expired. The majority shareholder who intends to make use of the right must declare its intention to minority shareholders and the NBS. The right of squeeze out is effective towards the minority shareholders only once approved by the NBS. The NBS grants the approval only if all the statutory conditions are met.

541. Minority shareholders must be given adequate compensation for their shares and it can be in a form of money, securities or a combination of the two. Compensation shall be regarded as adequate if it equals at least to one of the following amounts:

- where a mandatory takeover bid precedes the squeeze out, the consideration is fair where it is not lower than the consideration of that bid;
- if the mandatory takeover bid on a voluntary basis is launched before the right of squeeze out is exercised, the consideration is deemed fair, if the offeror has through this bid acquired shares carrying at least 90% of the voting rights in that part of the offeree company's share capital, which was subject to the takeover bid;
- where the compensation determined according to the rules applicable to mandatory takeover bids, in a case of expert appraisal, the appraisal may not be older than three months prior to the date when it was announced that the offeror will exercise its right of squeeze out.

542. Any lien on the shares transferred to the offeror expires as soon as the transfer is made. In the case of shares subject to a lien, the offeror shall provide the consideration to the lienor only insofar as is not otherwise provided for as a result of the agreement between the obliged person and the lienor.

§7. Insider Trading, Market Manipulation & Market Abuse

543. In the Slovak Republic and other transition economies, there was, mainly during the transformation phase, relatively large room form multiple unethical activities and practices on the capital market. For a fairly long period of time, only general civil or company law provisions were applicable and there were no laws, which would directly tackle the issue of insider trading, market manipulation or market abuse. In 2005, Act No. 747/2004 Coll. on Supervision of Financial Market (Supervision Act) was adopted. This Act lays down general rules of procedure for the supervision of the financial market in all respective areas that have been described in the above parts of this chapter. The Supervision Act states in its final part that it transposed the Market Abuse Directive;[52] however, reading through the

52. Directive 2003/6/EC of the European Parliament and of the Council of 28 Jan. 2003 on insider dealing and market manipulation (market abuse).

provisions of this Act, it is more of a procedural act than substantive. Thus, it is necessary to analyse some of the above-stated statutory acts as the Securities Act to find and define different types of market manipulations techniques, e.g., section 132 of the Securities Act.

Chapter 9. Commercial Contracts

§1. General Principles of Contract Law

544. In continental legal culture, where the legal system of the Slovak Republic belongs, the Slovak contract law does not include expressly stated basic principles on which the Slovak contract law is based. Various legal principles generated gradually throughout time and then were deduced from legal regulations. The courts create these principles. Historically it have been the courts of former Czechoslovakia or presently the Supreme Court of the Slovak Republic and Constitutional Court of the Slovak Republic, which have been developing the general principles of contract law.

545. First, the principle of equality of the parties is highlighted in the contract law. Further, the principle of contractual freedom of parties is the dominant principle of the contract theory and it can be seen in several ways. The principle of contractual freedom is based on the autonomy of the will of each individual party. In particular the following principles and freedoms have evolved:

(1) freedom of concluding contract;
(2) freedom of choice of contractual party;
(3) freedom to choose the type of contract;
(4) freedom of creating the actual content of the contract;
(5) freedom of choice forms of contract;
(6) principle of '*pacta sunt servanda*';
(7) principle of 'bona fides' and prohibition of abuse of individual rights; and
(8) principle of prevention of conflicts.

§2. Sale of Goods

I. International Sales Contracts

546. United Nations Convention on contracts for the international sale of goods of 1980 – CISG, published in Slovak Collection under No. 160/1991 Coll., was created in order to unify rules on international sales contracts in order to create a single legal regulation effective in all contracting states and thereby to replace different rules in various legal systems. This Convention applies to contracts of sale of goods between parties whose places of business are in different states when the states are contracting states or when the rules of private international law lead to the application of the law of a contracting state.

547. The scope of the uniform regulation is only the formation of the contract of sale and the rights and obligations of the seller and the buyer arising from such a contract. CISG expressly excludes from its application these issues:

– Validity of a contract or of any of its provisions or of any usage.

- The effect which the contract may have on the property in the goods sold.
- Liability of the seller for death or personal injury caused by the goods to any person.

548. CISG, although aiming to unify the substantive rules on international sale of goods, does not contain complete and exhaustive legal regulation of all matters related to these issues. The Convention is often not precise enough to resolve all particular issues, and in such cases the national court has to first use general principles upon which the Convention is based. However, the Convention does not enumerate these principles and their determination is upon judge in individual case. Slovak courts tend to turn directly to national law rules.

549. Special provisions of the Commercial Code apply to international sales contracts of entrepreneurs if two conditions are met. First, condition of contractual relationship with international aspect has to be met, and, second, such relationship has to be governed by Slovak law, which was either chosen by parties or it results from collision norms of international private law (e.g., Regulation (EC) No. 593/2008 of the European Parliament and of the Council on the law applicable to contractual obligations (Rome I)).

II. Domestic Sales Contracts

550. This part of the chapter solely focuses on domestic sales contract excluding the consumer contracts, which are covered by Chapter 5 of Part II.

A. Formation of the Sales Contract

551. The contract is established by agreement of the contractual parties on essential elements of the contract. The essential elements of the sale contract are:

(1) determination of the parties;
(2) specification of the subject matter;
(3) amount of goods;
(4) obligation of the seller to deliver the subject matter of the contract (movable goods) to the buyer and to transfer the respective property rights on the buyer;
(5) obligation of the buyer to pay the selling price.

552. The sale contract may be concluded in written or oral form; the Commercial Code does not specify the exact form of the contract.

553. Subject matter of the Commercial sale contract can be only the movable goods. In case of the immovable things, provisions of the Civil Code generally apply. However, the Commercial Code has to be applied in case of contract of sale of an enterprise involving immovable things as parts of the enterprise, and contract of sale of a leased thing (also lease contract or contract on financial lease).

B. Obligations of the Seller

554. The seller has the following three basic obligatory obligations:

(1) deliver the goods to the buyer;
(2) hand over to the buyer any documents relating to the goods; and
(3) enable him/her to acquire ownership title to the goods.

555. All the obligations are to be performed in accordance with a contract and the Commercial Code. Basically, the seller has to actually fulfil his/her contractual obligations. Payment of an agreed contractual penalty or damages has no prejudice to the contractual obligation of the seller to deliver the goods to the buyer, and enable him/her to acquire ownership title to the goods. The buyer can sue the seller in court to perform these obligations.

556. If the sending of the goods by the seller was agreed in the contract and the seller is not obliged under a sales contract to deliver the goods at a certain place, delivery of goods is performed by handing it over to the first carrier for carriage to the buyer. If the contract has no provision on shipping and goods in the contract are individually specified or specified by type, but the goods are delivered from a stock or to be manufactured, and the parties know where it is stocked or being manufactured, delivery is performed when the seller enables the buyer to dispose of the goods at that place. In other cases, the seller enables the buyer to dispose of the goods at the place where the seller has its seat.

557. The seller must deliver the goods either on the date specified in the contract or determined in the manner specified in the contract, or at any time during the period which is specified in the contract or determined in the manner specified in the contract, unless the contract or the purpose of the contract enables the buyer to set the time of delivery. The seller must deliver the goods in quantity, quality and specification required by the contract and must be packed or arranged for carriage in the manner specified in the contract.

558. If the contract does not determine the quality or specification of goods, the seller must deliver the goods in quality and specification that is suitable for the purpose specified in the contract, or if the purpose is not specified in the contract, for the purpose for which such goods are normally used.

559. If the quantity of goods specified in the contract is only approximate, unless the contract stipulates otherwise, divergence from the quantity given in the contract may not exceed 5%.

560. If the goods are delivered according to the sample or template, the seller has to deliver the goods according to the characteristics of the sample or template provided by the buyer.

561. If the contract does not specify how to pack the goods or arrange them for carriage, the seller is obliged to pack the goods or arrange them for carriage in the manner usual for such goods in commercial relationships, or, if such manner cannot be, in a manner necessary to preserve and protect the goods.

C. *Obligations of the Buyer*

562. The buyer is bound to pay the selling price for the goods and take delivery of the goods in accordance with the contract. With regard to payment of the selling price, the buyer is in the position of debtor and, in buyer's default, the seller has a right for payment of interest from delay in amount agreed in the contract or otherwise, if not agreed, in amount stated based on the Commercial Code.

D. *Transfer of Property and of Risk*

563. The Commercial Code distinguishes the moment when risk of damage passes from the seller to the buyer and the moment when ownership title is transferred.

564. The buyer acquires ownership title to the goods as soon as the delivered goods are handed over to him. Prior to taking delivery of the goods, the buyer acquires ownership title to the goods in transit when he acquires the right to dispose of the consignment. The parties may negotiate in writing that the buyer acquires ownership sooner.

565. The risk of damage to goods passes to the buyer at the time when he takes over the goods from the seller or, if he does not do so in time, when the seller makes it possible for him to dispose of the goods and the buyer breaches the contract by failure to take over such goods. Under the Commercial Code, the damage to a thing means the loss, destruction, impairment or devaluation of the thing.

566. If at the time when the contract is concluded the goods are already being transported, the risk of damage to the goods passes to the buyer when the goods are handed over to the first carrier. However, if the seller, when concluding the contract, knew or, taking into account all circumstances, ought to have known that the goods had been damaged, the seller is liable for such damage.

§3. Commercial Services

I. Distribution

A. *Exclusive and Non-exclusive Distribution Agreements*

1. Distribution Agreement

567. The distributor agreements are usually such agreements, which define framework conditions for a future conclusion of purchase contracts between the parties, usually governing the relationship between the manufacturer of goods, who is in the position of the seller, and distributor of products as the buyer. The agreement, however, is not restricted to the purchase of goods between the parties, but concluded for the long-term cooperation between the parties and provides obligations of the parties in relation to third parties. The subject matter of this agreement reflects often also some practical issues concerning the realization of sales in respect to national law and obligations that the law imposes on the seller. These framework agreements typically include prearranged content of (single, partial) purchase agreement, as well as may contain commercial terms and conditions, method of payment, limitation of property rights.

568. The purpose of the distributor agreement is to ensure that the goods reach the market. The manufacturer, however, often does not have adequate resources, skills, knowledge and permissions for it, on the market itself entered, so it is better to use a service of distributor that already operates in the market. A distributor is usually a company that meets all necessary legal, administrative and professional requirements for the operation of the market and the marketing of goods and services for sale. The manufacturer therefore enters into a contract to ensure the entry of goods into the market through the distributor.

569. National distribution agreement: The Slovak law does not complexly regulate a distribution agreement. The distribution agreement is not mentioned as a contract type in the Slovak law. The most common use of this is framework agreement with a partial purchase contract and often with the inclusion of an exclusive sale contract. Relationships of the distribution agreement are governed by general provisions of contractual relationships in the Commercial Code and by the principle of contractual freedom.

The distributor agreement is generally intended for cases of repeated identical or similar business operations, in which it is redundant to repeatedly negotiate and conclude all contractual conditions. Negotiation of terms and conditions is included in a framework agreement. A single purchase agreement has an easier form, e.g., confirmed orders with reference to the framework agreement. An order includes only the necessary specification of purchased goods. By reference to the framework agreement, the contractual relationship between the buyer and the seller is governed by the agreement. Terms of transfer of ownership and risk, insurance, etc. can be agreed according to the needs of the contractual parties who may use standard and generally recognized terms, e.g., 'INCOTERMS'.

The distributor purchases goods from the manufacturer (supplier) on his/her own name and risk. This form expresses the traditional marketing system, where the parties have only obligations regarding the purchase of goods. Such an agreement will be beneficial for traders who do not want to bind or be limited by such terms of, e.g., franchise agreement. Such distribution (framework) agreement means rather written negotiations of discount terms, agreed credit limit, the length of maturity of invoices. The provisions of the Commercial Code govern individual purchase agreements and their formation.

570. International distribution agreement: An exclusive sales contract governed by the Commercial Code can also be considered as a distribution agreement. Under the contract the supplier undertakes not to deliver the goods specified in the contract to a person in a particular area other than the customer. Based on the location of this contract in the system of the Commercial Code in part on special provisions on contractual relations in international trade, the exclusive sales contract may be used only in international trade and applies to cases where the distribution agreement will be governed by Slovak law. This agreement must be in writing and must clearly identify the area to which the sales exclusivity applies and goods covered; otherwise the contract is invalid. The Commercial Code closely regulates the terms of the contract.

During the contract's validity, the supplier may not supply the specified goods either directly or indirectly to persons in the agreed area, with the exception of the exclusive customer designated in the exclusive sales contract, and, if applicable, to other persons designated therein. The exclusive sales contract does not deprive the supplier of the right to publicize his/her products and engage in market research in the agreed area.

Individual sales within the framework of an exclusive sales contract are executed on the basis of separate sales contracts. Part of the contents of these contracts may be agreed when the relevant exclusive sales contract is concluded. If a contract does not specify the period of time for which it is concluded, the contract expires one year after the date of its conclusion. If it follows from the contract that the contracting parties intended to conclude the contract for an indefinite period of time and failed to agree on notice of termination, either party may give notice, which will take effect at the end of the calendar month following the month in which the notice of termination was delivered to the other party.

An exclusive sales contract may also bind the distributor not to buy goods from other manufacturers but it is not the main purpose of the legal regulation. If a customer fails to adhere to the schedule of deliveries of goods envisaged in the contract, or if he buys goods that are the object of an exclusive sales contract from another supplier, although such right does not apply to him under the contract, the supplier may withdraw from the contract, but he is not entitled to damages. If the supplier, contrary to the terms of the contract, supplies other customers, the exclusive customer may withdraw from the contract.

2. Influence of EU Competition Law

571. Exclusive distribution or exclusive customer allocations: Exclusive distribution or exclusive customer allocations are agreements whereby the supplier agrees to sell his/her products only to one distributor for resale in a particular territory or for resale to a particular class of customers. In those agreements, the distributor is usually also limited in his/her active selling into other exclusively allocated territories or classes of customers.

Such agreements may reduce intra-brand competition and lead to market partitioning, which may facilitate price discrimination between different territories or between different customers. When applied by several suppliers on the same market, such agreements may also facilitate horizontal collusion, both at the level of suppliers and at the level of distributors.

Whereas, despite the fact that the nature of the product is not particularly relevant to the assessment of possible anticompetitive effects, exclusive distribution may lead to efficiencies, especially where investments by the distributors are required to protect or build up the brand image. In general, efficiencies apply for new products, complex products, and products whose qualities are difficult to judge before or even after consumption. In addition, exclusive distribution may lead to savings in logistic costs.

572. Selective distribution: Selective distribution agreements, like exclusive distribution agreements, restrict on the one hand the number of authorized distributors and on the other the possibilities of resale. The difference with exclusive distribution is that the restriction of the number of dealers does not depend on the number of territories but on selection criteria linked in the first place to the nature of the product. Another difference with exclusive distribution is that the restriction on resale is not a restriction on active selling to a territory but a restriction on any sales to non-authorized distributors, leaving only appointed dealers and final customers as possible buyers.

Selective distribution is almost always used to distribute branded final products. The possible competition risks are a reduction in intra-brand competition and, especially in case of cumulative effect, foreclosure of certain type(s) of distributors and softening of competition and facilitation of collusion between suppliers or buyers. In an assessment of the possible anticompetitive effects of selective distribution, a distinction is being made between purely qualitative selective distribution and quantitative selective distribution.

Purely qualitative selective distribution selects dealers only on the basis of objective criteria required by the nature of the product such as training of sales personnel, the service provided at the point of sale, a certain range of the products being sold, etc. Purely qualitative selective distribution is in general not prohibited for lack of anticompetitive effects. Qualitative and quantitative selective distribution is exempted by the Block Exemption Regulation as long as the market share of both supplier and buyer each does not exceed 30%, even if combined with other non-hardcore vertical restraints, such as non-compete or exclusive distribution, provided active selling by the authorized distributors to each other and to end users is not restricted.

B. Franchising

1. Definition

573. The Slovak law does not define franchising nor does not govern a franchising agreement as a separate type of contract. The essence of a franchise is a long-term entitlement and obligation of a franchisee to use in its own business the strong position, trademarks, trade name, design, products and services of another person (the Franchisor).

574. Franchising is a system of marketing goods and/or services and/or technology, which is based upon a close and ongoing collaboration between legally and financially separate and independent undertakings, the Franchisor and its individual Franchisees, whereby the Franchisor grants its individual Franchisee the right, and imposes the obligation, to conduct a business in accordance with the Franchisor's concept.

575. The right entitles and compels the individual Franchisee, in exchange for a direct or indirect financial consideration, to use the Franchisor's trade name, and/or trademark and/or service mark, *know-how*, business and technical methods, procedural system, and other industrial and/or IP rights, supported by the continuing provision of commercial and technical assistance, within the framework and for the term of a written franchise agreement, concluded between parties for this purpose.[53]

2. Legal Protection of Franchisees

576. No Specific Protection: As was mentioned above, the legal regulation of franchising is missing in Slovakia. This fact, however, is not problematic in any way. Entrepreneurs, who in such situation cannot benefit from the statutory structure of franchising, must take higher attention to the formulation of their own franchise agreement that should regulate all aspects of the relationship between the beneficiary and provider of the franchise. An almost essential part of any franchise agreement is defining the mutual rights and obligations relating to IP objects, i.e., in particular, the conditions of the licence to the trademarks, transfer of know-how, providing franchise. The franchise agreement also usually includes provisions to ensure that the beneficiary has access during the term of the franchise agreement to all the necessary information – e.g., obligation of the provider franchise to train the beneficiary (its employees) and provide it with adequate support. Foreign franchisors should also expressly agree on the governing law and jurisdiction of general or arbitration court to decide any disputes in the agreement. Besides the text of the

53. European Code of Ethics for Franchising elaborated by the European Franchise Federation, available online: http://www.eff-franchise.com/spip.php?rubrique13 (accessed 31 May 2013).

franchise agreement as such, the manual is usually prepared and contains the important source of information for the franchisee, including relevant data to the franchise business, procedures and instructions. Manual is usually attached as an annex to the agreement.

577. *Influence of EU Competition Law*: Besides the provision of the business method, franchise agreements may contain a combination of vertical restraints concerning the sale of the products concerned, such as selective distribution, non-compete obligations, exclusive distribution or weaker forms thereof. The Block Exemption Regulation[54] covers licensing contained in franchise agreements where all the following five conditions are fulfilled:

(1) The IP rights provisions must be part of a vertical agreement, that is an agreement with conditions under which the parties may purchase, sell or resell certain goods or services.
(2) The IP rights must be assigned to, or licensed for use by, the buyer.
(3) The IP rights provisions must not constitute the primary object of the agreement.
(4) The IP rights provisions must be directly related to the use, sale or resale of goods or services by the buyer or its customers. In the case of franchising where marketing forms the object of the exploitation of the IP rights, the goods or services are distributed by the master franchisee or the franchisees.
(5) The IP rights provisions, in relation to the contract goods or services, must not contain restrictions of competition having the same object as vertical restraints, which are not exempted under the Block Exemption Regulation.

Those conditions are usually fulfilled as under most franchise agreements, including master franchise agreements, the Franchisor provides goods and/or services, in particular commercial or technical assistance services, to the franchisee.[55] In addition to these, the European Franchise Federation also adopted a European Code of Ethics for Franchising[56] that even though is not mandatory represents a common source of basic legal principles, to which also the Slovak franchise association subscribes.

As for the vertical restraints on the purchase, sale and resale of goods and services within a franchising arrangement, such as selective distribution, non-compete obligations or exclusive distribution, the Block Exemption Regulation applies up to the 30% market share threshold, subject to the following two specific remarks:

54. Commission Regulation (EU) No. 330/2010 of 20 Apr. 2010 on the application of Art. 101(3) of the Treaty on the Functioning of the European Union to categories of vertical agreements and concerted practices.
55. European Commission, *Guidelines on Vertical Restraints* (2010/C130/01) published in Official Journal of the European Union No. C 130, p. 1, of 19 May 2010.
56. Available online at: http://www.eff-franchise.com/spip.php?rubrique13 (accessed 2 Jul. 2015).

(1) The more important the transfer of know-how, the more likely it is that the restraints create efficiencies and/or are indispensable to protect the know-how and that the vertical restraints fulfil the conditions of exclusion from prohibition.
(2) A non-compete obligation on the goods or services purchased by the franchisee falls outside the scope of prohibition where the obligation is necessary to maintain the common identity and reputation of the franchised network. In such cases, the duration of the non-compete obligation is also irrelevant, as long as it does not exceed the duration of the franchise agreement itself.

II. Middlemen or Intermediaries

A. *Survey: Definition and Categories*

578. Intermediary activity is performed for remuneration, which is directed to that a natural or legal person may enter into a contract with a third party or conclude a certain business matter. Intermediary activity can be carried on the basis of:

(1) Brokerage Agreement, under the Commercial Code the broker undertakes to engage in activities aimed at providing the client with the opportunity of concluding a certain contract with a third party and the client agrees to pay the broker fee (commission).
(2) Commission Agent Agreement, under the Commercial Code the agent undertakes to arrange in his/her own name, but at the principal's account a certain business matter for the principal, and the principal undertakes to pay him/her a commission for his/her services.
(3) Mandate Agreement, under the Commercial Code the mandatary undertakes to arrange, at the mandant's expense and for a fee, a specific business matter by performing legal acts on behalf of the mandant, or by conducting other activity, and the mandant undertakes to pay him/her a fee for his/her services.
(4) Commercial Representation Agreement, under the Commercial Code the commercial representative as an independent entrepreneur undertakes to engage in long-term activity on behalf of the principal aimed at the conclusion of specified contracts or to negotiate and conclude transactions on behalf of the principal and on his/her account and the principal agrees to pay the representative a commission.

B. *Brokers*

1. Definition

579. Under the brokerage agreement the broker undertakes to engage in activities aimed at providing the client with the opportunity of concluding a certain contract with a third party and the client agrees to pay the broker fee (commission). The brokerage agreement (also an agreement with an intermediary) differs only slightly from an Agreement on commercial representation. The difference lies in the duration of the contract. A brokerage contract tends to be concluded for a single transaction or a short period, whereas an Agreement on commercial representation is usually concluded for a longer period.

2. Reciprocal Rights and Obligations of the Parties

580. The broker must inform the client, without undue delay, of any circumstances, which are important for the client's decision-making on the conclusion of the contract being negotiated, and the client is bound to keep the broker informed of all facts, which are of decisive importance for the conclusion of the contract. The broker is entitled to a commission upon a conclusion of the contract, which is the object of the intermediation.

581. If the parties agree in the agreement that the broker is only obligated to provide an opportunity for the client to conclude a contract of a particular content with a third party, the broker is entitled to a commission already by providing such opportunity for the client. If, under the brokerage agreement, the broker becomes entitled to a commission only after the third party has fulfilled the obligation ensuing to it from the intermediated contract, the broker also becomes entitled to a commission when the third party's obligation to the client is terminated, or postponed, due to a reason for which the client is responsible.

582. The broker is entitled to an agreed commission, or otherwise to the commission customary for the intermediation of comparable contracts at the time when the brokerage agreement was concluded. However, the broker is not entitled to a commission if the contract with a third party is concluded without his assistance or if, contrary to the terms of the brokerage agreement, he also acted as broker for the other (third) party with whom the intermediated contract was concluded.

583. The broker has the right to a commission in spite of the fact that a contract with a third party, or performance of a third party's obligation, is only concluded after the termination of his/her brokerage agreement, if he negotiated a contract with a third party.

584. The broker is obliged to keep the documents, which he has acquired when performing his/her negotiating (intermediating) activity for his/her client for as long as such documents may be important for the protection of the interests of the client.

585. The broker is not liable for the performance of third persons with whom he negotiated (intermediated) a contract; however, the broker may not propose to the client a conclusion of a contract with a party about which he knows, or ought to know, that there is a reasonable doubt whether such a party will duly and in time perform any obligations arising from the contract.

586. If the client so requests, the broker must provide him/her with data necessary to judge the credibility of a party with which the client should conclude the contract.

3. Termination of the Brokerage Agreement

587. The brokerage contract is discharged if the client's contract with a third party, which is the object of the intermediating activities, is not concluded within the time limit specified in the brokerage agreement. If no time has been specified, either party may terminate the contract by notifying the other party.

C. Commission Agents and Mandataries

1. Definition

588. The commission agent under the Commission Agent Agreement undertakes to arrange in his/her own name, but at the principal's account a certain business matter for the principal, and the principal undertakes to pay him/her a commission for his/her services.

589. The mandatory under the Mandate Agreement undertakes to arrange, on the mandant's account and for a fee, a specific business matter by performing legal acts on behalf of the mandant, or by conducting other activity, and the mandant undertakes to pay him/her a fee for his/her services.

2. Rights and Obligations of the Parties

590. The mandatory must proceed with due care when making arrangements for others and in accordance with the mandant's instructions and interests, and of which the mandatory is aware or ought to be aware. The mandatory is bound to inform the mandant of all the circumstances he becomes aware of while arranging a matter for the mandant and which might result in a change of the mandant's instructions. The mandatory may depart from the mandant's instructions only if it is necessary and in the interest of the mandant, and if it is impossible to receive the mandant's consent in time. However, even in such case, the mandatory may not depart from instructions, if it is prohibited by the contract or by the mandant.

591. The mandatory is bound to arrange a matter personally only if it is stipulated in the mandate. If the mandatory breaches this duty, he is liable for any damage caused in this relation to the mandant. The mandant is bound to hand over to the mandatory things and information necessary for the arrangement of a certain (specific) matter, unless their nature indicates that they are to be obtained by the mandatory. If the arrangement of a specific matter requires the performance of acts in law (transactions) on behalf of the mandant, the mandant has to issue a written power of attorney to the mandatory.

592. The mandatory is liable for any damage caused to things taken over from the mandant when arranging a matter on his/her behalf, and for any damage caused to things taken over from third persons on the mandator's behalf, unless he could not have averted such damage even when exercising due care. The mandatory must insure such things if the contract so provides, or if the mandant asks him/her to do so.

593. If the amount of remuneration is not agreed in the agreement, the mandant is bound to pay to the mandatory the remuneration, which was customary for an activity similar to that undertaken by the mandatory on the mandant's behalf at the time of conclusion of the mandate. Unless the agreement provides otherwise, the mandatory is entitled to his/her remuneration once he has duly performed the activity specified in the agreement, regardless of whether it has led to the expected result or not. The mandatory may ask for an appropriate advance on the conclusion of the agreement. The mandant has to reimburse the mandatory for all the expenses, which the mandatory reasonably incurred when performing his/her obligation, unless they are included in the mandatory's remuneration.

594. The mandant may terminate the mandate in part, or in full, at any time. Unless the notice of termination provides later day of effectiveness, it takes effect on the day when the mandatory learned of it, or on the day when he could have learned of it. As from the day when the termination notice becomes effective, the mandatory is not obliged to perform the activity to which the notice applies. However, the mandatory is obliged to warn the mandant of all measures, which must be taken in order to prevent any immediate threat of damage ensuing from the mandatory's incomplete performance in arranging a certain matter.

595. The mandatory can terminate the mandate; termination takes effect at the end of the month following the month in which such termination notice is delivered to the mandant, unless the termination notice sets a later date. The mandatory's obligation to perform activities on behalf of the mandant terminates on the day the notice becomes effective. If this termination of activities could cause damage to the mandant, the mandatory must inform the mandant of the measures to be taken to prevent such damage. If the mandant cannot take such measures, even by other persons, and he asks the mandatory to take them himself/herself, the mandatory is bound to do so.

3. Special Rights and Obligations Relating to Commission

596. When arranging matters, the commission agent must act with the due care in accordance with the principal's instructions. The commission agent may diverge from the principal's instructions only if it is in the interest of the principal and if he cannot obtain the latter's consent in time. If the commission agent breaches this obligation, the principal need not consider negotiations as being conducted on his/her account if he rejected such negotiations without undue delay after he learned of their contents.

597. No rights and obligations arise to the principal as a result of the commission agent's relationship with third parties. However, the principal may directly require a third party to hand over a thing or fulfil an obligation commissioned for him/her by the agent, if the commission agent cannot do so himself/herself due to circumstances concerning his/her person.

598. The principal holds ownership title to movable things entrusted to the commission agent for sale until title to them passes to a third party. Ownership title to movable things acquired for the principal by the commission agent passes directly to the principal at the time when such movables are handed over to the commission agent. After the commission agent has arranged a determined transaction, he is obliged to submit a report on the result to the principal and draw up a final account.

599. The commission agent must transfer to the principal, without undue delay, rights acquired as a result of arranging a certain business transaction on his/her behalf and take over to him/her everything that he has acquired as a result of such transaction, and the principal is bound to receive it.

600. If the amount of the commission has not been agreed upon, the commission agent is entitled to a commission corresponding to his/her accomplished activities and the achieved results, taking into account the commission customary for comparable activities at the time the contract was concluded. The commission agent is entitled to payment of his/her commission as soon as he fulfils his/her obligations.

4. Commission Agent Agreement to Procure the Purchase or Sale of a Security (Stockbrokers)

601. Under the Securities Act in a commission agent agreement to procure the purchase or sale of a security, the commission agent (stockbroker) undertakes to procure in its own name and for the account of the client the purchase or sale of a security, or to perform activities directed towards this objective, and the client undertakes to pay the agent a commission. The agreement must be made in writing.

602. Unless otherwise provided in the agreement, the client's instruction on the basis of which the commission agent procures the purchase or sale of a security has to be in writing. If the client's instruction is not made in writing, the commission agent is required to give the client, at its request, a confirmation of a received instruction.

603. Where a client instructs a commission agent to procure the purchase of a security, the commission agent may ask for an advance payment.

604. Unless otherwise stated in the agreement, and provided that the commission agent is able to do so, the commission agent is required, even without the client's consent, to sell the security for a price higher than that stated in the instruction or to buy the security at a price lower than that stated in the instruction. Otherwise the agent is liable for the damage incurred by the client. If the purchase price or the sale price is not specified in the client's instruction, the commission agent is required to buy or sell the security at the best price for the client, which can be obtained with due professional care.

605. Further, the provisions of the Commercial Code on commission agent agreement govern the agreement.

D. *Commercial Representation*

606. Agreement on Commercial Representation is similar to the distributor agreement. Other entrepreneurs can use both agreements for placing products on the market and both agreements are used in practice similarly. However, there are a few differences.

1. Definition

607. Under an Agreement on Commercial Representation the commercial representative as an independent entrepreneur undertakes to engage in long-term activity on behalf of the principal aimed at the conclusion of specified contracts or to negotiate and conclude transactions on behalf of the principal and on his/her account.

608. The agreement must be concluded in writing.

609. The Commercial Code specifies a person who can be a commercial representative. A first characteristic is that the service of the commercial representative is paid. The commercial representative is entitled to receive a commission for his/her services, which in most cases is specified in the agreement and should reflect the practices at the given place of business. The commercial representation may be non-exclusive, which means that the principal may authorize other persons to represent him/her in the area and also the commercial representative may perform the same activity for other principals. The commercial representation may also be agreed as exclusive. An exclusive contract can be semi-open on the part of the principal, and the principal undertakes not to have another representative for a given area, or semi-open on the part of representative when the representative undertakes not to represent any other person in the given area. If both parties undertake to the above-mentioned, it is the exclusive closed agreement. The law also offers the possibility to include a non-competition clause into the agreement. This clause is an agreement that the representative even after the termination of the representation for some time, no more than two years, in a particular territory or to a designated group of customers in that territory, is not entitled to carry out on its own or others' account activities which were the subject of the representation, or other activity that would have competitive nature of the business to the principal.

610. However, the Commercial Code expressly excludes:

(1) person who as an organ may bind a legal entity;
(2) partner or member of cooperative who under the law is authorized to bind the other partners or members; or
(3) liquidator, administrator, bankruptcy trustee, special trustee or trustee in restructuring of the represented person, from being a commercial representative.

2. Rights and Obligations of Parties

611. The commercial representative is obligated to pursue with due care in the specified territory, the commercial activity which is the object of his/her obligation. If the territory is not defined in the contract, it is presumed that the commercial representative has to pursue his/her activity on the territory of the Slovak Republic.

612. The object of the obligations undertaken by the commercial representative is to find parties interested in concluding such commercial transactions as are specified in the contract. The principal has to grant the commercial representative a power of attorney; otherwise the representative may not, on behalf of the principal, conclude commercial transactions, receive performance for him/her, or undertake other acts in law in the name of the principal.

613. The commercial representative has to carry out an activity which he has undertaken to do fairly, exercising due care, in good faith and has to heed the principal's interests, act in compliance with his/her authorization and the principal's reasonable instructions and advise the principal of all necessary information at his/her disposal. The commercial representative must keep the principal informed of trends on the market and of all circumstances, which are important for the principal's interests, and in particular for the decisions he makes concerning the conclusion of commercial transactions. If the agreement allows the commercial representative to conclude commercial transactions on behalf of the principal, the commercial representative must conclude them only on such commercial terms as are set by the principal, unless the principal agrees to another procedure. The commercial representative must notify the principal accordingly, without undue delay when he is unable to perform his/her activity.

614. The principal has to act fairly and in good faith in relations with the commercial representative. In particular, the principal has to:

(1) provide the necessary information on the commercial representative, relating to the transactions; and
(2) supply to the commercial representative the necessary information relating to the performance of the obligations under the agreement, in particular, within a reasonable time, inform the commercial representative, that he assumes a substantial reduction in the scope of activities in comparison to what could the commercial representative expected under normal conditions.

615. The principal is obliged to inform the commercial representative within a reasonable time that he/she accepted, rejected or failed to perform a transaction obtained by the commercial representative.

616. The commercial representative is also bound, within the scope of his/her obligations, to assist in the implementation of the concluded commercial transactions according to the principal's instructions and in the principal's interests, which are, or ought to be, known to the commercial representative, particularly when resolving discrepancies arising from the concluded commercial transactions.

617. The commercial representative may not, without the principal's consent, disclose information acquired from the principal to other parties, or use such information for his/her own benefit or for the benefit of other parties, if this is contrary to the interests of the principal. This duty remains binding even after the termination of the agreement.

618. The commercial representative is required to propose the conclusion of transactions or enter into transactions only with those who have prerequisites to fulfil their obligations. The representative is responsible for fulfilling the obligations of a third party with whom the representative proposed a conclusion of a transaction or adopted on behalf of the principal, only if he/she has undertaken to bear such liability in writing and if the representative receives extra remuneration for assuming such liability. In this case, the provisions on surety commitment govern the rights and obligations.

619. The commercial representative is entitled to the agreed commission or in amount customarily paid for comparable commercial representation in the field of activity of the place of its performance taking into account the nature of the transaction, which is the subject of the agreement. Commission is also remuneration of the commercial representative performed depending on the number or the level of transactions.

620. Unless agreed otherwise the commercial representative becomes entitled to a commission when:

(1) principal had executed the transaction; or
(2) principal should have executed the transaction according to the transaction concluded with a third party; or
(3) third party has executed the transaction.

621. However, regardless of the agreement, representative's right to commission must arise at the latest when the third party has executed his/her part of the transaction or would have done so if the principal had executed his/her part of the transaction. However, if a third party has to fulfil its commitment only after more than six months from the day when the transaction is concluded, the commercial representative is entitled to a commission after the conclusion of the transaction. Unless agreed otherwise, the commission must be paid to a representative not later than on the last day of the month following the quarter in which the entitlement to such commission arose.

3. Non-exclusive Commercial Representation

622. Unless the parties agree otherwise in the agreement, the principal may also authorize other persons to engage in the commercial representation which has been agreed with the commercial representative, and the commercial representative may engage in the kind of activity which he has undertaken for the principal also for other persons, or conclude commercial transactions which are the object of commercial representation on his own account or on another person's account.

4. Exclusive Commercial Representation

623. Exclusive commercial representation must be expressly agreed in the agreement. If an exclusive commercial representation has been agreed, the principal is obligated not to use another representative for commercial transactions within the specified territorial area and in the specified scope being the object of such representation, and the commercial representative is not authorized to take on commercial representation of another party within such scope, nor to conclude commercial transactions on his/her own account or on another person's account.

624. The Commercial Code, however, enables the principal to conclude commercial transactions on the territory to which an exclusive commercial representation agreement relates, without his/her exclusive representative's collaboration, but he must pay him/her the commission on such commercial transactions as if his/her exclusive commercial representative had assisted him/her in concluding them, unless the agreement states otherwise.

5. Termination of the Relationship with Commercial Representative

625. The obligation of the commercial representative terminates with the expiry of the time for which the agreement was concluded. However, if the parties continue to abide by the terms of the agreement, it is presumed that the validity of the contract has been extended by without limitation, i.e., for an indefinite period.

626. An agreement, which is concluded for an indefinite period of time, may be terminated by either party giving notice. The period of notice is one month for the first year of agreement, two months for the second year, and three months for the third year and subsequent years. The parties may agree to extend the notice period. If the parties agreed on the longer periods, the period of notice of the principal may not be shorter than the period of the commercial representative.

6. Distribution Versus Representation

627. Common for both agreements, either distribution agreement or agreement on commercial representation is that the subject matter of both is the intermediation of transaction. An agreement on commercial representation can be used also to a wider number of transactions that will be realized through a representative, while distribution agreement is specifically aimed to the distribution of goods, which means that it is primarily focused on the conclusion of sales contracts. Other differences are performing the agreements themselves. Distribution relationship is based on the fact that the goods become the property of the distributor and the property becomes property of the end user. Therefore, the distributor in the realization of end sales acts on its own account and not on behalf of the manufacturer. Whereas, the representative acts on behalf of the principal, so that the sales contract to the end customer include only one transfer of ownership title from the principal to the customer.

628. Another major difference is that representative receives commissions for his/her services. In the distribution agreement, the distributor is not paid for his/her services, but usually the price at which the distributor purchases goods is different from the price at which the distributor further sells the goods. The remuneration itself does not come from the distributor agreement, but it is a difference between the purchase price of goods and their sale price.

E. Financial Intermediation

629. Under Act No. 186/2009 Coll. on Financial Intermediation and Financial Counselling, the financial intermediation means pursuance of at least one of the following activities:

(1) Submission of offers to conclude a contract for the provision of a financial service, conclusion of the contract for the provision of a financial service and pursuance of further activities leading to the conclusion or to the amendment of the contract for the provision of a financial service.
(2) Provision of expert assistance, information and advices to a client in order to conclude or terminate a contract for the provision of a financial service.
(3) Cooperation at the administration of a contract for the provision of a financial service where the financial service character makes such cooperation possible.

(4) Cooperation at the handling and settlement of claims arising to a client from a contract for the provision of a financial service, in particular in connection with the events being crucial for the occurrence of such claims where the financial service character enables such cooperation.

630. Financial intermediation within the capital market sector includes also:

(1) provision of investment services, receiving and delegation of client's instructions concerning negotiable securities, mutual fund allotment certificates and securities of foreign subjects of collective investment, and their promotion;
(2) provision of investment counselling in relation to negotiable securities, mutual fund allotment certificates and securities issued by foreign subjects of collective investment.

631. Financial service means a service provided by a financial institution (e.g., bank, insurance company, reinsurance company, securities dealer, trust company, electronic money institution, etc.) or an activity pursued by the financial institution within the sector of:

(1) insurance or reinsurance;
(2) capital market;
(3) supplementary pension saving;
(4) receiving of deposits;
(5) granting credits.

632. The Financial agent means a person having located its registered office or place of business in the territory of the Slovak Republic and pursuing financial intermediation upon a written contract concluded with a financial institution or upon a written contract concluded with an independent financial agent. Only a financial agent may generally pursue financial intermediation in the territory of the Slovak Republic.

633. The investment agent means a person performing, on the full and unconditional responsibility of a securities dealer, financial intermediation within the capital market sector and further activities in accordance with a written contract.

III. Insurance

634. Under Act No. 8/2008 Coll. on Insurance as amended an insurance company, reinsurance company, branch of a foreign insurance company and branch of a foreign reinsurance company is obliged to use, for financial intermediation within the insurance or reinsurance sector, only the persons mentioned above under paragraph F who are entered in the Register of Financial Agents, Financial Advisers,

Financial Intermediaries from another Member State within the Insurance or Reinsurance Sector and Bound Investment Agents and authorized to perform such activities. Under the new Act No. 39/2015 Coll. on Insurance, this approach remains in force.

IV. Financial Services

A. General Observation

635. Financial services were originally understood as the business primarily consisting of taking deposits and providing loans made only by banks. Financial services include today not only banking services as defined in the preceding sentence but also other services provided by other financial institutions among which include beside banks also insurance companies, stock exchanges, investment companies, pension funds, and credit rating agencies, which offer a wide range of services. The basic structure of financial services consists of banking, insurance and investment services.

636. Directive No. 2006/48/EC of the European Parliament and of the Council relating to the taking up and pursuit of the business of credit institutions uses in relation to banking services term 'credit institution', which means an undertaking the business of which is to receive deposits or other repayable funds from the public and to grant credits for its own account. Whereas 'financial institution' means an undertaking other than a credit institution, the principal activity of which is to acquire holdings or to pursue one or more of the activities listed in an annex to the Directive.

637. The banking services provided by credit institutions and financial institutions are as follows:

(1) Acceptance of deposits and other repayable funds.
(2) Lending including, *inter alia*, consumer credit, mortgage credit, factoring, with or without recourse, financing of commercial transactions (including forfeiting).
(3) Financial leasing.
(4) Payment services.
(5) Issuing and administering other means of payment (e.g., travellers' cheques and bankers' drafts) insofar as this activity is not covered by point 4.
(6) Guarantees and commitments.
(7) Trading for own account or for the account of customers in:
   (a) money market instruments (cheques, bills, certificates of deposit, etc.);
   (b) foreign exchange;
   (c) financial futures and options;
   (d) exchange and interest-rate instruments; or
   (e) transferable securities.

(8) Participation in securities issues and the provision of services related to such issues.
(9) Advice to undertakings on capital structure, industrial strategy and related questions and advice as well as services relating to mergers and the purchase of undertakings.
(10) Money broking.
(11) Portfolio management and advice.
(12) Safekeeping and administration of securities.
(13) Credit reference services.
(14) Safe custody services.
(15) Issuing electronic money.

638. In addition to the activities listed above, the financial services also include all services of insurance companies related with insurance policies in life and non-life insurance, and investment services, i.e., services provided by brokers and investment companies, pension insurance services provided by pension funds and ultimately related to payments services across national borders.

B. Leasing

639. The essence of leasing is using of leased thing by a client of the leasing company during the term of the leasing contract. The client pays regular instalments, but the client does not own the leased thing but the leasing company owns it. After termination of the lease, the ownership of the thing changes depending on the type of lease. Generally, the person who used the leased asset during the lease agreement becomes the owner. Through the leasing of new and used cars, technology in the production or real property can be acquired.

640. In practice, there are two basic types of leases – financial and operative leasing. They differ mainly in:

- length of the lease;
- purpose it serves;
- transfer of ownership of the leased assets at the end of the lease.

Both types have common that the lessor owns the leased thing.

641. Financial Leasing: Financial leasing is a long-term lease, which is associated with the transfer of ownership to the lessee upon termination of the contract. The leasing company is the owner of the leased thing (e.g., a car) during the term of the lease, and after the end of the leasing contract and payment of the redemption price, the client becomes the owner of the thing. The Income Tax Act sets the minimum duration of the lease, which to be thirty-six months (three years). The client pays leasing instalments to the leasing company monthly or quarterly.[57]

*642. Operative leasing: O*perative leasing means a lease of the thing where the lessee does not want to become the owner of the leased thing. After the end of the lease the thing may remain the property of the lessor (leasing company). In this type of lease, the lessee must also pay the instalments, they may be lower than for financial leasing, because not paying off the entire value of the thing, but only wear that resulted from its use. The amount of these instalments is calculated based on the purchase price and the residual price, which should be the price at which the thing will be sold at the end of the lease to a third party.[58]

643. The term leasing or leasing contract is, however, not directly expressed in the Slovak legal system. In the Commercial Code the following contracts relates to leasing.

1. Contract for the Purchase of a Leased Thing

644. By a contract for the purchase of leased thing, the parties agree in the lease agreement or after its conclusion that the lessee is entitled to buy the leased thing during the term of the contract or after its termination. The contract must be in writing.

645. If the lessee has the right to purchase the leased thing during the period of validity of the lease contract, his/her right to purchase the leased thing under the said contract is asserted upon delivery of written notification that he/she will purchase the leased thing. This results in the termination of the lease contract, even if it was concluded for a fixed period.

646. If, according to the contract for the purchase of a leased thing, the tenant has the right to purchase such leased thing after the termination of the lease contract, this right becomes extinguished if the lessee does not notify the other party in writing and without undue delay, after the termination of the lease contract, of his/her intent to purchase the thing in question.

647. If the party which has the right to purchase the leased thing, in accordance with the contract for the purchase of the leased thing, notifies the other party that it is asserting its right to purchase the leased thing being the object of the lease contract, the contract of purchase is established upon delivery of the said notification. The party having the right to purchase the leased thing has the status of buyer, and the other party the status of seller.

---

57. For more *see* www.fininfo.sk – Portal financial education and consumer financial protection of the Ministry of Finance of the Slovak Republic.
58. *Ibid.*

2. Contract on Leasing a Means of Transportation

648. Under such contract the lessor undertakes to make available a means of transportation to the lessee for purposes of temporary use, and the lessee undertakes to pay a hire charge to the lessor. The contract must be in writing.

649. The lessor must provide the lessee with the means of transportation concerned, together with the necessary documents, at the time set in the contract, or else, without undue delay, following the conclusion of the contract. The means of transportation must be in working order and fit for the use specified in the contract, or else for the use to which such means of transportation is normally put.

650. The lessor is liable for any damage caused to the lessee if the leased means of transportation is not fit for the purpose. The lessee is entitled to use the hired means of transportation for the above-mentioned purposes. Unless the contract stipulates otherwise, the lessee may not let another person use the hired means of transportation.

651. The lessee is bound to take care that the hired means does not suffer any damage. The lessor is liable for damage, unless the damage is caused by the lessee or by persons to whom the lessee made the hired means of transportation available. The lessee must have the hired means of transportation insured only if the contract so specifies.

652. The lessee must maintain the hired means of transportation, at the expense of the lessor, in the condition in which he took it over from the lessor, allowing for normal wear and tear. The lessee must notify the lessor, without undue delay, of the need for any repairs, which the lessee is obliged to carry out. If the lessee fails to meet this obligation, he loses the right to reimbursement of the repair expenses; however, he may claim the amount by which the lessor has become enriched as a result of such repairs.

653. The lessee must pay the lessor the hire charge in the agreed amount or the charge customary at the time of conclusion of the contract, taking into account the nature of the hired means of transportation and the determined manner of its use.

654. Upon termination of the right to use a means of transportation, the lessee must return the means of transportation to the place where he took it over, unless the contract provides otherwise.

C. Factoring

655. Factoring normally means a contract on purchase of short-term claims incurred by the supplier as a result of supply for an unsecured loan. Common characteristics and the conditions which the claims assigned with the factoring relationship must meet are as follows:

- maturity of the claims cannot be longer than 180 days;
- the claim arose based on the supply of unsecured credit;
- no other rights of third parties are connected to the claim;
- it must be possible to transfer (assign) claims;
- the claim relates to a subject with an acceptable credit rating and from acceptable country to a factoring company;
- minimum turnover of invoiced claims must be usually met;
- claims should relate to a larger number of customers; and
- amount of claims from individual customer should not exceed a specified amount (usually max. 20%).[59]

656. These general conditions can be further specified in an individual agreement according to individual factors between a supplier and a factor. The factoring contract provides suppliers the possibility of three essential functions. These are the following options:

(1) Security guarantee – this feature applies in the case of non-recourse factoring, i.e., when the factor assumes the credit risk of the supplier. In this case, the factor has to pay the supplier the respective amount of the claim even if the customer does not pay the claim.
(2) Providing financing in advance – based on a contract factor provides suppliers of financial means in the agreed amount (usually 80%–90%) of assigned claims at the time of their assignment. The supplier has therefore a significant part of claims paid almost immediately, not waiting for the due date of the claim and the remaining amount to 100% of the claim is settled usually with fees, commissions and interest belonging to the factoring company.
(3) Ensuring management of claims – if agreed in the contract, the factoring company may secure accounting management of the claims, invoicing, collection and recovery of claims.

657. Factoring became fairly applied financial instrument through the Slovak market. The biggest banks have initiated their factoring ‘product’, which however is not generally regulated and is often signed in a form of innominate contract (contract of assignment of receivables respectively factoring contracts). In practice, the factoring contracts often differ, due to the fact that they need to be adapted to diverse circumstances.

V. Carriage by Land, Sea and Air

A. General Provisions

658. General provisions and regulation relating to the carriage of things are stated in the Commercial Code under the Contract on Carriage of a Thing.

59. Dvořák, P. Banking for Bankers and Clients. Linde: 2005. p. 564.

659. Under a contract on the carriage of things, the carrier undertakes to carry a thing or things (a consignment) from a determined place (the place of dispatch) to another determined place (the place of destination), and the consignor undertakes to pay him/her a carriage charge. This contract applies to carriage by different modes of transport.

660. In the field of international transportation, international treaties, which are binding to the Slovak Republic apply, e.g., Convention on the Contract for the International Carriage of Goods by Road of 1956, Convention for the Unification of Certain Rules Relating to International Carriage by Air of 1929 (Warsaw Convention).

661. The carrier is entitled to demand from the consignor confirmation of the transportation required in a document (a consignment note), and the consignor is entitled to demand from the carrier written confirmation of receipt of the consignment. If special documents are required for transportation, the consignor is obliged to hand them over to the carrier no later than the time the consignment is handed over for transportation. The consignor is liable for damage caused to the carrier by a failure to hand over such documents, or by the inclusion of incorrect facts in them. Unless the contract provides otherwise, the contract is terminated if the consignor has not asked the carrier to take over the consignment within the time limit set in the contract, or else within six months from the day of the conclusion of the contract.

662. The carrier may be bound under the contract to issue a bill of lading to the consignor on receipt of the consignment. The bill of lading is a document to which is attached the right to demand delivery of the consignment in accordance with the contents of the document. The carrier is bound to pass the consignment to the person so authorized under the bill of lading, if such person presents the bill of lading and confirms on it receipt of the consignment.

663. The carrier must transport the consignment to the place of destination with due care within the agreed time limit, or else without undue delay. Until the carrier has not passed over the consignment to the consignee, the consignor is entitled to require that the carriage be suspended and the consignment returned to him/her, or that it be disposed of in another manner, and it has to reimburse the carrier for all effective expenses relating thereto. The carrier is liable for damage caused to the consignment from the moment it is taken over by the carrier until its handing over to the consignee, unless the carrier could not avert the damage even when exercising all due care.

664. The carrier is entitled to be paid an agreed charge and, if no remuneration has been agreed upon, he is entitled to be paid the charge which was customary at the time of conclusion of the contract, taking into account the contents of the carrier's obligation. The carrier is entitled to payment of a carriage charge after completing carriage of the consignment to the place of destination, unless the contract specifies a different time as decisive. The consignor must provide the carrier with correct information about the contents and nature of the consignment and is liable for any damage caused to the carrier by breach of this duty.

665. In order to secure claims arising to him/her from the contract, the carrier has a lien on the consignment as long as he/she has the right to dispose of it.

666. Specific provisions relating to carriage by rail, air, road, inland waterways and sea, with regard to the formation of the contract, transport documents, exclusion of things from transport, receipt of consignments by carriers and their delivery to the consignees, and the scope of claims against carriers and their assertion may be stated in special regulations. However, the regulation of the carrier's liability for damage may not be restricted with regard to damage caused to the consignment.

B. Carriage by Sea and by Inland Waterways

667. The carrier is required to conduct a public waterway carriage under its transport regulations. Under Act No. 338/2000 Coll. On Inland Navigation as amended the transport regulations govern the requirements for carrying both persons and their baggage and goods in a public waterway carriage. The regulations include especially:

(1) details of the carriage of passengers and baggage, and of the contract on carriage;
(2) extent of the transport obligations;
(3) requirements for consignors.

668. Under Act No. 435/2000 Coll. On Maritime Navigation as amended, the owner of the seagoing ship is responsible for observance of agreed cargo transport conditions. International treaties govern conditions of the seagoing ship owner responsibility during the transport of cargo.

C. Road Transport

669. Under Act No. 56/2012 Coll. On Road Transport the carrier is obliged to issue the Transport regulations, which contain transport conditions of carrier necessary to concluding a contract on carriage, in particular:

(1) type of road transport and scope of transport services;
(2) manner of the conclusion of the contract on carriage of persons or the contract on carriage of goods; and
(3) rights and obligations of the carrier, in particular the extent of liability for damage and claims of passengers, consignors and recipients of things for damages or for a discount from the transport charge.

670. Transport regulations in transport of goods also include a range of services that the carrier provides consignors and consignees of things, and the extent of their cooperation with carriers, particularly the regulation of transport of different types of things and living animals, and conditions of manoeuvring with a vehicle for loading and unloading.

671. The carrier is obliged to publish its transport regulations on its website and by other appropriate means. Published transport regulations are part of the proposal of the carrier to conclude the contract on carriage, and after its conclusion, the regulations are part of the contractual rights and obligations of the contractual parties.

D. Air Transport

672. Under Act No. 143/1998 Coll. On Civil Aviation (Aviation Act) as amended an air carrier is liable to:

(1) perform air transport in the scope and terms and conditions stipulated in the licence or permission;
(2) perform passenger and cargo carriage with professional care and to regard the safety and order in his/her facilities and on board of aircraft, as well as to facilitate the carriage of handicapped persons;
(3) suitably inform the air transport users about tariffs and the terms and conditions of carriage, in case of scheduled air transport by a timetable, and where performed in collaboration with other air carriers to inform about the fact as well;
(4) consider public interest and the interests of air transport users;
(5) submit terms and conditions of carriage, tariffs for the regular international air transport and timetables in case of scheduled air transport to the Ministry for approval depending on the type of air transport performed; tariffs for scheduled air transport between the territory of the Slovak Republic and territory of other Member States have to be submitted to the Ministry for registration purpose pursuant to conditions laid down in a special regulation;
(6) inform the Ministry about the intended interruption or termination of scheduled air transport;
(7) in case of an aircraft accident, to pay advance compensation for the damage caused by either death or injury or any other damage to cover instant economic needs of damaged persons or their close relatives.

673. Air transport users – based on a carriage contract – have a right to be provided a proper course of carriage and in particular to have passengers and cargo transported to their destination in good quality and in time.

E. Rail Transport

674. Under 2014 amendment of Act No. 514/2009 Coll. On the transport on railroads, the rail transport might be carried out as public and private. Since the introduction of private rail carriers, the prices for transportation have been regulated through the regulatory body, which based on the application of the private carrier determines the maximum amount of travel cost. Furthermore, the rail carrier is obliged to issue transport regulations. The transport regulations comprise business terms of the carrier concerning the conclusion of the transport contract and the performance of the transport in particular the following:

(1) Type of offered transport services.
(2) Extent of transport obligation.
(3) Terms of conclusion of the transport contract.
(4) Method of the transport document reservation and sale in the stations, stops and railroad vehicles, the rules of transport document validity and invalidity and demonstration in case of an inspection and payment options in case of the loss of the transport document.
(5) Extent of passenger rights and obligations before the transport beginning, during the transport and immediately after the transport ending as well as in case of transport cancellation, incompletion or delay and the procedure for applying the claims when the conditions of carriage have not been observed.
(6) Extent of rights and obligations of disabled persons, passengers with reduced mobility caused by the involvement or the age and other passenger groups including accompanied persons.
(7) Conditions of carriage of the hand luggage, registered luggage, live animals and motor vehicles.
(8) Conditions of carriage of the dog having special training providing the aid for passengers with serious health damage.
(9) Extent of rights and obligations of goods consignors and consignees, in particular the requirements for the carriage of various types of goods, other things and live animals and the rules of delivery of wagons for loading and unloading.
(10) Procedure for the inspection of transport documents, the rights and obligations of persons authorized to inspect transport documents and to inspect the persons without valid transport document.
(11) Rights and obligations of the carrier, extent of carrier liability for the damage caused to the human or animal health, to the goods or luggage or other things, and the extent of claims of passengers and consignors and consignees of goods arising therefrom and concerning the compensation or allowance.
(12) Claim regulations.
(13) Fare tariff in public passenger transport.

675. The carrier is obliged to publish its transport regulations on its website and in other suitable ways.

F. Travel Contract

676. Under the Civil Code on the basis of an agreement on the transport of persons, the traveller who uses a means of transport for a stipulated fare has the right that the transporter duly and timely transports him/her to the place of destination.

677. In the course of transport, the transporter must in particular secure safety and comfort of the travellers and, in case of mass transport, enable them to use of social and cultural facilities. Details are regulated by transport regulations.

678. If the traveller has luggage, the transporter must transport the luggage together with the traveller and under his/her surveillance or separately. If the luggage is transported separately, the transporter is obliged to secure that the luggage is transported to the place of destination no later than at the same time with the traveller.

Chapter 10. Secured Transactions

§1. Introductory Observations

679. The secured transaction law in the Slovak Republic is governed by several acts. First of all, it is the Civil Code, which since 1 January 2003 has covered by its new provisions from 151a to 151md as amended both movable and immovable assets. This area of law has been highly evaluated both by the European Bank for Reconstruction and Development, which strongly influenced the current legal framework, and by international companies and conglomerates.[60] Besides the Civil Code, it is Act No. 162/1995 Coll. On the Real Estate Cadastre and the entries of ownership and other property rights to the real estate (Cadastral Act) which governs the securities over the real estate, Act No. 323/1992 Coll. On Notaries and Notary Activities, which governs the registration of different types of securities, and the Securities Act, which covers additional types of securities, which are used for securing the transactions, as certificates of deposit, passbooks, bills of exchange, bills of lading, warehouse certificates, warehouse warrants, goods warrants and others.

680. Despite the dichotomy of Slovak private law between the civil and commercial, where the Commercial Code applies generally to all business contracts concerning entrepreneurial and to contracts concluded by two or more business entities, the Commercial Code does not regulate the secured transaction law, and therefore it is always the Civil Code or the Securities Act which govern the formation, course and termination of the securities over collateral. The assets may be identified by a general description and may include assets to be acquired by the debtor at a future date. It is also possible to take securities over a group of assets, even where the group is constantly changing, such as receivables or inventory.

681. Mortgages are registered with the cadastral register, which is a publicized real estate register maintained by the cadastral office around the Slovak Republic. The online Cadastral Portal[61] was established by the government decree of Slovak Republic No. 540/2002. The online Cadastral Portal enables authorized access to land register data, obtain basic information instantly and without a personal visit to the respective district cadastral registry, for the authorized subjects obtaining summary and detailed information without complicated correspondence. Land register data publication over the Internet is supposed to bring enhanced database, improvement of property and legal relations transparency, drop of corruption, increase of the credit of the Slovak Republic abroad and the reduction of the workload of the district land registries and the Geodetic and Cartographic Institute in information service delivery.

682. Some of the other securities, mainly charges, are registered with the Central Notarial Register operated by the Chamber of Notaries of Slovak Republic. The

60. *See Secured Lending: Slovak Solution, Why Slovakia Has the World's Best Rules on Collateral*, The Economist (23 Jan. 2003).

61. Available online at: https://www.katasterportal.sk.

Central Notarial Register started operation on 1 January 2003 as a single centralized database. Each notarial office is equipped with software, which directly uploads the registered securities into the Central Notarial Register.

§2. SECURITIES UNDER CIVIL LAW

683. First, the securities under Civil Code will be briefly described as to their legal scope and character, formation, termination and where relevant, additional mandatory obligations of the parties will be provided. Given the fact that this area of law is very complex and broad, a reader should keep in mind that this is not an exhaustive analysis of the law.

I. Real Securities

A. Charge/Lien

684. According to the Civil Code a charge is deemed to secure a claim and its appurtenances by entitling the creditor to be satisfied, or claim satisfaction from the object of the charge – collateral – if the debt is not duly and timely paid. A charge is created by:

(1) written agreement;
(2) approved hereditary agreement of heirs;
(3) decision of a court or administrative body; or
(4) operation of law.

685. A written agreement is not required where the charge agreement concerns a movable thing, provided that the charge is created by physical delivery of the collateral. The charge agreement must specify the secured claim and the collateral. If the value of the secured claim is not specified in the charge agreement itself, the agreement must specify the maximum principal amount up to which the claim is secured. The collateral may be determined in the charge agreement individually, in terms of volume and type, or in another manner so that it is possible at any given time to identify the collateral.

686. A charge may secure both a pecuniary or non-pecuniary claim the value of which is determinate or determinable at any time throughout the duration of the charge. It may also secure a claim arising in the future or depending on a condition. Upon transfer or passage of a claim secured by a charge, the charge is transferred or passed on to the purchaser. The same applies also to any other change in the person entitled to the secured claim.

687. Concerning the character of collateral, it may be:

(1) thing;

(2) right;
(3) asset;
(4) residential or non-residential premises that are transferable, unless provided otherwise by the law;
(5) set of things, rights or assets;
(6) enterprise or part thereof, or any other collective thing;
(7) future thing, right or asset or if its creation depends on fulfilling a condition; or even
(8) number of individual collaterals;
(9) thus, it is possible to use everything as a collateral unless it is illegal or not freely transferable by law (e.g., under the Securities Act, it is prohibited to create a charge over certain types of securities (e.g., shares), which have already been charged). Any agreement prohibiting the creation of a charge has no effect as against third persons.

688. The fruits of the assets subject to the charge are automatically part of the charge till the moment they become separated. However, under the contractual autonomy principle, this rule may be modified by contractual agreement between the parties. In case of insured assets, any payment under the insurance forms as well a part of the charge.

689. Transfer of Charge: Upon the transfer or passage of collateral, the charge passes on to the purchaser of the collateral, unless the charge agreement provides that the chargor may dispose of the collateral or part thereof free of charge, unless provided otherwise. Furthermore, upon the transfer or passage becoming effective, all rights and obligations of the chargor under the charge agreement are passed on to the purchaser against whom the charge is effective. In the case of passing the collateral with charge within the scope of one's business, the situation differs. The charge is not effective against the purchaser of collateral, if the charger transferred the collateral in the normal course of business within the scope of its business activities or if the purchaser acting with due care was in good faith at the moment of transfer or passage of the collateral as to the fact that the collateral was free of charge. However, in case the charge was registered, it is presumed that the purchaser of the collateral is not in good faith, unless the purchaser proves otherwise. The chargor and the purchaser of the collateral have to register the change in the person in the registry.

690. Use of Charge: During the existence of charge, unless contractually provided otherwise, the chargor may use the collateral in a usual manner; however, the chargor must refrain from anything capable of being detrimental to the value of the collateral, except for the common wear and tear of the collateral. In case of the physical possession of the charge in the hands of the chargeholder, the chargeholder is obliged to take due care of the collateral and protect it from damage, loss and destruction. Moreover, the chargeholder may use the collateral only with the consent of the chargor. If due to the performance of obligations under subsection 2 expenses incur to the chargeholder, it may claim reimbursement of reasonably spent expenses from the chargor.

691. Enforcement of Charge: Regarding the enforcement of a charge, if the claim secured by charge is not duly and timely paid, the chargeholder may initiate the enforcement of the charge. In this respect, the chargeholder may satisfy itself in the way specified in the agreement or by the sale of the collateral by auction pursuant to a special law or may claim satisfaction by the sale of collateral pursuant to special laws (as under the Civil Procedure Code and Act No. 233/1995 on Executors). If the claim secured by charge is not duly and timely paid, the chargeholder may satisfy itself or claim satisfaction from the collateral even if the statute of limitations for the secured claim has expired. If the claim secured by charge is not duly and timely paid, the chargeholder may satisfy itself or claim satisfaction from the collateral even if the statute of limitations for the secured claim has expired. If the collateral is an enterprise or part thereof, the chargeholder is entitled to satisfy itself or to claim satisfaction from the enterprise or part thereof as a whole only if the charge was created over all parts of the enterprise or part thereof.

692. In case, there is more than one charge over the collateral, the order of satisfaction is determined by the order of their registration in the registry of charges, beginning with the earliest day of registration, or of the day of their entry in a special registry. If more charges have been created over a movable asset and one of them is created by physical delivery of the asset, the charges registered in the registry of charges have priority for the satisfaction of charges according to the order of their registration. If more charges have been created over the collateral, the chargeholders may agree upon a different order of charges determining the satisfaction. Such agreement becomes effective with the registration of the agreed order in the registry of charges or with the entry in a special register, if for creation of charge an entry in a special register is required by law, on the basis of application of all chargeholders participating in the agreement. Any agreement having a negative impact on the enforcement of the claim of a chargeholder not participating in the agreement has no effect as against this person.

The chargeholder has the obligation to notify the chargor and the debtor, if different than the person of the chargor, in writing about the commencement of the enforcement of the charge, and where a charge is registered in the registry, it has to notify the register of the commencement of enforcement of the charge in that registry. The chargeholder has to specify the mode of satisfaction or of claiming satisfaction in the written notification of commencement of enforcement of the charge. Following the notification of the commencement of enforcement of the charge, the chargor is prohibited of transfer of the collateral without consent of the chargeholder. The breach of this obligation does not have any effect as against persons who acquired the collateral from the chargor in the normal course of business within the scope of the business activities of the chargor, unless the purchaser knew or ought to have known of the commencement of enforcement.

The chargeholder may sell the collateral in the manner provided in the charge agreement or at auction after a period of thirty days from the date of delivery of the notification of the commencement of enforcement of the charge to the chargor and debtor, if different than the person of the chargor. If the charge is registered in the registry of charges and the date of registration of the commencement of enforcement is later than the date of delivery of the notification of the commencement of enforcement of the charge to the chargor and the debtor, if the debtor is different than the person of the chargor, the thirty-day period commences from the date of registration of the commencement of enforcement of the charge. The chargeholder may at any time during the enforcement change the manner of enforcement of the charge and sell the collateral at auction or claim satisfaction from the sale of the collateral pursuant to special laws. The chargeholder has to notify the chargor of the change in the manner of enforcement of the charge.

However, the chargeholder has also several obligations under the law, as to inform the chargor about the process of enforcement of the charge, in particular about all such facts that may have a negative impact on the price of the collateral when being sold.

Furthermore, the chargeholder has to proceed with the sale of the collateral with due care so that the collateral is sold for a price for which the collateral or a similar asset is normally traded under comparable circumstances at the time and place of sale of the collateral. At the end of the enforcement, the chargeholder has to serve the chargor with a written report about the enforcement of the charge without undue delay after the sale of the collateral stating in particular information about the sale of the collateral, proceeds of the sale of the collateral, expenses incurred in the enforcement of the charge and use of the proceeds of sale of the collateral. The chargeholder has to account for expenses incurred relating to the enforcement of the charge. If proceeds of sale of the collateral exceed the secured claim, the chargeholder has to hand over the surplus after deduction of the reasonably spent expenses.

In case that more charges have been created over the collateral, the chargeholder is obliged to notify in writing the other chargeholders, who have priority to the chargeholder enforcing the charge as to the order determining the satisfaction, of the commencement of enforcement of the charge. The chargeholder must include the manner of satisfaction or of claiming satisfaction from the collateral in the notification of the commencement of enforcement of the charge. Upon enforcement of charge by a chargeholder with a charge registered as the first in the order determining the satisfaction of charges – 'prior chargeholder' – the collateral is transferred free of the charges of other chargeholders. If the proceeds of sale exceed the secured claim of the prior chargeholder, other chargeholders are entitled to have their claims secured by a charge over the collateral being transferred satisfied from the proceeds of sale after deduction of expenses reasonably spent relating to the enforcement of the charge according to the order determining the satisfaction of charges by the prior chargeholder.

693. *Cessation of Charge*: A charge ceases under the following circumstances:

(1) secured claim ceases to exist;
(2) all assets or all rights encumbered with the charge cease to exist;
(3) the chargeholder gives up its charge;
(4) period of time for which the charge has been established lapses;
(5) upon return of the asset to the chargor, if the charge has been created by way of physical delivery;
(6) the chargor transfers the collateral in the normal course of business within the scope of its business activities or if the purchaser of the collateral at the time

of transfer or passage of the collateral acting with due care was in good faith that it was acquiring the collateral free of charge;
(7) the chargor transfers the collateral and the charge agreement provides that the chargor may transfer the collateral or part thereof free of charge; or
(8) by other means provided in the charge agreement or resulting from a special regulation.

After the charge ceases to exist, a deletion from the registry of charges or other special registry, if for creation of charge an entry in a special registry is required by law, is carried out; deletion is made as of the day requested in the application for a deletion of the charge, but no later than as of the day of cessation of the charge.

B. Mortgage

694. The law on charge stipulated by the Civil Code is very broad and applies on most of the assets, including the real property. Thus, the Civil Code applies, unless special provision is laid down, e.g., in connection with the registration of the real property (Cadastral Act). Mortgage as such is created by a contract in writing, otherwise absolutely void *ab initio.* The following content must be included within the mortgage agreement:

(1) identification of the parties;
(2) identification of the object of the mortgage; and
(3) claim that is secured by the mortgage.

695. In addition to the written mortgage agreement, the law requires the registration in the Cadastral Registry. Securing the mortgage on real property becomes legally effective by the approval of the Cadastral Registry. Thus, the approval of the creation of a mortgage over a real property is therefore constitutive, which means that the mortgage is created by the entry in the Register and not by the conclusion of the mortgage agreement. As for the creditors, the information of the Cadastral Registry is based on the substantive disclosure principle, under which certain cadastral date are credible until proven otherwise, thus the registered information and data form a refutable presumption. According to the jurisprudence of the Supreme Court, the facts of the matter always prevail over the facts registered in the cadastral register (limits of substantive disclosure).[62] Nevertheless, the acquisition of real property in good faith with respect to the facts entered into the cadastral register can therefore be ruled out.

696. The realization of the mortgage follows the general rules established by the Civil Code on charge.

62. Decision of the Supreme Court of the Slovak Republic of 27 Oct. 2000, 2 Cdo 67.

II. Personal Securities

A. *Surety*

697. Under a surety, a guarantor promises to satisfy the claim of a creditor if the debtor fails to do so. The surety is security for a third party's debt. Both Civil Code and Commercial Code regulate the legal institution of surety. Commercial transactions are always subject to the Commercial Code. As the loan agreement is a so-called absolute commercial transaction, the Commercial Code provisions also apply to banks. The regulations on surety under civil law are not applied in addition to the regulation under Commercial Code.

698. The surety is created by a written declaration of the guarantor addressed to the creditor and gives the name of the debtor in whose favour the surety has been assumed. The obligation, to which the guarantor subscribes, has to be specified in the written declaration. A unilateral letter of commitment of the guarantor creates the surety. The consent of the creditor or of the debtor is not required. Furthermore, it is not required that the surety is explicitly named as such. A surety can also be assumed for future claims can secure only valid claims and contingent claims.

699. Generally, the scope of the surety covers the principal debt between the creditor and the debtor, including any related interests. The guarantor is not liable for any contractual penalties (agreed between the creditor and the debtor) or any damages incurred by the creditor. Neither can the creditor demand reimbursement of legal fees. However, the guarantor has the right to enter into such an obligation in the letter of commitment or to accept liability as guarantor and payer. The creditor can only request the guarantor to satisfy a claim if the principal debtor fails to meet his or her obligations within an appropriate period of time after being requested in writing by the creditor. Only as of this time, can the creditor demand at the same time of both, i.e., of the debtor and of the guarantor that the claim be satisfied. If both are requested to satisfy a claim, each has to pay the same amount, with the obligation of one of the two parties being extinguished automatically when the other makes a payment. If the surety secures only part of the debt, the scope of liability is not reduced in the event of a partial payment as long as the debt is not repaid in the amount secured.

700. During the enforcement of the obligation against the guarantor, the guarantor has the right to raise all of the defences that the debtor is entitled to raise. Should the guarantor intend to satisfy the creditors, the guarantor has to inform the debtor of this immediately. The debtor must inform the guarantor thereafter immediately of any defences that he or she rises against the creditor. These defences must be well founded. Should the defences that the debtor has informed the guarantor of being ineffective against the creditor, the debtor is obliged to reimburse the guarantor for any legal fees. Should the guarantor have satisfied the creditor without informing the debtor, the debtor has the right to raise all defences against the guarantor that he or she would have been entitled to against the creditor.

701. The surety ceases to exist when the principal debt is redeemed. However, under the Commercial Code, there are two exceptions:

(1) surety does not cease to exist if the secured debt ceases to exist due to the impossibility of being satisfied by the debtor, but could still be satisfied by the guarantor; or
(2) debt perishes because a legal entity ceases to exist.

702. Claim of the creditor against the guarantor does not become time-barred before the claim against the debtor becomes time-barred. If the debtor acknowledges a debt, as of this time a new statute of limitation begins, which prolongs the statute of limitation of the surety. This happens if the surety is not defined as limited in time in the guarantor's letter of commitment. In case of a multiple surety with several guarantors, each of them is liable for the entire amount owed. The guarantors are liable as joint and several debtors. In the event of novation of the principal debt, the surety covers the new debt. If the guarantor does not consent the securing of the new debt, the security continues but covers only the amount of the original debt and the guarantor retains the right to raise all of the former defences.

B. Bank Guarantee

703. The bank guarantee is a special form of surety, which is common business practice and used frequently and effectively as means of securing debt. The bank guarantee is used regularly as well in international commercial transactions. The bank guarantee is created by a written declaration of the guaranteeing bank – the guarantor in the form of a deed of guarantee in which it promises to satisfy the pecuniary claim of the beneficiary bank – beneficiary up to a certain amount if the debtor fails to perform or based on other conditions under the deed of guarantee. The deed of guarantee contains all the details in the event of non-performance of the debtor. The bank guarantee is used mainly to cover pecuniary claims.

704. In case of higher amounts, which need to be secured by more banks, there are several banks guaranteeing the debt. In case of a bank guarantee, two banks providing security are jointly and severally liable. If the second bank pays an amount to the beneficiary, it has the right of recourse against the first guaranteeing bank. When a bank only informs the creditor that another bank is granting a guarantee in the creditor's favour, this does not create an obligation from the guarantee for the bank providing this information although the bank is liable for any damages resulting from false information.

705. Concerning the cessation of a guarantee, if a bank guarantee is limited by time, the bank guarantee expires if the creditor does not request payment in writing within the agreed time or does not present the required documents. Should the guarantor meet his or her obligations under the bank guarantee, the guarantor has the right of recourse against the debtor in the same as in the case of a surety.

§3. Securities under Securities Act

706. Under Slovak law, it is possible to create charge not only under the Civil law or commercial law but also under the Securities Act on different types of securities as shares, bonds, and warehouse certificates and other forms of securities, which are all governed by the Securities Act. Also, under the Securities Act, the majority of principles laid down by the Civil Code apply. First and foremost is the registration of all charges, which become valid upon their registration in a separate register of securities, which is organized by the CSD of the Slovak Republic (Central Depository), seated in Bratislava.

707. For a contractual charge to be established on a paper security transferable by endorsement, it is required that the owner makes a written statement on the security – charge endorsement. The charge endorsement has to identify the chargor. In addition, the charge endorsement must contain the appropriate particulars set out in the Securities Act:

- Signature of the endorser.
- Business name.
- Registered office.
- Identification number of a legal person, or the name, permanent residence and birth registration number of a natural person.
- If it is a foreign legal person, it must provide an identification number, if assigned. If a foreign natural person is the transferee, the date of birth has to be stated instead of the birth registration number.

708. The chargor may not further transfer a security containing a charge endorsement.

709. Unless specified otherwise by the Securities Act, contracts on creating charge over securities are governed by the provisions of the Commercial Code and Civil Code.

710. A contractual charge on a book-entered security in favour of the NBS is established by concluding a credit transaction with the NBS and it exists for the period of business relationship established by the concluded transaction. The central depository is obliged to register the contractual charge by order of the NBS. Simultaneously, the NBS is obliged to issue an order to register a suspension of the exercise of the right to use the security.

711. Contracts creating a charge over securities must be made in writing. In case of securities under the Securities Act, a charge may not be established on securities already subject to a charge. A contractual charge on securities creates or terminates the charge upon the registration in the Register. Upon registration of a change or termination of a charge on paper securities, the central depository is obliged to mark the change or termination on the paper security concerned.

I. Registration of Charge

712. An order to register a charge on a security may be given by a chargor, a chargeholder, or the NBS. The chargor or chargeholder has to attach to the registration order for the charge a written confirmation regarding the content of the contract to create a charge over the security. This does not apply if an order for registration of charge on a security is issued by the NBS.

713. Where details of the owner of a security are recorded in an owner's account maintained by a central depository or a member, or in records maintained by a stock investment firm, an order to register a charge on the security has to be submitted to that central depository, member or investment firm. A member or investment firm forwards this order to the central depository without delay.

714. In the event of a change in the information concerning a charge, the person whom this change concerns has to order an amendment to the registration in the register of charges, without delay after the date of the occurrence that gave rise to the change in the information regarding the charge. If a person whom the change in information concerns cannot be determined, this obligation falls to the chargeholder. If the obligation to order the registration of a change in the information falls to more than one person, this obligation is deemed discharged where the order is made by any one of these persons.

715. After grounds have arisen for the termination of a charge, the chargor has to without delay order the registration of the termination of the charge. The chargeholder may also make an order to register the termination of a charge, in which case he or she has to enclose with the order a written confirmation of the fulfilment of the obligation or another document, given by the chargor, proving a reason for the termination of the charge.

II. Use of the Securities as Collateral

716. With regard to the use of a collateral (securities over which a charge has been formed), the right of charge also applies to any transferee unless otherwise provided by Securities Act or a separate law. The chargeholder and transferee have to register the change of chargeholder in the register of charges. For any damage caused by the breach of this obligation, they are jointly and severally liable.

717. The chargeholder in regard to a contractual lien on a security must be the owner of the security. During the existence of a charge over a security, the right of charge also applies to any income from the security. The pledged security may not be traded in anonymous transactions except where a claim secured by a charge on a security is not paid in due and prompt manner; the chargor may sell the pledged security through an investment firm. The chargor has to notify the chargeholder in advance of the intended sale, unless otherwise provided in the contract on pledging of the security. This sale of securities, which are not stock exchange listed, has to be made through an investment firm for the highest price, which can be achieved with due professional care.

III. Transfer of Securities as Collateral

718. Contracts for the transfer of securities as collateral are governed by the provisions of Securities Act and the Civil Code on securing liabilities by the transfer of a right. Contracts for the transfer of securities as collateral has to be made in writing and, to a similar extent as when creating the charge has to state information on the debtor, the creditor, the securities transferred, and liabilities secured by the transfer of securities.

719. Transfers of securities as collateral are registered by the central depository in a separate register of securities transferred as collateral. Anyone who gives an order to register a transfer of securities as collateral without having proper authority to do so, or who gives such order incorrectly, incompletely or belatedly is liable for any damage arising as a result.

Part II. Economic Law

Chapter 1. General Principles

720. The Slovak Republic has been since 1993 establishing a democratic state with a market economy. Different governments have adopted numbers of new acts and implemented extensive number of market-oriented policies in order to form a prosperous market economy with a solid foundation. Between 2006 and 2008, before the world financial crisis, Slovakia experienced high rates of economic growth, which showed that the Slovak government was able to address also long-term structural challenges successfully.

721. Given the fact that Slovakia is a Member State of the EU, the sphere of economic law is greatly influenced by the EU law and EU market principles, which Slovakia subsequently implements within its national law. Under the auspices of the EU, the Government set out clear policy in which independent economic regulators, participants, consumers and investors can take an informed decision. Regulatory framework concerning the antitrust laws or consumer protection laws is highly unitized on the EU level.

§1. State Intervention in Economic Activities

722. State intervention in economic activities generally takes place only within the scope of either a high-profile industry (energy, healthcare or gas) or the State supervises the behaviour of other participants on the market and enforcement of the rules and regulations. Since the election in 2010, the Government with Prime Minister Fico has been regulating the market to a greater extent than the former governments. Given the fluctuation of the prices on the world markets, the Government controls the energy prices by providing additional powers to Regulatory Office for Network Industries, taking the ability to institute independent price changes from energy companies' boards. Besides the network regulation, the government influence is mainly on the supervisory level.

§2. Basic Principles of Economic Law

723. The basic principles of the economic law are set by the Constitution of the Slovak Republic, in its second part 'Basic Rights and Liberties', which does define not only the human rights or political rights but also the economic and socio-economic rights. These basic principles are further incorporated in the basic legal codes as the Civil Code or the Commercial Code and represent an inherent part of the entire legal framework.

I. Freedom of Trade

724. According to Article 37 and following of the Constitution of the Slovak Republic, everyone has the right to a free choice of profession and to training for it, as well as the right to engage in entrepreneurial or other gainful activity. Law can specify the conditions and restrictions with regard to the execution of certain professions or activities. Citizens have the right to work. Citizens who are unable to exercise this right through no fault of their own are provided for materially by the state to an appropriate extent. Given the fact that also citizens of the Member States of the EU have the freedom to travel and 'freedom of establishment', they are as well free to establish themselves in the territory of the Slovak Republic and the law applies to them in the same way that of Slovak citizens. Certain limitations might be laid down by the law; however, the EU together with the Court of Justice of the European Union follows and applies broad margin of appreciation for the discrimination in the EU between the home nationals and other Member State's nationals.

725. Besides the entrepreneurs, also employees have the right to equitable and adequate working conditions. The law guarantees, above all:

(1) the right to remuneration for work done, sufficient to ensure the employee's dignified standard of living;
(2) protection against arbitrary dismissal and discrimination at the place of work;
(3) labour safety and the protection of health at work;
(4) the longest admissible working time;
(5) adequate rest after work;
(6) the shortest admissible period of paid leave; and
(7) the right to collective bargaining.

726. Furthermore, everyone has the right to freely associate with others in order to protect his economic and social interests. Trade union organizations are established independently of the state. It is inadmissible to limit the number of trade union organizations, in the same way as it is inadmissible to give some of them a preferential status, be it in an enterprise or a branch of the economy. The activity of trade union organizations and the founding and operation of other associations protecting economic and social interests can be restricted by law if such a measure is unavoidable in a democratic society to protect the security of the state, public order, or the rights and liberties of others.

727. Under the Constitution, the right to strike is guaranteed and the conditions will be defined by law. This right does not extend to judges, prosecutors, members of the armed forces and armed corps, and members of the fire brigades. Currently, the Government wants to extend the types of professions where the right to strike would be excluded, namely medical doctors.

II. Free Movement

728. According to Article 23, freedom of movement is guaranteed; everyone who is rightfully staying on the territory of the Slovak Republic has the right to freely leave this territory. These freedoms can be restricted by law if it is unavoidable for the security of the state, to maintain public order, protect the health and the rights and liberties of others, and, in designated areas, also for reasons of environmental protection. Concerning the Slovak citizens, they have the right to freely enter the territory of the Slovak Republic. Given the European perspective, also all citizens of the Member States of the EU have the right to freely enter Slovakia, unless otherwise specified by law. A citizen must not be forced to leave his homeland and he must not be deported or extradited.

III. Freedom of Establishment

729. The freedom of establishment represents one of the core rights of the EU, which is central to the effective functioning of the EU Internal Market. The freedom of establishment is now set out in Article 49 of the Treaty:

> Within the framework of the provisions set out below, restrictions on the freedom of establishment of nationals of a Member State in the territory of another Member State shall be prohibited. Such prohibition shall also apply to restrictions on the setting-up of agencies, branches or subsidiaries by nationals of any Member State established in the territory of any Member State.
> Freedom of establishment shall include the right to take up and pursue activities as self-employed persons and to set up and manage undertakings, in particular companies or firms within the meaning of the second paragraph of Article 54, under the conditions laid down for its own nationals by the law of the country where such establishment is effected, subject to the provisions of the Chapter relating to capital.

730. This principle enables an economic operator (whether a person or a company) to carry on an economic activity in a stable and continuous way in one or more Member States. The principle of the freedom to provide services enables an economic operator providing services in one Member State to offer services on a temporary basis in another Member State, without having to be established.

731. These provisions have a direct effect. This means, in practice, that in the Slovak Republic, even if did not transpose in its legal system and into different laws this principle, the citizens could rely on this principle and in the case where necessary sue the state. However, usually Member States modify national laws that restrict freedom of establishment, or the freedom to provide services. Member

States may only maintain such restrictions in specific circumstances where these are justified by overriding reasons of general interest, for instance on grounds of public policy, public security or public health, and where they are proportionate. The Court of Justice of the European Union then enforces these exceptions. For the moment the bar is set relatively high, and Member State has to use all other possible legal tools before it restricts the freedom of establishment.

Under the Treaties, the Commission is responsible for ensuring that Community law and its correct application. As the guardian of the Treaty, the Commission has the option of commencing infringement proceedings against a Member State, which they believe to be incompatible with Community law.

732. The recently adopted Services Directive aims to create a legal framework for ensuring that both service providers and recipients benefit more easily from the fundamental freedoms guaranteed in Articles 49 and 56 of the Treaty. The Directive complements existing Community instruments and its provisions are, to a large extent, based upon the case law of the Court of Justice of the European Union.

IV. Equality

733. Along with the Constitution of the Slovak Republic, Act on Equal Treatment No. 365/2004 Coll. (Anti-discrimination Act) adopted in 2004 has established the basic legal framework of the Slovak anti-discrimination law. This Anti-discrimination Act stipulates in more detail the constitutional guarantees of equal treatment. The duty to observe the principle of equal treatment is defined as consisting in the prohibition of discrimination on the prohibited grounds:

- Sex.
- Religion or belief.
- Race.
- Colour.
- Language.
- Gender.
- Political view.
- Origin.
- Nationality.
- Ethnic group.
- Disability.
- Age.
- Sexual orientation.
- Marital status and family status.
- Property.
- Other status.

734. According to the EU law, the Anti-discrimination Act meets only the minimum standard determined by the anti-discrimination directives.[63] In addition, the duty to observe and follow the principle of equal treatment in particular spheres of life is regulated also by other laws and Statutes. Thus, all the participants of the market irrespective of their status should be treated equally and without any kind or type of discrimination.

63. Council Directive 2000/43/EC of 29 Jun. 2000 implementing the principle of equal treatment between persons irrespective of racial or ethnic origin and Council Directive 2000/78/EC of 27 Nov. 2000 establishing a general framework of equal treatment in employment and occupation.

Chapter 2. The Law of Establishment and Supervision of Economic Activities

§1. Introduction

735. The freedom of establishment is one of the four fundamental freedoms of the EU. As regards Articles 49 et seq. of the Treaty on the Functioning of the European Union (TFEU), it must be borne in mind that the right of establishment with which those provisions are concerned is granted both to natural persons who are nationals of an EU Member State and to legal persons. The right of establishment entails permanent installation in a Member State in order to pursue an economic activity in that state. Establishment of a person is characterized by the fact that he creates a permanent connection with the state of establishment, compared to a person who provides services in a state other than that of his/her permanent establishment. Subject to the exceptions and conditions laid down, it allows all types of self-employed activity to be taken up and pursued on the territory of any other Member State, undertakings to be formed and operated, and agencies, branches or subsidiaries to be set up (Case C-55/94 *Gebhard* (1995) ECR I-4165 section 23).

736. The Court of EU in *Reyners*(Dutch national prohibited from practising as an advocate in the Belgian courts) established the direct effect of Treaty provisions concerning the freedom of establishment (Case C-2/74 *Reyners* (1974) ECR 631 section 25). The Court held that any individual might on the basis of the above-mentioned Article 49 TFEU demand directly the same treatment as is applied to nationals. Therefore, no special European legislation is required. This means, in practice, that Member States must modify national laws that restrict freedom of establishment, or the freedom to provide services, and are therefore incompatible with these principles. Member States may only maintain such restrictions in specific circumstances where these are justified by overriding reasons of general interest, for instance on grounds of public policy, public security or public health, and where they are proportionate.

737. Article 53 TFEU provides that the mutual recognition of the diplomas and other qualifications, required in each Member State for access to the regulated professions, can be used to facilitate freedom of establishment and provision of services.

738. Directive 2006/123/EC on services in the internal market aims to create a legal framework for ensuring that both service providers and recipients benefit more easily from the fundamental freedoms guaranteed in Articles 49 (freedom of establishment) and 56 (freedom of services) TFEU. The Services Directive applies to the provision of a wide range of services – to private individuals and businesses except to a few specific exceptions.

739. The Services Directive facilitates the establishment of a business in a Member State. This concerns cases in which a legal or a natural person intends to establish in another country. But it also benefits to providers who want to establish in their own Member State, as they will take advantage of simplified rules and procedures. Under a general obligation for Member States to simplify procedures and formalities, some very specific obligations are established by the Directive (e.g., points of single contact, i.e., one-stop shops to obtain all relevant information and complete all procedures relating to business, prohibition of discriminatory requirements, such as nationality or residence requirements, and particularly restrictive requirements, such as 'economic needs' tests, etc.).

§2. The Establishment Act for Small-and Medium-Sized Undertakings

I. Survey

740. Slovakia's Small-and Medium-Sized Enterprises (SME) sector is characterized by a high proportion of SME, albeit to the detriment of micro-firms. The medium-sized group in particular makes above-average contributions to employment (23.3% compared to 17.2% in the EU) and value-added (22.3% as against 18.3%). Overall, however, the SME sector contributes less to value-added and employment than do its European counterparts on average. This may be the result of the Slovak economy's industrial structure. In terms of sectoral distribution, the trade sector is dominant, accounting for 39% of SMEs, compared with only 30% in the EU. The remaining SMEs are distributed among services (40%), manufacturing (13%) and construction (8%).[64]

II. Recognition of Foreign Persons

741. Business activities of foreign persons are governed by Commercial Code under which foreign persons may engage in business activities on the territory of the Slovak Republic under the same conditions and to the same extent as Slovak persons, unless the law stipulates otherwise. Citizens of Member States and their family members have the same rights for the performance of regulated professional activity and free provision of services in the Slovak Republic as persons who obtained the respective qualification in the Slovak Republic.

742. Recognition of professional qualification is governed by Act No. 293/2007 Coll. On the recognition of professional qualifications. Under this Act, the Ministry of Education has the competence to recognize education certificates for the purposes of carrying out a regulated job in the Slovak Republic.

64. The SBA Fact Sheet 2012 Slovakia, available at: http://ec.europa.eu/enterprise/policies/sme/facts-figures-analysis/performance-review/files/countries-sheets/2012/slovakia_en.pdf (accessed 31 May 2013).

III. Foreign Business

743. Foreign persons (individuals and entities) may engage in business activities on the territory of the Slovak Republic under the same conditions and to the same extent as Slovak persons, unless the law stipulates otherwise. A business activity on the territory of the Slovak Republic is understood as a business activity of foreign person if it has enterprise or a branch of the enterprise on the territory of the Slovak Republic. The authorization of a foreign person to undertake a business in the territory of the Slovak Republic is effective as of the day of entry of the enterprise of such a person or its branch in the Commercial Register in the extent of the scope of business entered in the Commercial Register. This does not apply to natural persons from EU Member States or OECD Member States, which are not compulsorily entered in the Commercial Register.

IV. Participation of Foreign Persons in Slovak Legal Persons

744. Under the provisions of the Commercial Code, a foreign person may participate in the establishment of a legal person or become a partner or a member in an already existing Slovak legal entity. Further, it may become the sole founder of a Slovak legal person or become the sole owner of a Slovak legal person, provided that the Commercial Code permits a sole founder or a single owner.

§3. The Professions

745. Literal professions, like notaries public, attorneys, architects, auditors, doctors, dentists, pharmacists, and performance of such professions are governed by special laws laying down conditions and requirements specific to the respective profession. Apart from the professional qualifications required for their establishment (a specific diploma of higher education, training under the supervision of an established member of the profession, etc.), the members of these professions must adhere to a professional organization (chambers) in which the law has vested the power to ensure that its members comply with the rules of professional conduct and ethics. Professional chambers like, e.g., Slovak Bar Association, Slovak Medical Chamber are non-governmental, independent, self-administrative professional organizations. Chambers usually include governing bodies as General Assembly, Council, Supervision and Disciplinary Committees. As a part of their independency, the chambers exercise the disciplinary power over their members and supervises the proper and due practice of the profession. The membership in chambers may be obligatory or voluntary; e.g., all Slovak attorneys must be members of the Slovak Bar Association, whereas membership in the Slovak Medical Chamber is voluntary.

§4. The Establishment of Aliens

746. The conditions for the entry and stay of foreign nationals in Slovakia are laid down in Act No. 404/2011 on Residence of Aliens. Based on an application and the purpose, a foreign national may be granted a permit for temporary (for the purpose of business; employment; study; special activity; research and development; family unification; performing service obligations by civil units of armed forces; who has the status of a Slovak living abroad; who has the status of a person with long-term residence in another Member State; the residence on the basis of a blue card of the EU), permanent (residence for five years; residence of unlimited duration; residence of a third-country national with acknowledged status of a person with long-term residence in the EU) or tolerated residence. The most significant category of aliens exempt from the obligation is the citizens of EU Member States. The residence of the EU citizen and the residence of the family member of the EU citizen is a permanent residence.

§5. Licensing Requirements in Various Sectors

747. Generally to exercise of economic activities in Slovakia it is necessary to comply with the conditions of sole trading governed by Act No. 455/1991 Coll. On Sole Trading (Trade Licensing Act) as amended. Trade authorization is the right to undertake a trade. This right is granted to natural persons and legal persons on the condition that they fulfil the general and particular conditions for undertaking a trade. Trades are divided according to the conditions for obtaining the trade authorization to:

(1) crafts, pursuit of which is conditional on certain professional qualification acquired through a relevant apprenticeship and listed in Annex No. 1 of Trade Licensing Act, e.g., cleaning and inspection of chimneys, cosmetic services, plumbing and heating, brewing and malting, watchmaking, etc.;
(2) regulated trades, pursuit of which is conditional on professional qualification acquired in a different manner and stipulated in Annex No. 2 of Trade Licensing Act, e.g., development and manufacture of weapons or ammunition, opthal optics, dental technics, driving school instructor, tourist guide, etc.;
(3) unregulated trades, pursuit of which is not conditional on stipulated professional qualification and which are not stipulated in Annex Nos 1 and 2 of the Trade Licensing Act.

§6. Supervision of Financial Market

748. Certain financial institutions, such as banks, credit institutions, investment companies, insurance companies, are subject to being duly licensed and being supervised by an NBS (*see* Chapter 8). In this relation supervision procedures, Slovakia implemented various EU directives, in particular the Basel II provisions of Directives 2006/48/EC and 2006/49/EC which represent the basic legislative and regulatory framework for supervised credit institutions and investment firms. The NBS conducts financial market supervision; i.e., it conducts supervision of banks, branch offices of foreign banks, investment firms, intermediaries of investment services, stock exchanges, management companies, mutual funds and collective investment undertakings, reinsurance undertakings, pension fund managing companies, pension funds, supplementary pension fund managing companies and other supervised entities of the Slovak financial market. The National Bank conducts supervision through its FMS ('Supervision Unit').

749. In the area of licensing, the Supervision Unit issued a total of 826 decisions in 2009, most of which concerned the capital market (357), the banking sector (163), the insurance sector (155) and the pension savings sector (124). Besides issuing decisions, the Supervision Unit received numerous notifications from supervised entities in all sectors of the financial market, approved securities prospectuses, and evaluated takeover bids. In 2009, a total of forty-five first-instance proceedings were held in regard to sanctions or remedial measures, resulting in twenty-eight decisions either to impose sanctions or remedial measures or to suspend the proceedings.

750. A substantial part of the Supervision Unit's activities consists of supervisory activities, i.e., the actual exercise of supervision over financial market participants through on-site supervisions and off-site supervision. In 2009, the Supervision Unit carried out a total of sixty-five on-site supervisions. Financial market participants are also subject to off-site supervision, the purpose of which is to periodically monitor and evaluate the financial position and risk profile of supervised entities.[65]

65. Report on the Activities of the Financial Market Supervision Unit of National Bank of Slovakia for year 2009, available at: http://www.nbs.sk/_img/Documents/_Dohlad/ORM/Analyzy/ReportsActivitiesFMS_2009.pdf/ (accessed 31 May 2013).

Chapter 3. State Incentives for Economic Activities

§1. General Remarks

751. One of the factors affecting the investor's decision on its investment localization is also the amount and the structure of the investment incentives, which may be obtained.

752. The Slovak Republic is characterized by considerable regional differences, which are given by various reasons. Investment incentives are one of the tools which are used to motivate investors to place their projects also in the less developed regions, i.e., the regions with higher unemployment, lower infrastructure quality, etc.

753. Slovak Investment and Trade Development Agency as a state-funded organization contributes to the acceleration of economic growth of the Slovak Republic by presenting the economic environment of Slovakia, attracting FDIs and the developing of the FDI projects up to their final stage.

754. Act No. 561/2007 Coll. on Investment Aid defines four categories of projects that can be supported by the investment incentives:

(1) Industrial production.
(2) Technological centres.
(3) Shared service centres.
(4) Tourism.

755. The incentives are provided in the form of:

(1) Subsidy for the acquisition of material assets and immaterial assets.
(2) Income tax relief.
(3) Contribution for created new jobs.
(4) Transfer of immovable property or exchange of immovable property at a price lower than a general asset value.

756. The provision of the State aid is governed in particular by the law of the EU, which forms the basic legal framework also for the Slovak authorities.

757. In accordance with Article 107 TFEU and Council Regulation (EC) No. 994/98 of 7 May 1998, the Commission may declare some State aid as being compatible with the common market and exempt it from the obligation to notify as laid down in Article 108 TFEU.

758. Commission Regulation (EC) No. 800/2008 declaring certain categories of aid compatible with the common market (General Block Exemption Regulation) thus defines the criteria for compatibility and the conditions for exemption from the obligation to notify as laid down for some categories of State aid, in line with Council Regulation (EC) No. 994/98.

§2. Incentives

759. Conditions for granting and using the incentives are stipulated in Act 185/2009 on Research and Development Incentives (Incentives Act). The Incentives Act further regulates the conditions for granting incentives to legal persons – entrepreneurs – for research and development in order to increase the level of research and development. Furthermore, the Act regulates the competence of state administration when providing incentives.

760. Under the Incentives Act, the following areas of research and development are supported:

- fundamental research, applied research or experimental development;
- feasibility studies of applied research and experimental research;
- industrial ownership protection; and
- temporary lease of highly qualified research and development staff.

761. Under the Incentives Act, there are two types of investment aid:

(1) subsidies for research and development projects from the state budget;
(2) income tax relief – at the amount incurred on research and development within the project for which incentives were approved.

762. The incentives are granted based on a written application. There are two providers of incentives in the Slovak Republic:

(1) The Ministry of Education of the Slovak Republic.
(2) The Ministry of Finance of the Slovak Republic.

763. An applicant for incentives might be:

(1) Micro-entrepreneur.[66]
(2) Small entrepreneur.[67]
(3) Medium entrepreneur, which is a legal entity and has an average of up to 250 employees and its turnover for fiscal or calendar year does not exceed EUR 50 million or its net asset value reported in its balance sheet does not exceed EUR 43 million.

---

66. *See* Art. 2 para. 3 of Annex 1 of the Commission Regulation (EC) No. 800/2008.
67. *See* Art. 2 para. 2 of Annex 1 of the Commission Regulation (EC) No. 800/2008.

(4) Large entrepreneur, which is a legal entity and has more than 250 employees and its turnover for fiscal or calendar year exceeds EUR 50 million or its net asset value reported in its balance sheet exceeds EUR 43 million.

An applicant for incentives becomes a beneficiary of the incentives based on a decision of the authorized body. There is no legal right or entitlement for the incentives.

Chapter 4. Competition Law

764. Competition law is generally divided into two branches: antitrust law, i.e., the law relating to restrictive practices, monopolies and mergers, and the law of unfair competition. Competition law was introduced in Slovakia in the early 1990s as a part of the market mechanisms aimed at the transformation from a centrally planned to a market economy. The main effort was accomplished in 2001 by the adoption of new Act No. 136/2001 Coll. on Protection of Competition (Competition Act), which represents the public law dimension of the competition law. The law on unfair competition is a part of private law, regulated by respective provisions of the Commercial Code and it is aimed at protection of private interests of the competitors and also at protection of consumers.

765. The Slovak competition law separates protection of economic competition and protection against unfair competition. The Commercial Code expressly delegates the protection of economic competition to the Competition Act. Further part of the law of unfair competition regulated by Act No. 250/2007 Coll. on Consumer Protection as amended (Consumer Protection Act) prohibits 'unfair commercial practices' in accordance the Directive 2005/29/EC concerning unfair business-to-consumer commercial practices in the internal market (Unfair Commercial Practices Directive). Specific area of law of unfair competition is the regulation of advertising governed by Act No. 147/2001 Coll. on Advertising as amended, and Act No. 308/2000 of Coll. on Broadcasting and Retransmission as amended.

§1. Antitrust Law

I. Introduction

766. Slovak competition law is basically structured like EU competition law. The Competition Act is compatible with Articles 101 and 102 TFEU (formerly Articles 81 and 82 of the EC Treaty) and of the EC Merger Regulation.[68]

II. Institutional Provisions

767. The Antimonopoly Office of the Slovak Republic (AMO) was established in 1990 by Act No. 347/1990 Coll. on Organization of Ministries and Other Central Bodies of State Administration of the Slovak Republic.

768. The exclusive activity of the AMO in the sphere of protection of economic competition is defined by the Competition Act. The seat of the AMO is Bratislava, the capital city of the Slovak Republic.

68. Council Regulation (EC) No. 139/2004 of 20 Jan. 2004 on the control of concentrations between undertakings (the EC Merger Regulation).

769. The main goal of the AMO is to promote and to protect the economic competition, to create conditions for its further development as well as to prevent the creation and maintenance of monopolistic or dominant position of entrepreneurs, if it precludes or restricts economic competition. Its competencies are defined by the Competition Act, which is a decisive instrument by assurance of the competition protection and creation system.

III. Scope of Application

770. The purpose of the Competition Act is to protect competition from any restriction and to create conditions for its further development to the benefit of consumers and regulating the powers and scope of activities of the AMO in supervising compliance with the provisions of this Act.

771. The Competition Act relates to the conduct of *undertakings*, defined as:

> an entrepreneur pursuant to special legislation, as well as natural and legal persons, their associations, and associations of these associations, with respect to their activities and conduct that are, or may be, related to competition, regardless of whether or not these activities and conduct are aimed at making a profit.

772. The Competition Act applies to all activities and conduct of undertakings that restrict or may restrict competition, except for competition restriction by undertakings providing services in the public interest pursuant to special legislation, provided that the application of Competition Act effectually or legally prevents them from fulfilling their tasks pursuant to special legislation (e.g., Postal Services, or Collective Bargaining).

IV. Substantive Provisions

A. Restriction of Competition and Restrictive Competition Practices

773. Restriction of competition means any restriction placed upon undertaking's freedom to act on a relevant market, especially the exclusion of existing or potential competitive activities, the actual or potential reduction of the scope of competitive activities, or distortion of conditions for competition.

774. Restrictive competition practices are those stated in Articles 4 and 8 of the Competition Act. Article 2 prohibits agreements restricting competition. Article 8 prohibits abuses of a dominant position.

1. Restrictive Agreements

775. An agreement restricting competition means an agreement and concerted practice between undertakings, as well as decisions of their associations, whose objective or effect is or may be restriction of competition. The agreement restricting competition is prohibited, unless this Act provides otherwise.

776. The Competition Act recognizes the following:

(1) Agreement between undertakings, which means any verbal or written positive expression of the will of the parties thereto, as well as any other positive expression of will derived from their conduct.
(2) Concerted practice between undertakings which means any coordination of their activities that does not bear signs of an agreement between undertakings referred to in (a) and cannot be identified as the natural consequence of the behaviour of another undertaking.
(3) Decision by an association of undertakings, which is any legal act of the association's body, as well as a recommendation of the association's body. Article 4(3) prohibits, in particular, an agreement restricting competition that involves:
   (a) direct or indirect fixing of prices or other trade conditions;
   (b) commitment to limit or control production, sales, technical development, or investments;
   (c) division of the market or sources of supply;
   (d) commitment by the parties to the agreement that different conditions relating to an identical or comparable performance will be applied to individual undertakings, which will or may disadvantage these undertakings in competition;
   (e) conditions stipulating that the conclusion of contracts will require the parties to accept further obligations that are not related to the subject of these contracts in terms of their nature or according to customary commercial practice; or
   (f) signs of collusive behaviour as a result of which undertakings coordinate their behaviour, especially in the process of public procurement.

777. However, the prohibition under Article 4 does not apply to the following:

(1) Agreement restricting competition where the combined market share of the parties thereto or the share of neither of the respective parties exceeds 10% of the total share for goods in question on the relevant market of the Slovak Republic ('*de minimis*' rule), except for:
   (a) agreements restricting competition referred to under (a) to (c) above; or
   (b) restriction of competition by means of the cumulative effect of agreements restricting competition, which contain a similar type of competition restriction and lead to similar effects in the relevant market, and their combined share exceeds 10% of the total share for goods in question in the relevant market.

(2) Agreements which contribute to the improvement of production or distribution of goods or to the promotion of technical or economic development; allow consumers an adequate share of the resulting benefits; does not impose on the parties to the agreement restricting competition such restrictions that are not indispensable to the attainment of the objectives of the agreement; does not afford the parties to the agreement restricting competition the possibility of excluding competition in respect of a substantial part of the goods in question on the relevant market. Whether the entrepreneur is eligible for exemption is evaluated by the entrepreneur himself/herself.
(3) Groups of agreements restricting competition that cannot influence trade between EU Member States, whose objective or effect is or may be restriction of competition on the domestic market and which meet the conditions for exemption from the prohibition pursuant to special legislation.[69]

778. Undertakings may ask the AMO to issue an opinion on whether or not their draft agreement or draft decision by an association of undertakings constitutes an agreement restricting competition.

2. Abuse of a Dominant Position

779. Abuse of a dominant position in the relevant market is prohibited. Abuse of a dominant position in the relevant market is defined as:

(1) direct or indirect enforcement of excessive prices or other unfair trade conditions;
(2) threat of restriction or an actual restriction of the production, sale or technological development of goods to the detriment of users;
(3) application of different conditions for identical or comparable performance with respect to the individual undertakings, through which the respective undertakings are or may be disadvantaged in the competition;
(4) tying the conclusion of a contract to the condition that the other party accepts further commitments, unrelated to the subject of the contract in terms of substance or according to customary commercial practice; or
(5) temporary abuse of economic power with a view to excluding competition.

B. Concentrations

780. Through control of concentrations, the AMO examines impacts of large mergers and acquisitions on the structure of markets. Concentrations are a tool of external growth of companies and of increasing the effectiveness of undertakings.

69. For example, Commission Regulation No. 330/2010 of 20 Apr. 2010 on the application of Art. 101(3) of the Treaty on the Functioning of the European Union to categories of vertical agreements and concerted practices.

They are not prohibited. The AMO assesses these operations from the view of potential creation of important barriers to effective competition on the markets.

781. Concentration under the Competition Act means the process of economic combining of undertakings through:

(1) merger or amalgamation of two or more separate undertakings; or
(2) acquisition of direct or indirect control by an undertaking or several undertakings over another undertaking or part of another undertaking or undertakings.

782. Concentration is subject to control by the AMO if:

(1) combined aggregate turnover of the parties to the concentration is at least EUR 46,000,000 attained for the closed accounting period preceding the establishment of the concentration in the Slovak Republic and at least two of the parties to the concentration attain a turnover of at least EUR 14,000,000 each in the Slovak Republic for the closed accounting period preceding the establishment of the concentration; or
(2) combined turnover attained for the closed accounting period preceding the establishment of the concentration in the Slovak Republic:
    (a) if it is a matter of concentration pursuant to point (1) at least by one of the parties to the concentration is EUR 14,000,000 and simultaneously the global combined turnover for the closed accounting period preceding the establishment of the concentration attained by another party to the concentration is at least EUR 46,000,000;
    (b) if it is a matter of concentration pursuant to point (2) by the party to the concentration over whose enterprise or part of enterprise the control is acquired is at least EUR 14,000,000 and simultaneously the global combined turnover for the closed accounting period preceding the establishment of the concentration attained by another party to the concentration is at least EUR 46,000,000.

V. Procedure

783. Proceedings commence on the AMO's own incentive or if petitioned by a participant in the proceedings. Proceedings in the case of an agreement restricting competition and in the case of abuse of a dominant position must always commence on the AMO's own incentive.

784. The AMO may initiate the proceedings on its own incentive and on the basis of a written petition by a natural or a legal person that is not an undertaking pursuant to the Competition Act. On the basis of a request submitted by a natural or a legal person filing a written petition, the AMO has to inform them in writing of further procedure regarding the matter within two months following the date of receipt of the request.

785. The AMO may end proceedings regarding an agreement restricting competition, Abuse of a Dominant Position and violation of the Articles 101 and 102 TFEU (formerly Articles 81 and 82 of the EC Treaty) by means of a decision imposing on an undertaking the requirement to fulfil the commitments submitted by the undertaking to the AMO for the purpose of elimination of possible restriction of competition. The AMO may issue this decision for a specific time period.

786. The AMO has to issue a decision within six months following the date on which the proceedings commenced. In complicated cases, the AMO Chairperson may allow, also repeatedly, an appropriate extension of the time limit for issuing a decision by a maximum of twenty-four months in total. If the AMO is unable to make a decision within six months, it is required to notify the party to the proceedings thereof and indicate the reasons. This time limit does not apply to the issuance of a decision on concentration.

787. The Office has to issue a decision on concentration within twenty-five working days following the date of delivery of complete notification of concentration. If the concentration requires in-depth analysis, the AMO has to issue a decision on concentration within ninety working days following the date of delivery of the written notification to party to the proceedings. This decision usually contains simplified reasoning with a list of parties to the concentration, sector or relevant market in which the parties to the concentration operate. The AMO issues a decision approving a concentration if the concentration does not significantly distort effective competition on the relevant market, mainly due to the creation or strengthening of dominant position. In opposite, the AMO has to prohibit a concentration, which would significantly distort competition on the relevant market mainly due to the creation or strengthening of dominant position.

VI. Sanctions

788. According to the Competition Act, the AMO can impose fine to undertaking up to 10% of its turnover for the preceding business year and a fine of up to EUR 330,000 on an undertaking that attained a turnover of up to EUR 330 or attained no turnover, or on an undertaking whose turnover is not able to be calculated, for violation of the prohibition of agreements restricting competition, abuse of dominant position and administrative offences related to the concentrations.

789. In order to set the specific amount of the fine within the limit set out by the Competition Act, the AMO has to take into consideration the criteria set out in the Competition Act, according to which it considers the gravity, nature and duration of the violation of provisions of the Competition Act, actual impact on the market and, where appropriate, the size of the market. In addition to the criteria of gravity and duration of the violation, AMO has to take into account other factors as well, especially the repeated violation by the same undertaking, refusal of undertaking to cooperate with the AMO, undertaking's position as the leader or instigator of the violation, gaining financial benefit as a result of a violation or failure to fulfil in practice an agreement restricting competition. AMO has to set the fine according to the above-mentioned criteria in order to fulfil not only its repressive function – punishment for breaching the Competition Act – but also the individual and general prevention.

790. The AMO may impose fines repeatedly. The AMO may impose fines within four years from the commencement of proceedings. However, the AMO may impose these fines within eight years from the day of the violation of the provisions of this Competition Act and/or Articles 101 and 102 TFEU (formerly Articles 81 and 82 of the EC Treaty), the failure to fulfil a condition or the violation of an obligation or commitment imposed by a decision of the AMO.

§2. The Law of Unfair Competition and Trade Practices

I. Introduction

791. The law of unfair competition in Slovakia is basically regulated in the Commercial Code which includes provisions on protection against unfair competition. An equally important part of the law against unfair competition is provided by the Consumer Protection Act, the substantial contribution of which is a detailed regulation of some forms of unfair competition and the availability of administrative action against them.

II. The Commercial Code

A. Survey

792. The Commercial Code contains general provisions, such as the definition of participants in economic competition (competitors), a ban on abuse of participation in competition, which it divides into unfair competition (Articles 44–52) and unlawful limitation of economic competition (the Competition Act).

B. Scope of Application

793. The Commercial Code in the first provision regulates the general clause, i.e., the general criteria of unfair competition and a listing of different categories of unfair competition. The Unfair competition means a conduct in economic competition, which is contrary to the good morals of competition, and which may be detrimental to other competitors or customers. Unfair competition is prohibited.

794. Unfair competition means in particular the following:

- Misleading advertising.
- Misleading marking of goods and services.

- Conduct contributing to mistaken identity.
- Parasitic use of the reputation of another competitor's enterprise, products or services.
- Bribery.
- Disparagement.
- Violation of trade secrets.
- Endangering the health of consumers and the environment.

795. The above-mentioned list specifies more precisely the possible manners of unfair competition. In this respect it is important to mention that the list is not exhaustive so that other unforeseen conduct may be also considered unfair competition, if it fulfils the conditions set forth in the general clause.

796. Concerning the misleading advertising, it is the advertising of products, services, real property, business name, trademark, indication of product origin and other rights and obligations, which misleads or is likely to mislead the persons to whom it is addressed or who it reaches and which by the misleading may affect the economic behaviour of such persons or which harms or is likely to harm a competitor or consumer.

797. In assessing the misleading advertising, all the characters are considered, especially the information it contains about:

(1) goods and services, their availability, appearance, composition, method and date of manufacture or delivery, suitability and usage, quantity, geographical or commercial origin or the results to be expected from their use, or the results of tests or controls;
(2) price or the method by which it is calculated, and the conditions under which goods and services are supplied or rendered;
(3) characteristics of competitor advertising, in particular, his/her identity, qualifications, its protected industrial property law, IP, prize or award.

798. False indication of goods and services is any sign which is capable of resulting misconception in business relations that goods or services marked by the sign come from a certain country, specific area or place or from a specific manufacturer or to have specific characteristics or special qualities, regardless of whether the sign was directly on the goods, packaging and business documents, etc. or whether the false indication was executed directly or indirectly and through which means.

799. Under the law, the conduct contributing to mistaken identity means:

(1) use of the trade name or designation of enterprise that has been used according to law by another competitor;

(2) use of special signs of business or special labelling or appearance of products, performances, materials of enterprise, which the customers connect with a certain enterprise or consider characteristic to such enterprise (e.g., packaging, forms, catalogues, advertising materials);
(3) imitation of foreign products, their packaging or performances, unless it was an imitation of the elements that are already in the nature of the product functionally, technically or aesthetically predetermined and imitator made all reasonable steps to exclude or at least substantially restricted the risk of confusion.

if these acts are likely to cause risk of confusion with businesses, business name, special designations or products or performances of another competitor. Conduct contributing to mistaken identity includes also choice of such business name, which is likely to risk of confusion with a public register (e.g., Commercial Register, Trade Licence Register, etc.).

800. Parasitic use of reputation means the use by a competitor of the reputation of another competitor's enterprise, products or services to gain extra benefits for its own or a third party's business activity which would not otherwise have been achieved by such competitor. Parasitic use of reputation often takes the form of exploiting another competitor's goodwill.

801. Bribery (corruption) means conduct whereby:

(1) competitor directly or indirectly offers, promises or renders benefits, to an individual who is a member of another competitor's statutory or similar body or employee (or an individual of similar status) to gain an advantage by means of unfair conduct for himself/herself or a third party (another competitor) to the detriment of other competitors, or an illegal competitive advantage; or
(2) individual mentioned above directly or indirectly demands or solicits or accepts any kind of benefit for the same purpose.

A benefit (bribe) may be material or non-material. Bribery is further subject to the provisions of the Criminal Code.

802. Disparagement means conduct whereby one competitor states or disseminates false information about the circumstances, products or services of another competitor, such false information being likely to be detrimental. Disparagement also involves stating and disseminating true information about the circumstances, products or services of another competitor, if such information is capable of causing detriment to that competitor. However, it is not considered unfair competition if a competitor is forced by circumstances to such conduct (e.g., in justified defence) or if it stated such information in comparative advertising.

Disparagement usually causes detriment by jeopardizing a particular competitor's reputation and goodwill. The Civil Code contains provisions enabling the harmed party to prevent unjustified interference, which harms the good name of a particular legal entity and seek satisfaction (moral satisfaction and/or just satisfaction).

803. Violation of a trade secret means conduct whereby an individual illegally informs another person about a trade secret or provides him/her with access to it, or exploits it for his/her own or another person's benefit, using it in competition, and of which the individual learned:

(1) as a result of having been entrusted with that secret, or by having gained access to it (e.g., through technical documentation, instructions, drawings, models or patterns) on the basis of an employment or other relationship with the competitor, or while performing a function to which it was appointed by a court or other authority; or
(2) through his/her own or another person's illegal conduct.

804. Endangering the health of others and the environment is an illegal conduct whereby a competitor distorts the conditions of economic competition by manufacturing and marketing products, or by carrying on activities, which endanger health or the environment as protected by law, in order to acquire benefits for himself/herself or for another person at the expense of other competitors or consumers (in particular by not observing a particular limit set for manufacturing (processing) or the sale of certain products).

Chapter 5. State Regulation of the Conditions of Commercial Transactions

805. Trading is the activity based on the autonomous decision-making of subjects. A good business is a result of a free decision of all present subjects and that is also favourable for all the subjects. Although the transformation of the economic system in Slovakia has been associated with business liberalization, including price liberalization and the process of business liberalization can be considered in principle to be closed, there are some fields where public authorities for various reasons affect the business and by specific legislation the state establishes specific rules for the business.

806. The state regulation of business may cover:

(1) determination of business rules for defined subjects, especially those that are of public nature or doing business under the supervision, or whose business is supervised;
(2) trading with certain commodities;
(3) organization of trading on certain business places.

807. Reasons for state intervention in the regulation of business relations are mainly the protection of health, environment protection, ensuring national defence and security, and also protection of persons in weaker position, namely consumers. These reasons often overlap, and it is neither possible nor necessary to specify any particular boundaries among them.

§1. Price and Supply Regulation

I. Legislative Framework

808. Rules of negotiation, implementation, regulation and control of product prices, performances, works, services, rent and property, measures to prevent adverse price developments and the competence of public authorities in the field of prices of goods on the Slovak market are governed by Act No. 18/1996 Coll. on prices as amended (the Prices Act). The Prices Act is supplemented by regulation of the Ministry of Finance of the Slovak Republic implementing the Price Act and number of ordinances of the Ministry of Finance of the Slovak Republic. Besides the Prices Act which forms the general legal regulation of prices, there are also special legal regulations of prices in specific fields, such as in energy sector – Act No. 251/2012 Coll. on Energy and Act No. 250/2012 Coll. on Regulation in Network Industries – postal services sector – Act No. 324/2011 Coll. on Postal Services – healthcare sector – Ordinances of the Ministry of Health of the Slovak Republic (prices of selected medicines, medical devices, dietetic food and services in healthcare), etc.

II. Price Regulation

809. Price regulation under the Prices Act is conceived primarily as an extraordinary measure, which is justified only if:

(1) extraordinary market situation with a direct impact on the prices of goods on the domestic market threatening the price stability or availability of the goods occurs;
(2) there is a danger to the market due to the underdeveloped competitive environment, and for assessing the competitive environment, the opinion of the AMO is required;
(3) it is required by the consumer protection or other public interest;
(4) in balancing the position of the buyer or the seller in respect of goods wholly or partly subsidized from public sources or on which financial aid is provided from abroad or from the EU;
(5) in change of the Slovak currency rate, tax laws, customs laws or subsidy laws;
(6) in network industries under a special regulation;
(7) it is a universal postal service or postal payment service.

810. The price regulation may be performed in the form of:

(1) official price determination;
(2) substantive guidance of pricing; or
(3) combination of both the above-mentioned methods.

811. Official price determination means determining the price for a particular type of product by the pricing authorities as a maximum or fixed price. Whereas, the substantive guidance of pricing means the determination of the conditions for negotiating prices by the pricing authority. These conditions are:

(1) maximum extent of acceptable price increases for a limited period; or
(2) binding procedure for establishing prices.

812. The Prices Act states that the price regulation is based on economically justified costs and a reasonable profit.

A. Main Areas of Regulation

813. Network Industries: The Act on Regulation in Network Industries governs the regulation of network industries, the status and competences of the Regulatory Office for Network Industries (*Úrad pre reguláciu siet'ových odvetví*), obligations of regulated entities, rules for the internal market of electricity and gas.

The network industries include electric energy, gas industry, thermal energy, and water management. The main framework of the Act is the performance of the price, substantive and extraordinary regulation and newly also quality regulation in network industries. The purpose of regulation under the Act is to ensure the availability of goods and related regulated activities at a reasonable price and specified quality in a transparent and non-discriminatory manner. Subject to regulation are:

(1) prices in network industries and their conditions of their claiming;
(2) conditions for conducting regulated activities.

The regulated activities include mainly the following:

(1) Generation, transmission, distribution and supply of electricity and related services.
(2) Production, transportation, distribution, storage and supply of gas and related services.
(3) Production, distribution and supply of heat.
(4) Production, distribution and supply of drinking water through public water supply.
(5) Collection and treatment of waste water in public sewer.
(6) Collection of surface water and energetic water from rivers and the use of hydropower potential of rivers.

814. Postal services: The Postal Regulatory Office (*Poštový regulačný úrad*) performs state regulation under Act No. 324/2011 Coll. on Postal Services. State regulation comprises:

(1) creation of conditions for establishing and maintaining the competitive environment on the market;
(2) setting general rules for providing postal services;
(3) setting the general conditions for providing interchangeable postal services and postal payment service;
(4) granting licences or imposition of the obligation to provide the universal service, setting conditions for providing the universal service and requirements for operating the public postal network;
(5) regulation of postal charges for the provision of the universal service ends the execution of postal payment service;
(6) regulation of financing of the universal service.

The state regulation of postal services is performed on the basis of the Postal Office's decisions which are general authorization, the postal licence and the decree on regulation of the postal charges.

815. Healthcare: The Ministry of Health of the Slovak Republic based on its Ordinance of 2003 stating the extent of price regulation in healthcare as amended regulates following:

(1) Fix prices of transfusion medicines prepared under Act No. 362/2011 Coll. on Medicines and Medical Devices.
(2) Conditions of price regulations of individually prepared human medicines under Annex No. 3 to the Ordinance.
(3) Maximum prices for professional pharmaceutical acts in the individual preparation of medicines in pharmacies (*taxa laborum*).
(4) Maximum prices for women's breast milk prepared in hospitals.
(5) Maximum prices of optical acts.
(6) Maximum prices of tissues and cells for transplantation under the Health Care Act.
(7) Maximum prices of business acts (*obchodné výkony*).
(8) Prices and terms of price regulation for selected acts of healthcare provided by healthcare facilities.

The Ministry of Health of the Slovak Republic further officially determinates price of selected items:

(1) Medicines which are not listed in the list of categorized medicines.
(2) Medicines which are listed in the list of categorized medicines.
(3) Radiopharmaceuticals.
(4) Medical devices.
(5) Special medical materials.
(6) Dietetic food.

An updated list of the above-mentioned regulated (officially determined) prices is available on the web page of the Ministry of Health of the Slovak Republic www.health.gov.sk (in Slovak).

B. Price Interventions of the Government

1. Price Authorities

816. Under the Prices Act, the Price authorities perform Price Interventions, i.e.:

(1) Ministry of Finance of the Slovak Republic.
(2) Ministry of Health of the Slovak Republic.
(3) Other state authority (Regulatory Office for Network Industries, Postal Regulatory Office, etc.).
(4) Higher territorial unit (e.g., determines after consultation with the municipality maximum prices for goods of local importance to the extent provided by the Ministry of Finance).
(5) Municipality (city) (e.g., determines the maximum prices of municipal tram and trolleybus).
(6) Financial control.

(7) Slovak Trade Inspection (performs the price controls under Act No. 128/2002 Coll. on State Control of Internal Market in the Consumer Protection Issues).

2. Breach of Price Discipline

817. If the price control authorities find that the controlled entity violated the price discipline under the Price Act, they must impose a fine:

(1) equal to the difference between the agreed price and the price that should be agreed upon in accordance with price regulations; or
(2) up to EUR 30,000 where the difference referred to in point (1) cannot be quantified or if it is a breach of price discipline, others as described in (1).

If the price control authority repeatedly found a breach of price discipline within twelve months, it may impose to the controlled entity a fine of up to EUR 60,000 and make a petition to cancel its trade licence under a special regulation.

§2. CONSUMER LAW

I. General Observations

818. In accordance with the EU law, the Slovak Republic follows the general principle of the Consumer Protection Policy, which include:

- health and security protection consumer right;
- right for consumer economic interests protection;
- information and education right;
- right for collective representation of consumer interests within consumer protection;
- right for indemnification of losses.

819. Slovak Consumer Protection law can be found in different codes and Statutes. Slovakia implemented the general principles within the Civil Code and laid down two specific Statutes, namely Consumer Protection Act No. 250/2007 Coll. (Consumer Protection Act), which governs consumer rights, obligations of producers, sellers, importers and suppliers and the scope of public administration in the area of consumer protection and Act No. 266/2005 Coll. on Consumer Protection in Financial Services at a Distance, which provides for consumer protection in financial service provided by the supplier by means of distance communication based on distance contracts and the obligations and rights stemming out of them.

A. Representation of the Consumer Interest

1. Government Level

820. Consumers in Slovakia are represented on the national level by the Ministry of Economy of the Slovak Republic (*Ministerstvo Hospodárstva Slovenskej Republiky*), which set up a specialized body – Information about Consumer Policy Department – which:

(1) works with competent Ministry units and other central state administration authorities on tasks relating to consumer protection;
(2) under its competence, supervises the observance of laws relating to consumer protection and, in accordance with the laws, implements necessary remedial measures;
(3) works, as needs arise, with the Spokesman and the Communications and Public Relations Unit in the preparation and realization of the Ministry media outputs;
(4) works with the Ministerial Coordination Group Secretariat in developing EU Council documents – framework position, instruction, opinion and mandate to the extent of its subject matter jurisdiction;
(5) works with the Legislative Department in drawing up the Ministry's opinions by drafting legal rules of central state administration authorities submitted for Government and National Council discussion, for discussion of the Legislative Council of the Slovak Government as well as of the Economic and Social Agreement Council and of the Economic Ministers Meeting;
(6) works with the Legislative Department on working out opinions on international treaties drawn up by other central state administration authorities;
(7) submits to the Legislative Department the intents of draft legal rules including the subject and contents of legislation;
(8) follows EU/EC legal rules relating to the department competence.

821. Furthermore, the department cooperates with civil associations to safeguard consumers' rights and economic interest and helps the civil associations with the creation of required conditions to develop their activities. Moreover, the department performs market supervision over consumer protection.

822. On 1 January 2019, the new Act No. 346/2018 Coll. on the Register of Non-Governmental and Non-Profit Organizations and on amending and supplementing certain acts came into force. The main rationale of establishing the Register is to create a reliable, up-to-date and unified source register of non-governmental and non-profit organizations. This decision was undertaken as the list of non-governmental organizations was scattered across diverse registers, collecting variate of diverse data.

Consumer Agencies

823. Besides the governmental bodies, there are a number of non-governmental organizations (NGOs) that are financed or co-financed by the Government from the state budget through the Ministry of Economy of the Slovak Republic. The main purpose of the NGO is to educate the consumers as to their rights and entitlements. The NGOs usually carry out seminars and training. However, in Slovakia the consumer agencies, which state in their basic legal documents that they protect and safeguard the rights of consumers (irrespective of their names), have the right under the Civil Code on Procedure to represent the consumers at the court or become an adjunct participant of the suit. Generally, for any entity to become an adjunct participant of the suit, the entity has to prove its 'legal interest on the outcome' of the suit. However, in the case of consumer agencies, the agencies do not have this obligation as the Civil Code on Procedure provides for special statutory rules on the consumer protection agencies.

§3. Consumer Protection Act

I. Survey

824. The Consumer Protection Act deals with some unfair competitive conducts in detail and allows their administrative sanctioning. The Act is primarily designed to protect consumers, while the Commercial Code is more dedicated to protect the competitive environment and the competition as such, but it protects customers as well. The Consumer Protection Act stands independently, and it has its own mechanism of sanctioning the conducts harming consumers.

II. Scope of Application

825. The Consumer Protection Act governs the rights of consumers and the obligations of producers, sellers, importers and suppliers, the competency of public administration authorities with respect to consumer protection, and the position of legal persons created or established for the purpose of consumer protection ('association'). Further, the Consumer Protection Act applies to the sale of products and provision of services, where performance is being delivered in the territory of the Slovak Republic or where performance concerns business activities in the Slovak Republic.

A. Seller

826. The seller is:

(1) entrepreneur offering or selling products to the consumer or providing services to the consumer;

(2) natural person selling plant and animal products to the consumer, which originate from his/her own minor agricultural activities;
(3) natural person selling his/her own used products, with the exception of food.

827. The seller is obliged to:

(1) sell products of the correct weight, measure or quantity and to allow the consumer to verify the correctness of these data;
(2) sell products and provide services of standard quality; where quality is not prescribed, the seller may sell products of substandard quality only after having notified the consumer of all the differences;
(3) sell products and provide services at agreed prices;
(4) correctly charge prices when selling products or providing services;
(5) ensure compliance with the hygienic conditions when selling products and providing services;
(6) when selling products and providing services, to comply with the product storage conditions stipulated by the producer or in a special regulation in order to prevent the deterioration of products;
(7) present the product to the consumer, where applicable in view of the nature of the product;
(8) ensure the sale of products and provision of services in a way allowing for their safe use;
(9) provide the necessary assistance to the European Consumer Centre in resolving a dispute between a consumer and a seller in handling cross-border complaints.

828. On the other side, the seller may not:

(1) impose obligations upon the consumer without legal grounds;
(2) deny the consumer's rights under the Act.

829. The seller is obliged to comply with the principle of equal treatment towards consumers in the provision of goods and services. If the product is displayed or otherwise prepared for sale, the seller may not refuse selling a product to the consumer, nor may he refuse the provision of a service, if it is possible in terms of operational capacity. It may not bind the sale of the product or service ('tying') for the sale of another product or to provide other services except to the seller sells goods or provides these services separately, or tying of sale is subject to the technical impossibility to separate sale of goods or provision of services.

830. The producer, seller, importer or supplier may not deceive the consumer; in particular, they may not state untrue, undocumented, incomplete, inaccurate, obscure or ambiguous information or withhold information concerning the characteristics of a product or service or concerning purchase terms and conditions.

B. Products and Services

831. A product is a new, used or modified movable item produced, extracted or otherwise obtained, regardless of its stage of processing, which is intended to be offered to the consumer or which can be assumed to be used by the consumer; it can be supplied for consideration or not; a product is also a movable item comprising part or accessories of another movable or immovable item, electricity, gas, water or heat intended for the consumer.

832. A service is any activity or performance offered to the consumer, whether for consideration or not, with the exception of activities governed by special regulations (Tax Advisors, Notaries, Attorneys, Patent Representatives, etc.), which are supervised by professional chambers or special state administration authorities.

III. Substantive Provisions

A. Denomination, Composition, Quantity and Labelling of Products and Services

833. Upon the sale, the seller is obliged to inform the consumer about the characteristics of the product being sold or the nature of the service being provided, on the method of use and maintenance of the product, on the hazards associated with its incorrect use or maintenance, on storage conditions and on the risk associated with the provided service. If necessary in view of the nature of the product and in view of the method and time of its use, the seller is obliged to ensure that the information also is intelligibly provided in an appended written manual.

834. The seller is obliged to ensure that the product sold by him/her is clearly labelled, indicating the producer, importer or seller, measure or quantity, method of product use and maintenance and the hazard associated with incorrect use or maintenance of the product, the product storage conditions, as well as the risk associated with the provided service, or information pursuant to separate regulations. Upon request by the supervisory authority or by the consumer, the seller is obliged to notify or document the product's data, if the product cannot be labelled.

835. The information must be provided in writing and it must be provided in the Slovak language.

B. Price Indication

836. The seller is obliged to inform the consumer about the price of the product sold or service provided and to clearly label a product or service with price or make the information on the price otherwise suitably accessible. If the condition of the purchase of the product or service is the purchase of another product or the provision of a service, the seller is obliged to inform the consumer about the price of another product or the price of other services along with the price of the product sold or service provided.

837. Information about the price, incomplete price, missing price information or the method of price determination cannot give the impression that:

(1) price is lower than the actual price;
(2) determination of the price depends on the circumstances on which it actually does not depend;
(3) price includes delivery of the product, performance, work or service which are actually paid separately;
(4) price is or may be increased, decreased, or unchanged, even if it may not;
(5) relationship of price and usefulness of the product or service corresponds to reality, even if this information is not true.

838. The seller is obliged to affix the selling price and the unit price. The unit price may not be indicated if it is identical to the selling price.

C. Advertising

839. The Law of Advertising is regulated by Act No. 147/2001 Coll. on Advertising ('Advertising Act').[70] Under the Act, advertising must comply with competition rules and good morals. Advertising must not be misleading, hidden and should not have signs of unfair commercial practices.

840. Further the advertising must not:

(1) abuse the trust of the consumer's lack of experience or knowledge;
(2) present the products whose production, sale, supply or use is prohibited;
(3) contain anything that detracts from human dignity, national feelings or offends religious sensibilities, as well as any discrimination on grounds of sex, race or social origin;
(4) promote violence, vandalism, vulgarity and abet the offence with his/her express consent;
(5) present naked human body in a scandalous way;
(6) present products, which are environmentally harmful or detrimental to life or health of humans, animals or plants, without explicitly and clearly noticing the harmfulness;
(7) threaten physical health or mental health of the citizen;
(8) present products as being beneficial to the health of humans, animals or plants, unless proven by experts;

70. This law reflects all enforceable EU directives and regulations adopted in this field.

(9) present the food and nutritional supplements as if they had medical effects;
(10) use sensory perception, which affects the memory of humans, without realizing it ('Subliminal perception');
(11) contain personal data, data on the financial situation of people without their prior consent;
(12) refer to the statements of others without their prior consent;
(13) interfere with the rights of others without their consent;
(14) abuse the trust of minors.

841. Advertising must meet the requirements for public speech acts, the principles of culture, language, spelling and grammar rules, pronunciation rules of the Slovak language and established technical terminology. Advertising must not distribute automatic telephone call system, fax and e-mail without the prior consent of the person who is the recipient of advertising. Advertising cannot be distributed if the recipient refuses delivery of advertising in advance.

842. Advertising special offer products must contain:

(1) date of commencement of the period during which the special offer will last, if that period has not yet begun to run;
(2) date of expiry of the special offer period or indication that the special offer is valid until the stock ends.

D. Unfair Commercial Practices

843. Unfair commercial practices are prohibited. A commercial practice is considered unfair, if:

(1) it is contrary to the requirements of professional diligence;
(2) it materially distorts or may materially distort the economic behaviour of the average consumer with regard to the product or to the service whom it reaches or to whom it is addressed, or of the average member of the group when a commercial practice is directed to a particular group of consumers.

844. The misleading actions, misleading omissions and aggressive commercial practice are considered to be the most common unfair commercial practice. The list of commercial practices, which are in all circumstances considered unfair, is contained in Annex I of the Consumer Protection Act.

E. Regulated Trade Practices

1. Announcements of Price Comparisons and Discounts

845. When announcing the price comparisons and discounts, the seller has to comply with the following obligations. The Consumer Protection Act states, *inter alia,* that a commercial practice is also regarded as misleading if it causes or is likely to cause the average consumer to take a transactional decision that he would not have taken otherwise, and it involves the marketing of a product, including comparative advertising, which creates confusion with any products, trademarks, trade names or other distinguishing marks of a competitor. Under the Advertising Act, a comparative advertising is advertising that directly or indirectly designates another competitor or his/her products. Comparative advertising is only allowed, if it:

(1) compares products, services, or real property that satisfy the same needs or are designed for the same purpose;
(2) compares without prejudice one or more concrete, typical, essential and provable characteristics of products, services or real property including their price;
(3) does not discredit or bring into disrepute trademarks, business names, other distinguishing marks, goods, services, activities or circumstances of a competitor;
(4) does not misuse the advantage of product goodwill, goodwill of trademark or other competitor's distinguishing feature of competitor or indication of origin of competing products;
(5) does not present product or services as an imitation or product or service copy which is protected by trademark or business name;
(6) does not create interchange among traders, among advertisers and a competitor or between trademarks, business names, other distinguishing marks, goods or services of advertiser and competitor;
(7) is not misleading;
(8) does not include an unfair commercial practice.

846. Announcement of discounts must comply with rules on price information. The seller is obliged to correctly charge prices when selling products or providing services. The Consumer Protection Act states that price information, incomplete price, missing price or information about the method of price determination may not invoke the impression that: (i) the price is lower than it actually is; (ii) the price determination depends on circumstances on which it in fact does not depend; (iii) the price includes the delivery of a product, performance, work or service, which is in fact charged separately; (iv) the price is or may be increased, reduced or may remain unchanged although it is not true; and (v) the value for money ratio of the offered product or service corresponds to reality, although such information is not true.

2. Clearance Sales

847. The Consumer Protection Act defines commercial practices as any act, omission, course of conduct or representation, commercial communication including advertising and marketing, by a seller, directly connected with the promotion, sale or supply of a product to consumers. The clearance sales fall therefore within the scope of application of the Act, and consumers are consequently protected against unfair and misleading practices in regard to clearance sales. Slovak law does not require any prior approval of the clearance sales. The clearance sales as a commercial practice are not listed among prohibited practices in the Annex of the Act (or Annex I of Directive 2005/29/EC) and cannot, as such, be considered unfair in all circumstances. A commercial practice ('clearance sale') is not covered by Annex I of Directive 2005/29/EC and cannot be prohibited solely because prior authorization has not been granted by the competent authority, without itself carrying out an assessment of the unfairness of the practice in question against the criteria set out in Articles 5–9 of that Directive (*see* Case C-206/11 *Georg Köck v. Schutzverband gegen unlauteren Wettbewerb* (2013), paragraphs 46, 51).

3. Financial Services Offers

848. Consumer protection in the financial services provided by the supplier by means of distance communication is regulated in Act No. 266/2005 Coll. on Consumer Protection in Distance Financial Services as amended. Under the Act, provision of distance marketing financial services means the provision of financial services by a supplier to the consumer exclusively through means of distance communication. Means of distance communication means the means, which can be used without physical contact of the supplier with the consumer at the provision of distance financial services, in particular the electronic mail, phone, fax, addressed letter, offer catalogue.

849. The Act also exactly defines what is being understood under a financial service. Financial services include services which are being provided by insurance companies, including insurance companies from other Member States, securities agents, banks and foreign banks, pension companies, etc. The Act defines a supplier as a person who within the scope of its business activities provides contractual financial services through means of distance communication on the basis of a distance contract.

850. In order to offer its financial services to a customer, the supplier can use the means of distance communication, which enable direct communication only with a clear and articulate consent of a consumer or when the consumer does not explicitly object their use. Automatic phone system and fax can be used by the supplier only upon prior consent of the consumer. At unrequested communication, the supplier is obliged to offer financial services in the manner, which would not cause any costs to the consumer.

851. Before concluding a distance contract, the supplier is obliged to provide the consumer together with the offer of financial services also with the information in the extent stated in the Act. The supplier must in particular inform a consumer on: (i) the supplier and/or intermediary, (ii) the financial service (including total price of the service, notice of risks, information on taxes not paid by the supplier), and (iii) the distance contract (including the right to withdraw, minimum term of the contract, choice of law and court, the manner of dealing with complaints, the possibility of out-of-court settlement of a complaint and on the existence of guarantee funds, etc.). The information must be current, complete and accurate.

852. The supplier must inform the consumer of the conclusion of the distance contract without undue delay. The supplier is obliged at the request of the consumer to provide him/her with more information about financial services for financial services under special laws (Insurance Act, Securities Act, etc.) in paper form or in the form of registration on another durable medium, at any time during the term of the contract. The consumer has the right to change the means of distance communication, unless it is contrary to concluded distance contract or the nature of the financial services excludes it.

853. The consumer is entitled to withdraw from the distance contract without paying penalty and without giving any reason within fourteen calendar days from the conclusion of a distance contract or the receipt of the above-mentioned obligatory information in paper or other durable forms.

854. Consumer rights cannot be contractually excluded or limited in advance, and irrespective of the governing law. Distance contract may not contain provisions on waiving consumer's rights in advances, and the provisions of that burden of proof on the fulfilment of all or part of obligations of the supplier lie with the consumer.

4. Gift Vouchers

855. The Consumer Protection Act defines commercial practices as any act, omission, course of conduct or representation, commercial communication, including advertising and marketing, by a seller, directly connected with the promotion, sale or supply of a product to consumers. The sale of gift vouchers falls therefore within the scope of application of the Act, and consumers are consequently protected against unfair and misleading practices when they purchase or use gift vouchers. In particular, traders cannot display misleading information on the gift vouchers (such as a misleading expiry date). The omission of material information the consumer needs (in this case to be able to use the gift voucher) is also prohibited: e.g., taking into account the product and circumstances, the omission of the period of validity could be considered a misleading practice. In addition, practices contrary to professional diligence and affecting consumers' behaviour are also considered unfair under the Directive. For example, national enforcement authorities may consider, depending on the context and the product, that a very limited period of validity of the gift voucher constitutes an unfair commercial practice.

5. Auction Sales

856. Auction sales at an Internet auction (e.g., eBay auction) are not necessarily protected by distance selling legislation. New Directive No. 2011/83/EU of the European Parliament and of the Council of 25 October 2011 on consumer rights will, from 2013 (EU Member States have to transpose the Directive to their national law at the latest by 13 December 2013 and apply those measures from 13 June 2014), introduce important changes to the law as it affects consumers and those who sell goods and provide services to them, especially in the online environment. As currently, a consumer will be entitled to withdraw from a distance or off-premises contract. However, the cooling-off period during which a consumer may withdraw from a sales contract will be extended to fourteen calendar days (from seven days currently). The period will be extended to circumstances including online auctions (provided that the counterparty is an entrepreneur).

857. Whereas, auction sales between individuals themselves are regulated by general provisions of the Civil Code on the sales contract that defines the terms of ownership from the sales contract, delivery of the purchased item, payment of the purchase price as well as the right to withdraw from the contract. These sales do not fall under the Consumer Protection Act and are not considered a contract between the seller (entrepreneur) and the buyer.

6. Unsolicited Sales

858. The Consumer Protection Act expressly states demanding immediate or deferred payment for or the return or safekeeping of products supplied by the trader, but not solicited by the consumer except where the product is a substitute supplied under a special law, among the aggressive commercial practices.

7. Pyramid Selling

859. Under the Consumer Protection Act, establishing, operating or promoting a pyramid promotional scheme where a consumer gives consideration for the opportunity to receive compensation that is derived primarily from the introduction of other consumers into the scheme rather than from the sale or consumption of products is considered misleading commercial practice and represents a practice listed in the list of commercial practices which are in all circumstances considered unfair.

8. Door-to-Door and Distance Selling

860. Special consumer protection is regulated also in the field of door-to-door and distance selling by Act No. 108/2000 Coll. on Consumer Protection in Door-to-Door and Distance Selling, as amended.[71]

861. Doorstep selling can be done only in working days from 08.00 to 19.00 and in the non-working days from 10.00 to 15.00.

862. The seller must fulfil the following special obligations:

(1) Demonstrate to consumers and other interested parties if they require it.
(2) Inform consumers in writing about where and how the consumer can complain about defects in the goods or services provided.
(3) Inform the consumer in writing at the latest before the conclusion of the contract about his/her right to withdraw from the contract in writing within seven working days of receipt of goods or of conclusion a contract for services and give the name and address of the person against whom that right may be exercised.

863. The distance contract is a contract concluded by the seller and the consumer for mail sales of goods or provision of services at a distance only by means of communication (in practice in particular electronic communication).

864. The seller must, prior to the conclusion of a distance contract together with the offer of goods or services, inform the consumer about:

(a) his/her identity and address;
(b) a description of the goods or services;
(c) the price of the goods or services provided;
(d) the delivery terms and costs of delivery;
(e) the terms of payment;
(f) the right to have the consumer to withdraw from the contract;
(g) the price for the use of means of distance communication, where the price is determined by other than the basic rate;
(h) the period during which the seller is bound by its offer, including the price; and
(i) the minimum period for which the contract can be concluded.

865. The consumer is entitled, without giving any reason, to withdraw from the contract within seven working days of receipt of goods or of conclusion a contract

71. This Act has been amended a number of times in order to be in compliance with the EU law. This law reflects all the changes brought by Directive 2011/83/EU of the European Parliament and of the Council of 25 Oct. 2011 on consumer rights, amending Council Directive 93/13/EEC and Directive 1999/44/EC of the European Parliament and of the Council and repealing Council Directive 85/577/EEC and Directive 97/7/EC of the European Parliament and of the Council.

for services, if the seller timely and properly complied with his/her information obligations mentioned above. Otherwise, the consumer may exercise his/her right to withdraw within seven working days from the date on which the seller additionally meets his/her information obligations, but not later than three months from the receipt of goods or of conclusion a contract for services.

F. Honest Business Practices

866. Under the Consumer Protection Act, professional diligence means the standard of special skill and care which a trader may reasonably be expected to exercise towards consumers, corresponding to the honest business practice or to the general principle of good faith in the trader's field of activity.

867. Seller must not act contrary to good morals. Acting contrary to good morals means particularly conduct that is contrary to established traditions and showing clear signs of discrimination or departure from the rules of morality recognized in selling products and services, or may cause harm to the consumer for breach of good faith, honesty, custom and practice, especially misusing error, deceit, threat, significant inequality of the parties and violations of contractual freedom.

868. The Act also mentions a code of conduct. Code of conduct means an agreement or set of rules which defines the behaviour of traders who undertake to be bound by the code in relation to one or more particular commercial practices or business sectors, unless such rules are imposed by law, regulation or administrative provision of a public administration authority.

869. The use of unfair commercial practices may also be inspected by code creator or persons and associations through the code creator. Such activity may be performed irrespective of court proceedings or administrative proceedings.

IV. Interim Measures

870. If the seller harms the collective interests of consumers, the Consumer Protection Association may under the Consumer Protection Act submit a petition to the supervisory authority for interim measures. The petition must include a description of actions which under the opinion of the association lead to harm of the collective interests of consumers, a description of the facts justifying the issuance of preliminary injunction and reasoning, what is the urgency of the petition and the need for immediate abandonment of activities affecting the collective interests of consumers. The petition for interim measures may be brought only if the seller does not refrain from harming the collective interests of consumers within two weeks of receipt of written notice from the association to abandon such action containing the same elements as the petition for interim measures pursuant to the preceding sentence.

871. If the supervisory authority finds a violation of consumer rights, which harms the collective interests of consumers, it may issue an interim measure to order the seller to refrain from such breach of consumer rights and must initiate administrative proceedings for violation of the Consumer Protection Act or a special law. The interim measure has to be notified by the supervisory authority in writing, to subject against whom it is directed, stating the facts upon which it issued the interim measure.

872. The interim measure may be challenged within three days of a written objection. The objections have to be decided by the superior authority of the supervisory authority within five days of their receipt, and it may reject the objection, confirm the measure or revoke the interim measure.

V. Sanctions

873. Where the obligations laid down in the Consumer Protection Act or in the law of EU are breached, the supervisory authority has to fine the producer, seller, importer or supplier up to EUR 66,387.84; where the breach repeats within twelve months, the authority has to impose a fine of up to EUR 165,969.59.

§4. Consumer Sales

874. Consumer Sales are generally governed in the Civil Code, and special regulation is presented in Act No. 250/2007 on Consumer Protection as amended. The Slovak law defines a consumer contract as any contract regardless of the legal form, which was concluded with a consumer by a supplier.

875. The provisions on consumer contracts, as well as all other provisions governing the relationships involving a consumer, are always used, if it is in favour of the consumer. Different contractual arrangements or agreements, whose content or purpose is to circumvent this rule, are invalid. The Civil Code states that on the one hand the supplier is a person who in concluding and performing contracts held as part of its trade or business and on the other hand the consumer is a natural person who in concluding and performing the contract does not act within the scope of his/her business or profession.

876. If a consumer contract is made in writing, subject matter and price may not be smaller than the other part of that contract, except for the name of the contract and designations of its parts. The contract entered into contrary to this provision is null and void.

877. Consumer contracts must not contain provisions that cause a significant imbalance in the rights and obligations of the parties to the detriment of consumers. Such provisions are called 'unfair condition'. This does not apply to the terms and conditions relating to main contractual consideration and appropriateness of price if the contract terms are expressed in specific, clear and understandable manner, or if unacceptable conditions were individually negotiated. Provision with which the consumer has the opportunity to become acquainted before signing the contract, but had no influence on their content, is not considered individually negotiated contractual provision. If the supplier does not prove otherwise, contractual provisions agreed between the supplier and the consumer are not considered to be individually negotiated. The law expressly states that the unfair terms in consumer contracts are invalid.

878. The unfairness of a contractual term is assessed having regard to the nature of the goods or services for which the contract was concluded, and all the circumstances connected to the conclusion of the contract at the time of contract conclusion and all other terms of the contract or of another contract on which it depends.

879. If the court determines any contract terms in consumer contracts which are to be concluded in several cases, and it is usual that the consumer does not substantially influence the content of contract or in the general business conditions, to be invalid due to unfairness of such terms, or did not award consideration to the supplier due to such conditions, the supplier is obliged to refrain from the use of such terms and conditions with the same meaning in all its contracts with consumers. The same obligation has to apply to any successor of the supplier.

880. The Civil Code states particularly the following examples of unfair conditions in consumer contracts:

(1) Provision which the consumer is obliged to perform and which the consumer had no opportunity of becoming acquainted before the conclusion of the contract.
(2) Provision that allows the contractor to transfer rights and obligations under the contract to another supplier without the consent of the consumer, if the transfer had a negative effect on enforcing or securing consumer claims.
(3) Exclusion or limitation of the liability of the supplier for any act or omission which caused to death or bodily injury of the consumer.
(4) Exclusion or limitation of the rights of consumers in application of responsibility for defects or damage.
(5) Provision allowing the supplier to withdraw from a contract without contractual or legal reason and not allowing the same to a consumer.
(6) Provision allowing the supplier to unilaterally change the terms of the contract without reason agreed in the contract.
(7) Determination of the price of goods or services at the time of fulfilment, or entitlement of the supplier to increase the price of goods or services without the right of the consumer to withdraw from the contract, if the price agreed at the time of conclusion of the contract is substantially exceeded at the time of fulfilment.
(8) Provision requiring any consumer who fails to fulfil his/her obligation to pay a disproportionately high sum in penalties as sanction for failure to meet his/her obligation.

(9) Restricting access to the evidence available to the consumer or imposing the obligation to bear the burden of proving that the other party should bear.
(10) Provision which in the case of partial or complete failure by the supplier unreasonably restrict or exclude the possibility for consumers to enforce his/her rights against the supplier, including consumer rights to set off against the supplier.
(11) Unreasonably short period for expression of consent of the consumer to an automatic extension of the term of the contract.
(12) Entitling the supplier to decide that its performance is in accordance with the contract or agreement conferring the right to construct the contract only to the supplier.
(13) Arbitration clause requiring all disputes with the supplier to be settled exclusively by arbitration.

881. Sale of goods in the shop: The Civil Code includes special regulation for the sale of goods in the shop (consumer sales contracts). If the seller has to deliver under an agreement with the buyer or due to the nature of goods, the thing at the place specified by the buyer, the buyer is obliged to take over the goods at the moment when the goods are delivered. In other cases, the buyer is obliged to take over the goods at the moment of the sale, if not agreed otherwise.

By the moment of taking over of the property, the ownership title to the goods passes to the buyer. In the distance sale, ownership passes to the buyer at the moment when the buyer takes over the goods in the place of destination specified by the buyer. In self-service sale, the ownership title is passed by the payment of price for the purchased goods. Before this moment, the buyer can return the goods to the selected original place.

The sold goods must have a quality, amount, measure and weight required or lay down by legal regulations and must be free of defects; in particular, it must be in accordance with technical norms. If special rules are to be kept in using the thing, in particular if the thing is to be used according to directions for use or to a technical norm, the seller must inform the buyer of such rules unless they are generally known. The warranty period is twenty-four months. If the purchased item, its packaging or instructions attached to it contain the deadline for use, the warranty period will not end before that time. If it is a used item, the buyer and seller may agree on a shorter warranty period, but not less than twelve months. At the request of the buyer, the seller is obliged to provide a guarantee in writing (warranty certificate). If the nature of things allows, it is sufficient to issue a bill instead of the warranty certificate. In a declaration in the warranty certificate or in advertising, the seller can provide a longer guarantee than is provided by this Act. Terms and scope of the guarantee are set in the warranty certificate.

Rights from liability for defects of goods to that a warranty period applies terminate unless they were applied during the warranty period. Rights from liability for defects of quickly perishable goods must be asserted no later than on the day following the purchase; otherwise, these rights become extinct.

882. Door-to-Door and Distance Selling: Special consumer protection is regulated also in the field of door-to-door and distance selling by Act No. 108/2000 Coll.

on Consumer Protection in Door-to-Door and Distance Selling, as amended. Doorstep selling can be done only in working days from 08.00 to 19.00 and in the non-working days from 10.00 to 15.00.

The seller must fulfil the following special obligations:

(1) Demonstrate to consumers and other interested parties if they require it.
(2) Inform consumers in writing about where and how the consumer can complain about defects in the goods or services provided.
(3) Inform the consumer in writing at the latest before the conclusion of the contract about his/her right to withdraw from the contract in writing within seven working days of receipt of goods or of conclusion a contract for services and give the name and address of the person against whom that right may be exercised.

A distance contract is a contract concluded by the seller and the consumer for mail sales of goods or provision of services at a distance only by means of communication (in practice in particular electronic communication).

The seller must, prior to the conclusion of a distance contract together with the offer of goods or services inform consumer about the following:

(1) His/her identity and address.
(2) Description of the goods or services.
(3) Price of the goods or services provided.
(4) Delivery terms and costs of delivery.
(5) Terms of payment.
(6) Right to have the consumer to withdraw from the contract.
(7) Price for the use of means of distance communication, where the price is determined by other than the basic rate.
(8) Period during which the seller is bound by its offer, including the price.
(9) Minimum period for which the contract can be concluded.

The consumer is entitled, without giving any reason, to withdraw from the contract within seven working days of receipt of goods or of conclusion a contract for services, if the seller timely and properly complied with his/her information obligations mentioned above. Otherwise, the consumer may exercise his/her right to withdraw within seven working days from the date on which the seller additionally meets his/her information obligations, but not later than three months from the receipt of goods or of conclusion a contract for services.

Selected Bibliography

Fekete, I. *Občiansky zákonník – Komentár.* 1st edn. Bratislava: EPOS, 2012.

Ovečková, O. et al. *Obchodný zákonník – Komentár*, 1–2 Part. 2nd edn. Bratislava: Iura Edition, 2008.

Patakyová, M. et al. *Obchodný zákonník – Komentár.* 3rd edn. Praha: C.H. Beck, 2010.

Statistical Office of the Slovak Republic, Social Trends In The Slovak Republic 2012, available online at: https://www.employment.gov.sk/files/slovensky/ministerstvo/analyticke-centrum/report-on-social-situation-2016.pdf lastly visited 22 September 2020.

Slovak Statistical and Demographical Society, The Views on the Slovak Economy, 2011, available online at: http://www.ssds.sk/publikacie/pes/pes2011.pdf lastly visited on 31st May 2013.

Vojčík, P. *Právo duševného vlastníctva.* 1st edn. Plzeň: Aleš Čeněk, 2012.

Selected Bibliography

Index

The numbers here refer to paragraph numbers.

Abuse of dominant position. *See* Antitrust law
Acts contrary to honest business practices, 866–869
Advertising, 765, 794, 796–797, 839–842, 847
Annual accounts, 199
Antitrust law, 764, 766–790
Assets of the estate. *See* Bankruptcy
Auction sales. *See* Sales
Auditing, 212–213
Aval. *See* Bill of exchange

Bank account, 189
Bank guarantee, 703–705
Bankruptcy, 334–389
Bill of exchange, 391–444
Bookkeeping, 199–200
Broker, 579–586
Business, 44–53, 132–135, 214–217

Carriage, 642–663
Chambers of commerce. *See* Professional organizations
Cheques, 390, 445–456
Clearance sales. *See* Sales
Collateral, 679–719
Commercial activities of public bodies, 69–72
Commercial acts, 44–67
Commercial agency, 578, 589–595
Commercial agent. *See* Commercial agency
Commercial arbitration, 145–166
Commercial company. *See* Company
Commercial contracts, 544–679. *See also* Commercial services and Sales contracts
Commercial law, 37–43
Commercial obligations, 62–68, 169–213
Commercial pledge. *See* Pledge
Commercial property rights. *See* Intellectual property rights
Commercial Register, 49–50, 170–184
Commercial securities, 471–472, 679–719
Commercial services, 567–678
Commission agency, 588–605
Company, 85–115
Competition law, 577, 764–790. *See also* Antirust law
Concentrations. *See* Antitrust law
Consumer contracts, 218, 874–882
Consumer information, 827
Consumer law, 818–882
Consumer protection, 55, 765, 818–882
Contract law (General principles of), 544–545
Cooperative, 121–131
Copyright, 312–321
Corporation. *See* Company
Credit institutions (supervision of), 748
Currency exchange, 467

Denomination of products and services, 833–835
Designations of origin, 239, 845
Designs, 239, 277–282
Discounts (announcements of), 845–846
Distance sales. *See* Sales
Distribution, 567–570

Equality, 63, 545, 733–734
Exclusive distribution agreements. *See* Distribution
Exclusive purchasing agreements, 569–570

Factoring, 655–656
Financial markets, 457–543

Index

Financial services, 635–656. *See also* Factoring and Leasing
Franchising, 573–577
Freedom of trade, 724–727
Free movement, 728

General Partnership. *See* Partnership
Gift vouchers, 855
Goodwill, 800

Honest business practices, 866–869

Indication of quantity, 827, 834
Information duty, 664
Insider trading, 543. *See also* Stock exchange
Insurance, 487–497
Insurance companies (supervision of), 748–750
Intellectual property rights, 236–333. *See also* Copyright, Designs, Models, Know-how, Patent, Plant breeder's right and Trademark
Intermediary, 578–633. *See also* Broker, Commercial agency
International sales contracts. *See* Sales contracts
International treaties, 244, 660, 668
Invoice, 202

Know-how, 322–325

Labelling of products and services, 799, 833–835
Leasing, 639–654
Liabilities of the estate. *See* Bankruptcy
Liability (product). *See* Product liability
Licensing requirements, 747
Limited partnership. *See* Partnership
Liquidation of a company, 92. *See also* Bankruptcy

Married people, 76–82
Maximum prices, 809–816
Merchant, 74–84
Middleman. *See* Intermediary
Models, 239, 266–276

Negotiable instruments, 390–456. *See also* Bill of exchange, Cheques

Partnership, 85–131
Patent, 245–261
Plant breeder's right, 283–294
Pledge. *See* Collateral
Price interventions of the government, 816–817
Price regulation, 809–817
Product liability, 880
Professional knowledge, 48, 745, 747
Professional organizations, 132–137
Professions, 745
Promissory notes, 392–393
Public bodies (commercial activities of), 69–65
Pyramid sales. *See* Sales

Quality of goods and services, 827

Real securities. *See* Commercial securities
Restrictions of minor importance. *See* Antitrust law
Restrictive agreements. *See* Antitrust law
Restrictive competition practices. *See* Antitrust law
Restructuring, 373–389

Sales, 550–566, 845–865, 874–882
Sales contracts, 550–566
Sales of goods, 550–566
Sales representative, 606–628
Securities, 683–719. *See also* Stock exchange
Selective distribution, 572
Small-and medium-sized undertakings, 740–744
State incentives for economic activities, 751–763
State intervention in economic activities, 722
State regulation of the conditions of commercial Transactions, 805–882
Stockbroker, 601
Stock exchange, 471–472, 499

Supervision of credit institutions. *See* Credit institutions Supervision of economic activities
Supervision of insurance companies. *See* Insurance companies
Supplementary protection certificates, 262–263
Surety, 697–702

Takeover bid regulation, 524–536
Trade association, 135–137
Trademarks, 295–311
Trade name, 326–330
Trade practices, 845–869. *See also* Unfair competition
Transfer of property, 563–566. *See* Sales contracts
Transfer of risk, 563–566. *See* Sales contracts
Transparency regulation, 25, 225, 524. *See also* Stock exchange
Transport. *See* Carriage
Travel contract. *See* Carriage
Trustee. *See* Bankruptcy

Undertaking, 169–213. *See* Annual accounts
Unfair competition, 791–804. *See also* Trade practices
Unfair consumer contract terms, 877–880

Warehouse certificate, 391, 679, 706

www.ingramcontent.com/pod-product-compliance
Ingram Content Group UK Ltd.
Pitfield, Milton Keynes, MK11 3LW, UK
UKHW020137290926
15471UKWH00003B/549

9 789403 530109